P9-DFJ-032

Chicken Soup
for the Soul.

The
Magic
of Cats

Chicken Soup for the Soul: The Magic of Cats
101 Tales of Family, Friendship & Fun
Amy Newmark

Published by Chicken Soup for the Soul, LLC www.chickensoup.com
Copyright ©2020 by Chicken Soup for the Soul, LLC. All Rights Reserved.

No part of this publication may be reproduced, stored in a retrieval system or transmitted in any form or by any means, electronic, mechanical, photocopying, recording or otherwise, without the written permission of the publisher.

CSS, Chicken Soup for the Soul, and its Logo and Marks are trademarks of Chicken Soup for the Soul, LLC.

The publisher gratefully acknowledges the many publishers and individuals who granted Chicken Soup for the Soul permission to reprint the cited material.

Front cover photo courtesy of gettyimages.com/MAIKA777 (©MAIKA777)
Back cover and Interior photos: cat reaching courtesy of iStockphoto.com/Leoba (©Leoba), black cat reaching courtesy of of iStockphoto.com/EEI_Tony (©EEI_Tony), cat tied up in yarn courtesy of iStockphoto.com/101cats (©101cats), cat playing with toy courtesy of iStockphoto.com/Stephanie_Zieber (©Stephanie_Zieber)
Photo of Amy Newmark courtesy of Susan Morrow at SwickPix

Cover and Interior by Daniel Zaccari

Distributed to the booktrade by Simon & Schuster. SAN: 200-2442

Publisher's Cataloging-In-Publication Data
(Prepared by The Donohue Group, Inc.)

Names: Newmark, Amy, compiler.
Title: Chicken soup for the soul : the magic of cats : 101 tales of
     family, friendship & fun / [compiled by] Amy Newmark.
Other Titles: Magic of cats : 101 tales of family, friendship & fun
Description: [Cos Cob, Connecticut] : Chicken Soup for the Soul, LLC,
     [2020]
Identifiers: ISBN 9781611590661 | ISBN 9781611593013 (ebook)
Subjects: LCSH: Cats--Literary collections. | Cats--Anecdotes. | Human-
     animal relationships--Literary collections. | Human-animal
     relationships--Anecdotes. | LCGFT: Anecdotes.
Classification: LCC SF445.5 .C45 2020 (print) | LCC SF445.5 (ebook) | DDC
     636.8002--dc23

Library of Congress Control Number: 2020933859

PRINTED IN THE UNITED STATES OF AMERICA
on acid∞free paper

25 24 23 22 21 20   01 02 03 04 05 06 07 08 09 10 11

The Magic of Cats

101 Tales of Family, Friendship & Fun

Amy Newmark

CSS

Chicken Soup for the Soul, LLC
Cos Cob, CT

Changing lives one story at a time®
www.chickensoup.com

Table of Contents

❶

~Magical Miraculous Cats~

1. Moonlight, *T.J. Banks*.. 1
2. Westward Ho, *Lori Shepard*.. 3
3. A Letter to Bubba's First Family, *Beth Cato*................ 6
4. Twelfth Night in St. Bethlehem, *Anne Oliver*................10
5. Ben the Benevolent, *Jan Rottenberg*.......................... 13
6. A Christmas Cat, *Liz SanFilippo Hall*........................ 16
7. Zelda Finds a Hidden Killer, *Maureen Boyd Biro*.......... 20
8. A "Catastic" Tale of Hope, *Nancy Sevilla*................... 23
9. The Siamese Connection, *Mackenzie Donegan*.............. 26
10. Nine Lives and a Sixth Sense, *Lori Kempf Bosko*........... 29

❷

~Clever Cats~

11. Pack Rat Meets Fat Cat, *Sergio Del Bianco*................. 33
12. My Cat, the Stalker, *Diane Stark*............................. 36
13. Tinkle Terror, *Debbi Mavity*.................................. 39
14. The Magic of Baber, *Kashana Douglas*...................... 41
15. Who's Watching Whom? *William Clark*...................... 44
16. The Doorknob Treatment, *Ronica Stromberg*................ 47
17. Foster Moms, *Kathleen A. Gemmell*......................... 49
18. The Cat Behind the Toilet, *Terilynn Mitchell*.............. 51
19. Johnny Cat, *Connie Kaseweter Pullen*...................... 55
20. Clairvoyant Cat Communications, *Donna L. Roberts*.......... 57

21. In Sputnik's Orbit, *Dave Fox* 61
22. The Cat Who Wasn't There, *Linda J. Wright* 64
23. A Tale of Meatloaf, *Christine Grecsek* 68
24. Not Without My Mama, *Jessica Reed* 71
25. How to Acquire a Cat Without Really Trying, *Debra I.* 73
26. Demands Attention, *Morgan Rondinelli* 75
27. In a Black Cat's Path, *Emily Dill* 78
28. Tummy Tickles, *Donna L. Roberts* 81
29. Enter Love, *Cynthia Carter-Trent* 84
30. A Proper Introduction, *Jeanne Blandford* 87

❹

~What a Character!~

31. Zen Master, *Garrett Bauman* 92
32. Othello, The Amazing Black Cat, *Helen Krasner* 96
33. Paying for My Sins, *Sharon McGregor* 99
34. To Catch a Mouse, *Melissa Abraham* 101
35. Cat in a Tree, *Michaele Jordan* 103
36. Harley the Cat, *Les Davies* 107
37. When Tuxedo Let Go, *Bonnie Compton Hanson* 109
38. Cory T. Cat's Special Ornaments, *Sheila Embry* 112
39. Feline Fetish, *Jill Burns* 116
40. Elvira Ever Changing, *Jeffree Wyn Itrich* 118

❺

~Cat Therapy~

41. Healing Kitty, *Carrie Cannon* 123
42. Calvin's Best Friend, *Susan C. Willett* 126
43. Nurse Cats, *Shawn Marie* 130
44. Sufi and Groucho, *J. Truluck* 133

45. Sweet Talk, *Kate E. Anderson*................................136
46. Sammy the Supercat, *Carrie Roope*.........................140
47. Tenderhearted Tickles, *Janet Haynie* 144
48. Not Quite Purrfect, *Bobbie Lippman*......................147
49. Mabel Made This Family, *Jessica Parkinson*..........151
50. The Cat Named Blessing, *Mary M. Alward*.........155

❻

~Oh So Naughty~

51. Cat with a Conscience, *Rachel Evangeline Barham* 159
52. Does Insurance Cover That? *Debi Schmitz Noriega* 162
53. A Puzzling Choice, *Megan Nelson*...................................166
54. Lesson from Larry, *Brook-Lynn Meijer*.............................169
55. Convicted Feline, *Nancy Saint John*................................171
56. The Houseguest, *Connie Kaseweter Pullen* 175
57. Perfect Angels, *Barbara LoMonaco* 178
58. Attack Cat, *Lisa Mackinder* 181
59. Squeak, *Alex Lester* 184
60. Stuck in a Tree, *Irene Maran* 188

❼

~Four-Legged Friends~

61. One Special Friend, *Karleen Forwell* 191
62. Sibling Rivalry, *Carolyn Barrett*.....................................193
63. Gizmo to the Rescue, *Ann Morrow* 195
64. Friendship Is the Best, *Connie Kaseweter Pullen* 198
65. War and Peace, *Pat Wahler*..202
66. Yours, Mine and Ours, *Cheryl Krouse*............................204
67. Cat and Little Red Hen, *Jeannie Clemens* 207
68. Foe or Friend, *Helen Heavirland*....................................210
69. Bons Amis, *Rebecca Edmisten* 213
70. How Many Cats? *Judy Dykstra-Brown* 216

~Tricks & Traits~

71. Frankie vs. Blitzen, *Butch Holcombe* 218
72. The Cookie Snatcher, *Teresa Hoy*......................................221
73. Cat Burglars, *Connie Goldsmith*..225
74. Day-Trippers, *Barbara Blossom Ashmun* 228
75. The Pot Has Eyes, *Kristi Adams*..231
76. Our Water-Loving Kitty, *Kimberly Lowe*............................234
77. The Diva, *David-Matthew Barnes*......................................236
78. In a Flash, *Jan Bono* 238
79. Far Worse Things, *Joshua J. Mark*....................................241
80. The Perfect Pair, *Monica A. Andermann* 245
81. Walking Willy, *Deb Biechler* 248

9

~Learning to Love the Cat~

82. My Purrfect Match, *Danielle Kosecki*..................................251
83. Nobody Moves In While I'm Away, *Vickie McEntire*............254
84. Say Again? *Kathleen A. Gemmell* 257
85. Lucky, *Sandra Martin* 259
86. Catastrophe, *James A. Gemmell* 262
87. Hedgehog, *Tim Ramsey*...265
88. Ode to Frankie Cat, *Rebecca Gardyn Levington*...................269
89. Yin Yang, *Dorann Weber* 272
90. Don't Count Your Chickens, *Renée Vajko-Srch*...................275
91. My Husband Did Not Want a Cat, *Katherine L. Mitchell*.....278

10

~Brave Cats~

92. Six Legs Between Them, *Linda Sabourin*.............................282
93. A Cloud in Our Hearts, *Laura Savino*................................286
94. The Bat Fanatic, *Susan A. Hoffert*.....................................290

95. A Special Independence Day, *Diane Stark* 294
96. Roger the Wonder Cat, *Valerie Archual* 298
97. Watson to the Rescue, *Jennie Moore Ivey* 302
98. Loving Blue Eyes, *Teresa Hoy* 305
99. Home Is Where the Cats Are, *Carolyn M. Trombe* 309
100. Angel in Cat's Clothing, *Carolyn Donnell* 313
101. Xena — A Story of Courage, *Helen Krasner* 317

Meet Our Contributors 320
Meet Amy Newmark 333
Thank You 335
About American Humane 336
About Chicken Soup for the Soul 338

**Chapter
1**

Magical
Miraculous Cats

Moonlight

In ancient times, cats were worshipped as gods;
they have not forgotten this.
~Terry Pratchett

You walk between worlds
between dreams
a lilac lynx
stepping out of the shadows
to sit by my side.
You are the white-gold light
against the winter-bare trees
come morning
a promise a whisper
a morning-glory of a cat
wrapping yourself round my heart.
You shimmy & you shimmer
beckoning with citrine eyes;
you conjure & cajole
purring, burbling stories
a feline Scheherazade
an Empress
all smoky mauve, steel, and grace,
sashaying toward sunrise

dismissing the night
with a flick of your elegant tail.

— T.J. Banks —

Westward Ho

There is something about the presence of a cat...
that seems to take the bite out of being alone.
~Louis J. Camuti

I started second-guessing myself as I drove into the evening in my dusty car. What the heck was I thinking dragging Libby across the country? After eight weary hours of driving, we had completed the first leg of the "Big Adventure," from Orlando, Florida, to the quaint, little town of Monroeville, Alabama. We were westward bound, exploring as many states as possible along the way.

One middle-aged lady in a Subaru with a cat.

I had settled into a lazy life of retirement at age fifty-six. Ten years after officially retiring as a Detective Police Sergeant, I had an epiphany. I was not living my Best Life. My whole purpose in retiring at such a young age was to travel. I wanted to explore foreign countries in far-flung places. I dreamed of road tripping the entire United States. National Park Geek would be my new nickname. It was time for a major life change, or I would be too old, too infirm, or just too afraid to do it.

I sold my townhome at market peak and paid off all my bills. It was now or never. I got rid of loads of junk and put my "must keeps" into storage. My two faithful dog companions had passed away within months of each other, so I could hit the proverbial road. No current relationships. No responsibilities. Nothing should hold me back. Oh, wait, I had been talked into adopting a skinny black-and-white kitten named Libby. Flash forward three years to a full-grown, sassy boss of a cat. How could I leave her for two months?

My sister said, "If you leave her with me, you will not get her back." Well, that was not an option. It was currently hip to travel with a dog everywhere — to the grocery store, public library, or even the doctor's office — so why not a petite, sweet feline as a trusted companion?

On the first night of our journey, anxiety flooded through my body as I lay on the hotel bed. I was exhausted from driving. It was a challenge carrying Libby's litter box and my overpacked suitcase to our room. I knew it would be the first night of many. *What if there were stairs?* I told myself. *Maybe we should just drive back to Florida and hang out by my sister's pool.* I asked Libby in a shaky voice, "Should we turn around and go home? What do you think?" Her response was a cool, green-eyed stare. The Queen had her own comfy, giant hotel bed. She was not going anywhere. I decided I would reassess in the morning.

The arrival of a new day ended all that paralyzing fear. Life was once again full of endless possibilities.

Away we went checking off items on our "must-visit list." There were national parks to explore, local delicacies to try, and delightful independent bookstores to visit. Libby settled in quite nicely. I had bought a giant Pet Tube that fit the entire back seat of my Subaru. It was a cylindrical, deluxe cat house fit for the Queen.

Each new stop was a plethora of weird smells and odd spaces to pad around. Hotel room windows became Libby's favorite perching spots. She startled a couple of young cleaners in a fancy bed-and-breakfast in Mississippi, who thought she was a cute stuffed animal until she skittered under the bed. She made many friends along the way, including vacation rental owners, pet-friendly hotel concierges, and delighted children looking for a break from long backseat travels. It was a toss-up as to whether people thought I was cool bringing my cat along on my big trek or a "Crazy Cat Lady." One of the best things about this trip was it taught me not to care about what people think.

Many times, self-doubt would creep back in, especially when we made it to Utah and I realized that I was more than 2,000 miles from home. Now we had to drive all the way back! I learned to focus on one day at a time, to live in the moment. Each morning brought fresh, new adventures. This was a trip of a lifetime, and I was doing it all by myself. Libby was the best of company; I never felt truly alone. She was my backseat driver, cuddle buddy and best friend. She was a trooper. If she could persevere through the insecurities of what came next, then I could, too.

We drove through majestic scenery that took my breath away. We traveled switchback roads through snowy mountains and dusty deserts where my palms sweated and my knuckles turned white. In many places, we lost our GPS and cell-phone reception. During these times, I would tell Libby, "We've got this, girl!" I'd receive a meow of approval from the back seat. Each new challenge made me feel strong, independent and resourceful.

Libby and I were on the road for forty-seven days. We traveled 8,443 miles through thirteen states. We explored five national parks, an ice cave, a volcano, and the birthplaces of Harper Lee and Elvis. We drove on Historic Route 66 and made side trips to funky museums. A sing-along with a trio of handsome mariachis was an unexpected highlight in Albuquerque, New Mexico. I got lost hiking in Sedona, Arizona for three hours on a trail misnamed "EASY BREEZY." I had no water or map but I never even considered panicking. I knew I had to survive and get back to Libby, who was window napping in our pricy, pet-friendly hotel.

Whenever my anxiety reared its ugly head, I would encounter friendly fellow travelers who shared experiences and tips for the road. In Bryce Canyon, Utah, a retired nurse gave me her spare pair of hiking boots because my worn-out sneakers were not cutting it through the snowy, rocky terrain.

With each leg of the journey, my self-confidence grew steadily. Yes, I could have made this fantastic trip all by myself, but it was so much better with Libby, my steadfast companion.

— Lori Shepard —

A Letter to Bubba's First Family

A beating heart and an angel's soul, covered in fur.
~Lexie Saige

To the former family of the orange tabby cat named Bubba, who left him
with Sun Cities 4 Paws Rescue:

I don't know who you are or where you're living now, but I have a strong
hunch that your family often wonders where Bubba is and if he's doing okay.

He's more than okay. He's a loving bundle of furry awesomeness — but
you already knew that. You helped him become the cat he is today.

I visited the rescue, desperate to ease my heartache after losing my
seventeen-year-old cat to kidney disease. I walked around the adult
cat room, looking into the spacious cages along the walls. I probably
circled the carpeted cat tree in the middle of the room twenty times
before noticing the orange cat asleep in a nook.

"Oh, that's Bubba," the shelter attendant told us as she gave the
cat a scratch. He leaned into her touch. "He's so easygoing that he has
the full run of the place, but he usually stays right here on these cat
trees. This condo actually belongs to him." She motioned to a nearby
four-foot-tall post with perches.

"He comes with a cat tree?" I echoed. Most cats in the room didn't
even come with a name, much less a big, expensive sleeping place.

"Oh, yes. And a green snake." She pointed to an empty cage. A green cloth snake poked out from a blanket.

My husband Jason picked up Bubba. The lanky orange tabby melted into the nook of his arm and purred.

Our attendant continued with Bubba's story. His previous family had a job transfer that forced them out-of-state to company housing that didn't allow cats. They had raised Bubba from a kitten, and the whole family was heartbroken to leave him behind. They wanted to be sure his cat tree and favorite green snake toy stayed with him.

His backstory proved he'd been loved, and I could tell he was well loved at the shelter, too. Every worker who walked by crooned his name and had to pet him. He was the shelter heartthrob, and he basked in the attention.

"How long has he been here?" Jason asked, hoisting Bubba onto his shoulder. The malleable cat gladly took in his new vantage point. I could tell by Jason's smile that this cat was coming home with us.

"About six months," she said.

Our jaws dropped. "How has a cat this loving been here that long?" I asked.

"He's an adult cat, about three years old. That makes him hard to adopt." She gave an apologetic shrug. "He's also sleeping in a cat tree most of the time. People don't see him."

We had seen him. We had to take him home.

The shelter workers gathered around to say goodbye to Bubba. They were happy he had a new family, but judging by the tears in some eyes, I could see he'd be missed, too.

I expected Bubba to hide as soon as we released him at our house. Instead, he strolled casually from his cage as if he'd always lived there. After a jaunt around the place, he settled in on his old-familiar cat tree, paws hugging his green snake. He handled the change to his new name of Finn with the same graceful aplomb and began answering to it within days.

I've known a lot of cats. I have never known any others with Finn's easygoing confidence. Nothing bothers him. I can vacuum around his cat tree as he sleeps there, and he barely flicks an ear. He blisses out when he curls up in a lap for hours on end, but never sulks if he needs to be moved aside. I was baffled that he didn't come running when I opened up cat food cans. Soon, I found out that he expected to be carried to his food dish. Even then, he didn't deem most foods to be worthy of his palate. I undertook a grand effort to find a food he liked, and after forty different kinds (I kept a spreadsheet), I finally found one he enjoyed, though he prefers to lap up the gravy rather than eat the chunks.

If I could talk to you, family who loved him so, I'd like to know what you fed him and what he enjoyed so I could buy it, too!

I would also like to know how much trouble he caused as a kitten because he's still a force of destruction and mischief as an adult. He tries to get in my grocery bags — with the groceries still inside. He shreds receipts. He sniffs in disdain at most canned cat food, but he wants to eat apple pie and other fresh-baked goods.

Most amazing of all, he jumps onto the wooden railing along our staircase landing, and then proceeds to bend over to attack his own tail through the gap, yowling for attention all the while. He practically gave me a heart attack the first few times he performed the stunt. I began to take pictures and videos — and then stopped when I realized the attention only encouraged him. Now, I try to ignore his balancing act and the panicked racing of my heart.

I've also discovered that he loves when I make the bed. He dives onto the mattress as I fluff out blankets and purrs like mad as they settle over him. He'll stay there for hours, completely covered by thick layers. It's a wonder he doesn't suffocate!

Every day, I wonder what mischief our Finn will get into. Every day, I'm blessed by his loving, mellow manner and easy purr.

Though over two years have passed, I imagine that you still think of your Bubba and miss him. His old cat tree was worn to shreds and has since been replaced, but he still jumps onto the platforms to cuddle his careworn snake. We'll keep that with him forever. We hope that it helps him remember you.

I hope this letter eases the guilt and grief you surely felt when you left Bubba behind. Thank you for nurturing him to be so loving and trusting, and for leaving him with a great shelter where we could find each other.

I would write more, but I think he's into something he shouldn't be. He's yowling, and something is rattling. I better go check on him. You know how that goes....

With gratitude,
Beth Cato and the entire Cato family

— Beth Cato —

Twelfth Night in St. Bethlehem

If light is in your heart, you will find your way home.
~Rumi

Our family made its eighth Army move during the summer of 1987. We were to wait in Clarksville, Tennessee, while my husband George completed a thirteen-month unaccompanied tour in Korea. Our six-year-old son Rick, our four-year-old daughter Starr, Barney the Sheepdog, our large long-haired gray cat named Q, and I were in a rental house near a place called Two Rivers.

My task was to have a house built for us and have it ready when George returned in the late summer of 1988. He would be assigned to the 101st Airborne Division at Fort Campbell, Kentucky, which is adjacent to Clarksville.

We had decided to build in an area known as St. Bethlehem. To arrive at our lot, we had to pass a neighborhood called Rudolphtown. Every morning, the kids and I would drive from Two Rivers to our lot to take pictures. Every afternoon, we would go to the St. Bethlehem post office to mail pictures of the progress to Daddy in Korea.

As we went back and forth between Two Rivers and St. Bethlehem, the kids and I would sing, "Over Two Rivers and through the woods..." On passing Rudolphtown, we would launch into "Rudolph the Red-Nosed Reindeer." I even joked that our daughter was the little Starr of St. Bethlehem.

If we were lucky, we would be in our new house before Thanksgiving. Even though Daddy would not be there for Christmas, we would make a home and memories. He would be home by summer.

The days passed. The house rose. The pictures were mailed. Shortly before Thanksgiving we loaded ourselves and Barney into our car. Q, protesting, was loaded into a pet crate in the back of our Jeep. The move was an adventure. We slept on the floor for a week until the movers arrived.

Barney adjusted quickly, but Q spooked easily and was skittish. When the workers and movers arrived, I put Q in his crate in the basement. I asked everyone not to enter the basement. If they had to go there, they were told not to let the cat out of the crate.

Well, it happened anyway. Somehow, Q disappeared.

Thanksgiving was subdued. We had much to be thankful for, but no Q to enjoy turkey with us. Q was Starr's special friend, and his loss hurt her most of all.

An odd thing happened one day. In the grocery store, I ran into a real-estate agent who told me we were lucky to have left the rental when we did. Someone had broken a window in the basement and gotten into the house. (I recalled that when we lived there, the window had been cracked.) There was no real damage from the break-in, but blood and gray hair were all over the window and basement floor.

Then, I knew. Q, our large gray cat, must have somehow found his way back, crossing two large rivers. It was perhaps a seven-mile journey. Finding no one home, he must have been frightened. I went to the rental house, but I couldn't find him.

As the Christmas season approached, the kids and I would read stories and legends surrounding the magic of Christmas. They loved the story of Twelfth Night, when the Star of Bethlehem led the Wise Men to their destination.

Christmas came and went, as happy as Rick, Starr, Barney and I could make it with George still in Korea and Q who knows where.

We had cousins in Nashville, Tennessee, whom we visited for the day on January 6th. While returning to St. Bethlehem late that night,

Starr kept nagging me to hurry. "We have to be home by midnight," she said.

"Why, baby?" I asked her.

She replied, "It's Twelfth Night, and Q is following the star of St. Bethlehem home. We have to be there to greet him."

While she had garbled the story and misunderstood much, she had the unshakable belief that Q would come home that night.

I was sick with dread, wondering how I could explain it her. Q had never been outside the Two Rivers rental house. He had never seen the outside of our new house in St. Bethlehem, having been transported there in a crate. I had to admit, however, he did seem to have found his way back to the old house, given that gray cat hair in the basement.

Oh, me of little faith, and she of great faith... our little Army family needed a miracle, and we received one. For one little girl named Starr, on Twelfth Night, it happened. Just before midnight, in St. Bethlehem, Tennessee, Q came home.

— Anne Oliver —

Ben the Benevolent

One sees clearly only with the heart.
Anything essential is invisible to the eyes.
~Antoine de Saint-Exupéry, The Little Prince

My small cat hospital was busy enough, but rescues kept it really hopping. So when the door chimed just before closing on a Friday night, and a man walked in carrying a shoebox, I wasn't really surprised. "I have a cat," he said with a Spanish accent, "a little cat."

"Oh," I said, "have you tried taking it to the shelter?" After a brief conversation in broken English and broken Spanish, I learned that he had tried, but the shelter would not take the cat because it was too sick. He had tried another animal hospital but they did not accept strays.

I peered into the box and found a scrawny kitten whose nose and eyes were plastered shut with mucus, and of course there were fleas. "Okay," I said. "I'll take the kitten," knowing that I wouldn't be leaving the office on time. "Can you make a donation to the hospital?" I asked sheepishly. Fifty dollars later, I was in charge of saving this male kitten and his road to recovery began.

Months later, after plenty of good food and lots of TLC provided by a dedicated and nurturing staff, the kitten blossomed into an adorable, rambunctious ball of fire. His left eye had become large and painful and had to go, but he didn't seem to notice. And since he had arrived close to the fourth of July, I chose to name him after one of our founding fathers, Benjamin Franklin.

Eventually, the time came to find Ben a forever home. He was healthy and ready to be adopted, but there was a small problem: After months of toting him back and forth from office to home in order to feed and medicate him, Ben had become more to me than just another rescue. Whoever was going to adopt him not only had to pass my rigorous scrutiny, but also had to walk on water.

Ben was placed in the adoption cage in the waiting room. Every morning when I arrived at the office, that one eye would follow me, and I would feel a tug at my heartstrings. So when Andrea, one of my favorite clients, inquired, "What's his story?" I was elated. Andrea already had three cats, one a youngster who needed a playmate. Quickly, I recounted Ben's history and placed him on Andrea's lap. She was interested but not ready to commit. "I'll let you know in a week," she promised, and I was hopeful.

Over the course of the week, I found myself becoming less and less excited at the prospect of Ben's potential adoption. So, when Andrea phoned the following Saturday with her decision, I had mixed feelings. "I've decided a fourth cat would be too much for us," she said.

"I understand," I responded, trying very hard to sound disappointed.

There was only one rule of fostering: You could not keep an adoptable cat or kitten. But rules are meant to be broken, so why should this one be any different? That night, Benjamin was loaded into his carrier for a one-way trip to his forever home — mine.

In no time at all, Ben claimed the upstairs of my small ranch house. Like any kitten, he got into everything and pestered all the other feline residents. He became "Benamin" when he was sweet and "Ben!" when he was naughty. Very quickly, he learned what he could get away with.

One day, when Ben was big enough to scale the baby gate across the bathroom door, I watched with apprehension as he jumped over. The bathroom was Spirit's domain, my paraplegic Tortoiseshell who had lost her freedom when I could no longer get her diaper to stay on. Spirit didn't mind much as she had always been a loner anyway, never interacting with the other cats. Nevertheless, I had always felt bad about her isolation. To my amazement, she scooted over to Ben immediately and lowered her head. Ben wrapped his front legs around her neck and began grooming her vigorously. Tears filled my eyes as I watched Spirit with her new friend. This became a daily ritual, even though his primary motive for hopping the gate was to see what food he could steal from Spirit's dish.

Since then, Ben has similarly welcomed two rescue kittens, and while he wasn't my first foster failure and likely will not be my last, I am so glad I kept him. Ben not only earned his keep, but is also proof that every homeless kitten deserves a chance.

— Jan Rottenberg, D.V.M. —

A Christmas Cat

*Until one has loved an animal, a part of one's soul
remains unawakened.*
~Anatole France

muffled meow startled me awake at nine o'clock. I fumbled through the darkness of my new bedroom and cracked open my door to let in the hallway light. I heard another muffled meow.

The garage was below me. Maybe that's how a cat had gotten in. Or was I dreaming? I had wanted a cuddly cat to call my own forever, but my parents had yet to relent, claiming pets were a lot of work.

I called over the bannister. "Mom? Did you hear that?"

I heard another meow, this time as clear as day. I turned around. A black-and-white cat sat in the hallway, his tail swishing and green eyes gleaming.

"Mom!" I yelled, not even considering I might wake my younger sisters. "There's a cat in the house!"

My mom bolted up the stairs. "It's okay! He must have escaped from my room," she whispered. She scooped up the chubby cat, who curled up against her. "He's a Christmas present for you and your sisters. Someone is going to watch him until Christmas Eve, but I can't bring him over there until tomorrow. Can you keep a secret?"

Thrilled beyond belief at finally having a cat, I nodded.

Although I had agreed, I couldn't contain my excitement. The next night, while getting ready for bed with my sister Katie, I said,

"Don't tell Mom I said anything, but we're getting a cat for Christmas. Act surprised, okay?"

Christmas morning flew by. As the oldest kid, I was in charge of handing out gifts. My youngest sister Maggie always opened hers first, followed by Katie, and then me. One by one, we unwrapped our presents, but all I could think about was that cat: a real, live cat. My parents didn't seem to notice my anticipation, though, wrapped up in their robes, sleepily drinking their coffee at the crack of dawn.

After we opened the last wrapped gift, my mom said, "I think we may have one more present," and headed down the hallway.

Katie and I exchanged looks. My dad took out the video recorder and hit Record as my mom walked back into the living room. She carried a long white box with three holes along each side. The box shook slightly as she set it down. "This is for all three of you," she said.

My sisters approached the box. I stood behind them, figuring that since I was the only one who was supposed to know, I should let them open it.

As they popped open the box top, the black-and-white cat leaped into the air, his long tail arcing behind him. We all screamed... even me. He scurried down the hallway, his claws trying to gain traction on the wood floor.

"A cat!" Maggie squealed. We ran after him, sliding down the hallway in our Christmas socks. Our dad followed, the camera bobbing.

Not knowing the house, the cat turned left, past the bathroom and into a dead end: the laundry room. We took a quick glance around; he was nowhere in sight. But in such a small space, there were only so many options. Sure enough, his green eyes twinkled from behind the washing machine, giving away his location.

"Come here, kitty," I called.

Nothing. Not a peep. Not a squeak. Not a meow. We waited for a while, hoping that, if we were quiet enough, he would come out and greet us properly. But the minutes ticked by, and he didn't budge. Disappointment at not being able to hold him started to bother me, but I forced away the feeling.

It turned out my mom had adopted the cat from a shelter, and his old owner had been an elderly lady who was not as loud as three young girls. The poor cat had to have been so scared.

When he finally emerged hours later, he slunk out from the laundry room. He took tentative steps down the hallway. We acted like statues in the open dining- and living-room area, watching him, worried any sudden movements would send him right back into hiding.

He stopped to watch us, his tail swishing. He took a few more steps, rubbed his chubby body against my leg, and purred. We giggled, but he didn't take off running... until the doorbell rang, signaling the arrival of my mom's family. At the sound of the chime, he took off, tearing down the hallway and returning to his spot behind the washing machine.

While he hid, the family gathered: six of my mom's siblings along with their significant others and a whole lot of kids. Mostly, we stayed in the back of the house, where the adults gathered to eat and drink and the kids could shake their presents. The volume of our talking and laughter became increasingly louder. I checked on the cat every once in awhile, but he was clearly most comfortable in the quiet confines of his dark hiding spot.

When we sat down to dinner, we quieted down. The adults gathered around the long dining-room table. Some of my cousins went downstairs to eat. A few cousins, along with myself, stayed in the back room to eat near the tree. As we were busy devouring our turkey and sweet potatoes, the cat must have assumed it was safe to come out. Once again, he ventured down the hallway, a little more confident than earlier. But he froze when he reached the dining and living area; even his tail stopped swishing.

"What an adorable cat!" an aunt declared.

Milliseconds later, the cat zipped to the closest hiding spot he could find: the Christmas tree. He bounded over the gifts and climbed as high as possible on the nine-foot tree, shaking the colorful lights as he went. I tried coaxing him down, but he clearly wasn't coming down with so many people around. So there he stayed while we finished dinner and unwrapped presents, surveying all of us from his perch.

When everyone left a couple hours later, and the only sounds came from the TV, the cat scrambled his way down the branches, sending a few ornaments crashing in the process. We didn't move from the couch. When he reached the floor, he stared at us again. I wanted to reach out to him and tell him how much I loved him already, but I didn't want to scare him.

In the dimly lit room, he jumped onto the couch, strolled across our laps, and curled up in my lap. As I petted him, he started purring again. "We should name him Purcy," I said. His purr was so loud that my family quickly agreed.

He spent the rest of the night in my lap. His arrival — and hiding — weren't what I expected when a cat finally joined our family, but that was okay. He was, by far, the very best Christmas present ever.

— Liz SanFilippo Hall —

Zelda Finds a Hidden Killer

*Cats are mysterious kind of folk — there is more
passing in their minds than we are aware of.*
~Sir Walter Scott

My cat Zelda is acting strangely, pacing and meowing as if she's in distress. Now, she talks to me. "You need to find Killer," she says. Killer — our neighbor's cat? "Hurry!" Zelda urges. Now, Scout, my Beagle, barks. I dash outside but don't see Killer anywhere. Zelda runs over to our seldom-used side yard and paws at a pile of autumn leaves. I dig through the leaves and find Killer, worried for a moment when he doesn't move. I scoop him up. He's all right! I've gotten to him in time, but I wouldn't have without Zelda's help.

What a funny dream, I thought nervously on waking. In real life, my cat Zelda couldn't stand Killer, the big, gray-striped tomcat who lived next door, so named because his owners hoped he would be a good mouser. Killer loved to hang out in our yard and would spend hours lazing on our redwood deck in the sun, much to Zelda's dismay.

Killer tolerated Zelda's daily hiss. He'd roll over contentedly, ignoring her unless she came too close. I didn't blame Zelda. She was there first. Scout was the buffer between them.

The dream didn't ring true. It hardly seemed likely that Zelda would worry about Killer's wellbeing, but I felt a twinge of alarm regardless and made a mental note to check on Killer before I left the house for the day.

As I gathered up my keys and stashed my laptop in my briefcase, I heard Zelda meowing somewhere in the house. That was odd. Zelda rarely meowed. Impatient to get going, I walked outside and scanned the empty yard for Killer, shivering a little in the crisp air. At first, I didn't see him, but then I spotted him, lying on the bottom stair of the deck beside a pot of yellow petunias, just where the early morning sun was shining. Relieved, I walked back indoors, closed the sliding glass door firmly behind me, and called to my pets to be sure they were both inside before I left. Immediately, Scout came scampering, but now I couldn't find Zelda. Oh, no! Had she darted outside while I was looking for Killer? I didn't want her to be out all day, especially alone with Killer.

"Zelda!" I called. "Where are you, kitty? Come here, Zelda." I checked all her usual places—behind the family-room couch, under my office desk, on top of the living-room chair. No Zelda. Where was that darn cat? If I didn't get going, I'd miss my morning meeting. "Scout," I called, remembering now that Scout had barked in my dream when I was looking for Killer. "Where's Zelda? Show me where Zelda is."

Scout bolted down the hall to the door of our guest bathroom and barked. For the first time, I noticed the door was slightly ajar. We rarely used this bathroom, and Zelda never went in there. I pushed the door open carefully. An eerie light greeted me. I opened the door wide, astonished to see Zelda perched on the edge of the sink, her image reflected in the mirror like a glowing, silvery ghost. Beside her flickered a wax candle my husband had lit that morning and forgotten to blow out before he left. In the wee hours, unbeknownst to me, our power had gone out briefly. The candle was nestled among a decorative wreath of fall leaves and had burned nearly all the way down.

If I'd left the house as planned that morning and not returned until evening, the leaves would surely have caught fire. Shaken, I blew out the candle and scooped Zelda up in my arms, nuzzling her warm, gray fur. I was stunned as I thought of what might have happened and remembered her strange meowing, both in my dream and later in the house.

My dream *had* been a warning—just not the one I thought it was when I awoke. This "Killer" was hidden in my home, a candle burning unattended among dry, autumn leaves. If not for Zelda and Scout, I might never have known. My sweet cat had not only kept a fire from burning down my house that morning, but she may have saved her own life.

I have always had a healthy respect for the messages that come to us in dreams, but rarely has one been so urgent and literal. As for Killer the cat, he never left his perch in the sun that morning, but Zelda had her favorite dinner of fresh prawns that night and even got to be queen of our the deck the next day when a vet appointment kept Killer away.

—Maureen Boyd Biro—

8

A "Catastic" Tale of Hope

When you have lost hope, you have lost everything.
And when you think all is lost, when all is dire
and bleak, there is always hope.
~Pittacus Lore, I Am Number Four

With our sons grown and raising their own children, our house was feeling empty. My husband Mike and I adopted two feral kittens, orange tabby brothers who we named Hunter and Buddy. They're now four and a half years old and a huge part of our lives and family. Hunter is my big boy, weighing twenty-three pounds. Buddy is smaller at eighteen pounds.

We love to camp and hate the thought of leaving the "boys" at home, so we've turned them into our "camping cats." In our car, they travel in a pet playpen so they can watch the world go by. We also travel with a trailer, and they love being in it. It's a five-hour drive to our main camp, which is on an acre of land we own in the Sierra Nevada Mountains in Plumas County at a place called Little Grass Valley, California. We set up camp in May once the snow has melted and leave it up until October when the weather gets cold. Hunter and Buddy love exploring during the daylight. We keep them indoors at night.

On July 19, 2019, we decided to leave after work for our week in the mountains instead of waiting until morning. It's a long drive, and we wanted to get it over with. We arrived at our camp at ten. The cats went from the car to the trailer as usual. I asked Mike to tether them since we were unloading, and it was dark. He tethered Buddy and was reaching for Hunter when Hunter jumped out the trailer door and into the darkness. We didn't think much of it because he never strays far from us. We called him and went looking with flashlights in hand, but found no Hunter, not even a peep. We went to bed, expecting him to show up during the night, but he didn't.

The next day, we hiked the mountains, calling and calling, still nothing. We didn't know until the next night that there had been a bear near our camp whose smell must have scared Hunter. We went cabin to cabin talking with people. Everyone was very kind and said they would keep an eye out for him. After a week of searching, we had no choice but to go home without him.

I was devastated, to say the least. Two weeks passed before we could go up again and resume our search. I printed fliers with his picture and the location of our camp; there's no cell phone service there, which makes communication difficult. People would drive by asking if we'd found him yet. They were putting out bowls of cat food on their decks. One man was carrying cat treats in his pocket "just in case."

The most frustrating thing was that Hunter wouldn't show himself! We weren't sure where to continue searching; it was like trying to find a needle in a haystack. We came home empty-handed again and again. We contacted a pet psychic, who said he was still alive. Buddy was crying for his brother and losing weight from stress. People started telling me to "face reality, he's gone for good" and "he's perished," but I had to keep searching! I could feel in my heart that he was still alive, and I had to find him before winter.

On Labor Day, September 2, we received a call in the afternoon from a Forest Ranger named Sierra. She had spotted Hunter in a campground three miles from our camp. I packed up my gear and left the next morning, ready to stay as long as it took. I wasn't going to come home without him again. I drove straight to the Little Beaver campground site #25 where she had seen him. I brought clothes and towels with Buddy's and Mike's scent on them and placed them around the campsite. I set up my tent, scattered cat treats around, and set out a bowl of food. For seven hours, I called and called him. No response. As the sun went down, I sat in my chair, crying.

Then I reached into my pocket and pulled out a bead I had picked up off my dresser before leaving home. It's a silver bead with the word HOPE spelled out. I had found it on one of our campouts years before. As I held it in my hand, I realized I needed to have enough hope for both Hunter and myself, that we would find each other again. I walked to the bathroom to wash away my tears.

As I walked back to my campsite, calling him, he showed himself! I called to him, and he popped into a culvert. I grabbed my flashlight, his bowl of food, and a towel with his brother's scent. I couldn't see Hunter; he was too deep inside the pipe. I sat down on the ground, talking calmly to him the whole time. Hunter was crying but wouldn't come out. I sat there talking to him, telling him I wouldn't leave without him, and I would sit there as long as he needed to feel safe. I pushed the food further into the pipe, talking and soothing him. After half an hour, he finally came to eat the food, but he wouldn't let me touch him yet.

Slowly, I pulled the food bowl out of the pipe as he continued eating. I touched his neck to pet him, and he started purring. When he finished eating, I wrapped him in the towel and carried him to his kennel. He struggled to get free, but I refused to let him go. I decided then that we were going straight home. I didn't want to take the chance that he'd get away again. He talked in the car, telling me his tale as we drove 200 miles home in the night. I only stopped to call Mike to let him know we were on our way, together again. Hunter had lost half his weight, but the saving grace was that he had made it to the lake, which meant he had water to survive.

It's been three weeks since he returned to our family. He's regaining weight, spending time with his brother and our beloved grandkids. He's back to sleeping on his favorite chair, and he cuddles more than he ever did before. He has nightmares sometimes, which I wake him from. He is definitely our miracle cat!

— Nancy Sevilla —

9

The Siamese Connection

A bond between souls is ancient —
older than the planet.
~Dianna Hardy

've had a Siamese cat for as long as I can remember. They are my absolute favourite breed. Having one makes me feel complete, like having my own sidekick. When I moved away from the family home, I brought my Chocolate Point Siamese cat with me. When Tucker passed away at age seventeen, I knew moving forward was going to be difficult.

After a couple of weeks passed and I was tired of being miserable, I decided to get in touch with the breeder who had sold us Tucker. I wanted to see if it was possible to trace his bloodline and maybe have a part of him back in some way.

When I heard back, the news wasn't good. The breeder had stopped her business eight years earlier. There was no way for me to find another cat in Tucker's family.

My husband helped me realize that even though we couldn't get another cat with Tucker's bloodline, we could still fall in love with another cat. After searching online, I discovered that a woman who lived five blocks from us bred Siamese cats. One of her cats had just given birth to five kittens a month prior. I thought it was pretty cool that the kittens were just down the street, so I contacted her and asked if she would mind if my husband and I came by for some "Siamese therapy." She obliged happily, and off we went to meet the Siamese babies.

We showed up at her place with no expectations. We had a blast watching all the babies crawl around. The timing of their birth was perfect as they were just starting to explore and play. While chatting with the breeder, Jane, we asked her how long she had been in the business of breeding.

She told us, "Over twenty-five years."

I mentioned the town where I had gotten Tucker seventeen years earlier. I didn't provide her with any other information.

She said, "It's funny you say that. I used to live about forty-five minutes away from there." Nineteen or twenty years ago, she told us, she had sold two Siamese cats (from different litters) to a woman in the same location.

"The woman also bred Bouviers," said Jane.

I froze because the biggest coincidence in my life had just happened. The kennel that Tucker was from also bred Bouvier dogs. They had a huge farm property, and the big black Bouviers were running free in the farmyard as we pulled in to pick up Tucker. It had to be the same place.

"Do you remember what kind of Siamese cats you sold the kennel?" I asked.

"A male Lilac Point and a female Chocolate Point, I think," said Jane.

Tucker's parents were a male Lilac Point and a female Chocolate Point. The ages of Tucker's parents correlated perfectly with what Jane had said, too. Jane pulled up photographs she had stored on a hard drive. To our amazement, there they were: Tucker's long-lost family. We had found them! She had a picture of a cat named "Gorgeous George" who, as it turns out, was Tucker's grandfather. The kittens that Jane had now were descendants of George's bloodline through their mother. This means they are cousins to our beloved Tucker — and living right in our own neighbourhood!

"May I hold them?" I asked.

"I'm not sure how they'll respond," said Jane. "They really haven't had any human contact, but you can go ahead and try picking them up."

Carefully, I picked up one of the little boys and felt an immediate connection. He was the only one willing to let me hold him. As I brought him close to my chest, he did what Tucker had done when I first met him. He put his tiny paws around my neck, and I looked at my husband and said, "He's the one."

My husband nodded in agreement. "He's definitely the one." We had a part of Tucker back again, living on in a beautiful little boy, and we were overjoyed.

Tucker and I could have ended up anywhere in our journey together. We lived in a multitude of different cities, travelled in cars and across the country in moving trucks, and even flew in airplanes together. After I graduated university, we moved away again, and I met my husband. It was an amazing coincidence that Tucker's parents were born a few blocks from the home where we eventually settled.

It's been a month and a half since we fell in love with baby Huxley. We are so happy that he is officially home. We decided to name him after author Aldous Huxley, as he too had Siamese cats who would sit on his shoulders while he created his art. Perhaps our Huxley will do the same. My husband and I are both artists and we loved it when Tucker would do that. Either way, we are excited about getting to know Huxley and embracing his little personality.

— Mackenzie Donegan —

10

Nine Lives and a Sixth Sense

Don't give up before the miracle happens.
~Fannie Flagg

My very first fur baby was a fluffy white, part-Persian cat named Rebel. We got him as a kitten from the SPCA, and he quickly took over the house and our hearts. He was almost six months old when he disappeared, and I was heartbroken.

We had already made an appointment to get him neutered, but it was too late. He must have been in the mood to prowl, so when we had company one day, he snuck out while they were walking in.

We searched for him everywhere, canvassing the neighbourhood, putting up posters, and even offering a reward. I checked the pound and the emergency vet clinic to see if he had been injured or picked up. No one had seen him, so we kept searching.

We lived in the city, close to a high-traffic road, and Rebel didn't have "street smarts" because he was an indoor cat. We also suspected that if he got lost, he wouldn't be able to find his way home. Every time we went out, I would search for him as we drove down the road. Nothing.

Weeks went by with no sign of our cat. Everyone said I had to accept the inevitable — either he was dead, or someone else had him and was giving him a good home. I didn't accept that. I just couldn't.

After two weeks with no sign of him, we put his bed, toys, food, bowls, and litter box into storage so we wouldn't have to walk by the sad reminders every day. But I still wasn't ready to give up.

One morning, I left for work a few minutes early and started walking to the bus stop a block away. It was a nice autumn day, crisp and sunny — a good day for a walk. I arrived at the bus stop and checked to see if the bus was coming, but I was still a little early.

Something told me to keep going, so I decided to walk to the next bus stop. I got there and saw the bus coming, but I just kept walking, watching the bus whiz by, knowing I was going to be late for work. But something told me to keep going.

I continued to walk for another twenty minutes, veering into a neighbourhood I wasn't familiar with — and walked right up to my cat! He was sitting by a fence and he was filthy, no longer white, more of a dirty brown colour. He was matted and stinky, and had a scab on a ragged torn ear. He was so scrawny.

I called his name as I scooped him into my arms. His motorboat purr was as loud as I remembered, and he pushed his dirty face into mine. I teared up with happiness because I had found my cat.

I turned around and carried him home. He purred all the way. When we got there, I refilled his bowls with food and water and set up his litter box. I cuddled him some more and then phoned to tell my boss I was on my way, promising to make up the time I had missed. I had another quick snuggle with my cat, washed up, grabbed my bags, and ran to catch the next bus.

Work was busy, so I didn't have a chance to call my husband and tell him that I had found our cat. When he came home from work that afternoon, he was shocked to find a dirty, smelly cat in the house — one he didn't recognize.

At first he thought it was a stray that had somehow gotten into the house. But after a minute he realized it was really our cat, so he gave Rebel a bath, getting rid of most of the dirt and bad smell.

When I finally walked through the door an hour later, I told him the story about getting a weird premonition and walking until I got to a strange neighbourhood — and found Rebel.

He just shook his head. "After I bathed him, I finally believed it was really our cat. But when I first saw him, all matted, dirty and skinny, I wouldn't have recognized him in a million years. I can't believe you did!"

I'm so glad I was blessed with a sixth sense that day and kept walking past bus stop after bus stop on my way to finding our wayward cat. We took him to the vet to make sure he was okay and arranged to get him fixed as soon as possible. After that, Rebel stayed put, never wandering away again, which was a good thing because I have a feeling he had already used up most of his nine lives.

— Lori Kempf Bosko —

Chapter 2

Clever Cats

11

Pack Rat Meets Fat Cat

Always the cat remains a little beyond the limits
we try to set for him in our blind folly.
~Andre Norton

I was climbing up the stairs at home and heard some rustling behind our bedroom door. I already knew what it was. Our cat Felix has an affinity for money. Shiny coins don't interest him, but he is crazy about paper money. Maybe it is the scent that attracts him or the interesting design. Whatever the case, whenever I leave loose change and a few bills on the dresser, I can usually find him there later, flipping through the money with his paws. He can keep it up indefinitely. I think of him as a rich, fat cat who loves to play with money.

Our family has always had an unusual relationship with money. My father never really trusted banks, so he socked away piles of banknotes in odd places around the house. When he passed away, we searched a long time before finding his hidden cash reserves. My mother is just as frugal, having had her home in France destroyed during World War II. We call her a pack rat because she lets nothing go to waste. She also squirrels away wads of money in different places to make sure that she's covered in any eventuality.

One spring day, my ninety-year-old mother decided to splurge and go for a one-day sightseeing bus trip with her friends. Without mentioning anything to us, she hid a quantity of cash and jewelry before heading out. On her return in the evening, she called us in a panic because she couldn't find her stash.

We drove to her place immediately to calm her down and get the whole story. She related that she didn't think that she had been burglarized. She was just so excited about her trip that she had absent-mindedly hidden her treasure trove and now couldn't remember where she had put it.

We helped my mother search her home for hours but came up with nothing. She was just too good at hiding things. We tried to prompt her memory with questions, but she still drew a blank. The stash had to be hidden somewhere, but it was going to take some doing to find. We promised to return the next day to continue the search.

On our way home, my wife wondered out loud if we should bring Felix back with us when we continued the search the next day. I thought she was kidding, so I laughed out loud at the idea. But once I realized she was serious, it didn't seem like such a bad idea. He was nuts about paper money and had a nose that was much more sensitive than ours to sniff things out.

So the next day we drove back to my mother's place with Felix. He was curious about where this outing was taking him and quite excited once we arrived. My mother spoils all of our pets, so they love her madly and enjoy spending time at her place.

Once we opened up the cupboards and closets, it wasn't long before he began sniffing around. He couldn't believe his luck, being able to roam and dig at will in this previously forbidden territory. My mother has household rules and usually doesn't allow pets in certain areas of her house. Soon, he was scratching at a shoebox in the bottom of the closet. Sure enough, when we opened it, we found a wad of banknotes hidden under the shoes inside.

And so it went. There was cash hidden in a cereal box in the kitchen cupboard. More banknotes turned up hidden between folded sheets in the bedroom dresser. Before long, Felix had unearthed a half-dozen stashes of cash. It was all money my mother had hidden over time and forgotten about. We knew she liked to hide a little cash, but never suspected she had hidden so much. Thanks to Felix, we recovered a lot of money.

Giving Felix a much-deserved break and taking one ourselves, we made some coffee and slumped onto the couch to enjoy some cookies. The seating seemed a little lumpy, so we tried adjusting the pillows. By now, Felix had jumped up to join us and was frantically flailing at the cushions. We discovered the mother lode zipped into the back of the couch cushions.

Rejuvenated by our successful treasure hunt and the refreshments, we handed over the goods to my grateful mother, who promised to write down every hiding spot from then on.

Felix had enjoyed his day, performing admirably while showing just what a smart cat is capable of. As a reward, house rules at my mother's place were loosened. From that day forward, Felix was allowed to nap on the couch and could even sneak onto her bed when she went to sleep. Both Mom and Felix were quite happy with their new arrangement.

— Sergio Del Bianco —

12

My Cat, the Stalker

If there is one spot of sun spilling onto the floor,
a cat will find it and soak it up.
~J.A. McIntosh

"Tigger, you're in my way," I said, rolling my eyes at the black cat who was lying on my treadmill belt. "I can't work out unless you move."

He meowed at me without lifting his head. Every morning for the past year, I'd driven my kids to school and then come home and exercised on the treadmill. And every morning, I'd found Tigger lying in that exact spot.

"Every single day, I have to pick you up and move you," I told him as I did just that. "You would think you'd know the routine by now."

After my walk, I'd head to the kitchen for a cup of coffee. While it was brewing, I'd usually unload the dishwasher. And without fail, I'd find Tigger lying on the kitchen counter, in the exact space I needed to unload the dishes.

And I'd move Tigger for the second time.

After cleaning up in the kitchen, I'd always head to my desk to work on the computer. And there would be Tigger, my faithful companion, lying on my desk, literally on my computer keyboard.

"You need to move, Tig," I said.

He looked right at me and meowed. Clearly, he had no intention of relocating.

I sighed, sat down in the chair and scooped the cat into my lap.

"You're always in my way, you know," I said as I stroked his back.

After a few hours on the computer, I left the house to pick up my kids from school. When we got back, the three of us sat at the kitchen table, ate a snack, and then started on their homework. And, of course, Tigger was right there.

"Mom, he's lying on my math paper," my son Jordan complained.

"Tigger, get off my book," my daughter Julia whined.

I picked up the cat and kissed his head. "You're a pest. No, actually, you're a stalker," I said.

"What's a stalker?" the kids asked.

"It's someone who follows you everywhere you go," I explained. They nodded. "Yep, he's a stalker, for sure."

Tigger the Stalker. Every day, that cat followed me through my routine. Everywhere I needed to be, he was always there first. On the treadmill. On the kitchen counter and the table. On my computer.

"This cat is absolutely crazy about me," I told my husband. I explained how he followed me throughout the house each day. "He loves me so much that he stalks me all day."

Then one weekend, I had to go out of town. When I came home, my husband asked me about my daily routine.

As I explained how I walked on the treadmill each morning, cleaned the kitchen and then worked on the computer, my husband smirked.

"What's so funny?" I asked.

"About what time each day do you do each of those things?"

As I answered his question, his smirk turned into an outright grin. "Guess where Tigger was yesterday at nine? Guess where he was at noon? Guess where he was at four?" I shrugged, and he said, "He was on your treadmill at nine. At noon, I spotted him lying on the computer desk. And at four, he was lying on the kitchen table."

"So he followed our routine even though I wasn't here?" I asked. "That's so sweet."

My husband shook his head and motioned for me to follow him upstairs.

He pointed at my treadmill and said, "At nine in the morning, the sun is shining through that window, right onto the treadmill belt.

At noon, it's shining through the window by the computer desk. And around four, the sun is shining through the windows in the kitchen and right onto the table."

My mouth dropped open. "Are you saying he's not following me? He's just chasing the sun?"

He nodded. "Sorry. I know you thought he loved you that much."

I was so disappointed. I had friends who talked about their aloof cats. I was proud that my cat loved me and wanted to be everywhere I went.

But all along, he hadn't been stalking me. He'd been chasing the sun throughout the house each day.

The next day, I decided to switch up my routine. At nine, I worked on the computer while Tigger lay on the treadmill. Then at noon, while he was lying on the sunny spot on the desk, I walked on the treadmill.

Oddly, I missed having to move him out of my way. I missed thinking my cat loved me.

The truth was, Tigger was an aloof cat after all. It was a sad realization.

A few days after learning that he was chasing the sun and not me, I took a break from my daily routine and lay on the floor in front of the window, right in the sunshine. The warmth did feel nice. Maybe I couldn't really blame Tigger.

Not long after I lay down, Tig curled up beside me in the sunshine, purring loudly.

I ran my hand down his back and smiled. Tigger wasn't aloof. He did love me. Just not as much as he loved the sun.

— Diane Stark —

13

Tinkle Terror

*A cat is the only domestic animal I know who toilet
trains itself and does a damned impressive job of it.*
~Joseph Epstein

ooking over my shoulder, I watched in the mirror as my sun-bleached tresses shimmied down my back when I shook my head. After wetting and blow-drying my hair twice, my locks were finally straight and silky enough to withstand the scrutiny of my teenage peers. Unfortunately, I knew my short bangs would stick straight up as soon as they were blasted by the notorious Florida humidity.

I turned around and leaned over the vanity to bring my face closer to the mirror. Then I picked up my mascara, twisted the top, and pulled the loaded wand out of the container. I would never leave the apartment until my thin, blond lashes were at least visible. As I raised the small brush to my eye, I heard what sounded like somebody urinating in the toilet.

I froze! My heart started racing. I was the only one home!

The bathroom was behind me and slightly to the right. The door was open, but I was unable to see the toilet from my vantage point. The front door of our apartment was just a few steps from the bathroom. Was it possible somebody had walked in without me seeing him or her in the mirror? I was fifteen years old and weighed about ninety-eight pounds. What if it was a big, burly man? I wouldn't have a chance.

To make my escape, I would have to pass in front of the bathroom.

Surely, the home invader would hear my heart pounding. Slowly, with only my mascara wand for a weapon, I crept toward the front door. My plan was to poke the trespassing tinkler in the eye should he try to grab me.

As I got to the bathroom, I peeked around the doorframe. My jaw dropped. It took a moment or two for my brain to process what I was seeing. After my fight-or-flight response diminished, I started laughing.

The intruder had his rear end hanging over the bowl, four paws on the seat, and tail twitching. It was my sister's gray tabby, Tom! He looked up at me, gave one more flick of the tail, hopped down, and strolled casually from the room. Nobody had taught him to use a toilet, so he must have been a very smart, observant kitty. He did forget to flush, though.

— Debbi Mavity —

14

The Magic of Baber

I regard cats as one of the great joys in the world.
I see them as a gift of highest order.
~Trisha McCagh

It's long been thought that cats possess the power of intuition, though I wasn't sure I believed that until we had Baber.

Baber was a little puffball of a Calico kitten who barely had her eyes open when my mother found her in a field. She was a lovable but very quiet cat, rarely making any noise at all. When she would go into heat, she would retreat to the dark corners of the basement and yowl alone. She would only return to the family when it was over. If one of us was sick, she would come and sit on the person's chest nearly face-to-face and stare. Every single time we sniffled, she would send out a weird, muffled, concerned kind of purr! It was like no other purr I had ever heard before. She would lie there with the patient until he or she got up or got better. Other than that, she was silent... until one day.

My mother was getting ready to go to work, and Baber started crying and following her around the house. This was such an odd thing for her to do that my mother knew something must be wrong. She checked Baber all over to make sure nothing was abnormal physically. After being satisfied that was not the cause, she proceeded with her morning routine. Baber was relentless. Mom picked her up once again, petting her and scratching her head while talking to her. Figuring that was what she wanted, she put her back down and tried to return to what she was doing. As soon as Mom put her down, she started crying again.

Quite concerned at this point, my mother ran down a checklist of kitty needs. She gave her fresh food, both wet and dry. Baber didn't eat… and the meowing didn't stop. Mom changed her litter and gave her fresh water. She even gave her a treat and stopped to play with her a bit. Baber didn't want water, a treat or to play. She continued following my mother closely, still crying nonstop. Finally, in frustration, my mother sat down, threw her hands up and exclaimed, "What is wrong? I have tried everything I know to do, and I don't know what is wrong!" Still, Baber continued without pause.

My mom left that day for her appointment in a hurry, a little late, and very frustrated. As she walked out, our strictly inside cat tried to squeeze out the door with her even though it was a cold, snowy day.

Baber's incessant cries didn't stop when my mother left. In fact, they seemed to get a little worse. My father tried to console her, to no avail. My brother and I tried, too. Nothing stopped her from pacing and meowing in this agonizing way. We were all confounded and upset by this time. This went on all day… and then the phone rang.

It was my mother calling to inform us that she had been in a car accident and would be riding home in the tow truck. Luckily, she was okay, but the car was undriveable. When she returned home, she came in and threw her coat on the back of the couch. Baber climbed up on her coat almost immediately, lay down, and fell asleep. Finally, she was quiet, and now we knew why. She had been trying to alert us to the impending doom, and we just didn't understand.

Baber returned to her quiet nature, and all was well until about a year later. It was another nasty winter day, and again my mother woke up and began to get ready for an appointment. Baber began crying and following her around everywhere again. My mother started to do the same things she had done before, but in the middle of the feeding and petting, she realized something. This had occurred the year before on a snowy day and she'd had an accident. She cancelled her appointment and stopped getting ready for work. She said to Baber, "I hear you, and I'm not going!" Instantly, Baber settled down and went to sleep.

I have no doubt that if my mom had gone to work that day, it would not have ended well. One could speculate what might have happened. Personally, I am content not knowing.

This kind of phenomenon never happened again in Baber's life. Out of all the animals my kindhearted mother had rescued and saved, this was the first time I had ever seen one of them save *her* life in return.

— Kashana Douglas —

Who's Watching Whom?

The smart cat doesn't let on that he is.
~H.G. Frommer

I call out, "Boots!" I wonder where my nature-loving tuxedo cat is. I turn to look down the trail, which is guarded by red oak, American beech, sassafras, loblolly pines, white oak and hickory. I tell friends I have so many hickory trees that I would be wealthy if I invented a beneficial product made from hickory nuts.

There are plenty of fallen branches and trees that keep Boots busy with her own obstacle courses. In another seventy yards, I look over to my right and see Boots walking on a large, fallen red oak. I continue with my hike in the Tennessee foothills for another quarter mile. I stop and turn around to look for Boots. In a couple of seconds, I see her walking over the rise.

I can tell that Boots is walking a little faster to catch up with me. I walk around a curve that goes downhill into a holler. I stop and wait for Boots. She walks up to me, and I bend over to pet her and say, "Good girl. You're a good walker." She walks between my legs, and we continue into the holler.

When we walk out of the holler, I can still see the lake and distant ridge of hills now and then between the trees. After early spring, the foliage will block the scenic view. As I begin to walk a fairly straight trail next to a horse pasture, I lose sight of Boots. Hopefully, she knows where I am. I hear the fluttering of wings, and I look up to see two tufted titmice navigating through the trees.

I don't see a lot of birds in the woods, but sometimes I see a red-bellied woodpecker or a white-breasted nuthatch climbing up and down the tree trunks. Now and then, I see a red-tailed hawk gliding over the treetops. Looking up at the trees, I laugh to myself, thinking about Boots. Sometimes, when I'm near a tree, Boots will run up the tree until she gets to my height, and then she stops and looks at me eye-to-eye.

I walk past the end of the horse pasture and wonder what Boots is doing now. Sometimes, she will lose track of me when she starts digging or chasing something. When she finishes her task, she starts crying out and looking for me. At times, I stop walking to listen for her. It worries me when she starts crying because there are coyotes in the area.

People say that coyotes are more afraid of us than we are of them, but I certainly don't trust them in the same area with my favorite feline. As soon as I hear Boots crying, I start backtracking toward her. It's almost time for us to turn around and head back anyway.

Looking at the position of the sun and the brightness of the sky, I'm guessing it will be dark in two hours. As we start heading back, I think about when Boots started coming in the house after dark. I knew that male cats were bothering her, but one attacked her mercilessly one night. I found her early the next morning, scared, defensive and in pain. My wife and I took her to the vet, and she required major surgery. After that incident, she had two more late-night rendezvous. After the final one, she was taken back to the vet with a minor injury. Since then, she has come inside by nightfall.

Boots is now about four years old. After she recovered, she was able to run again and climb trees. She is smaller than average, more into flight than fight. Even though she's not a champion fighter, she's a good tree climber and runner. I don't think they have an IQ test for cats, but if they did I know she would be near the genius level.

Finally, I see her taking one of her shortcuts through the woods. She knows my routes, and she likes shortcuts and the occasional siesta.

Now that she's getting close to me, I stop to greet her. I say, "What have you been doing? Let's go back; it's almost time for supper."

I'll be back at the house in fifteen to twenty minutes, and I hope that Boots will follow me. As I take one of the winding paths, I knock some twigs and small limbs off the trail with my walking stick. Since I'm not fifty or sixty anymore, I'll be glad to get back, drink some water and fix some coffee. If I remember, there's a Honeycrisp apple on the kitchen countertop with my name on it.

I look back for Boots and see that she's still following me, but she's lagging behind a good thirty yards. I notice that the redbuds are near full bloom. They look good against the deep, blue sky. I'm getting close to the trailhead. As I walk around some boulders on the side of the hill, I pass two eucalyptus benches that I assembled for scenic viewing. About twenty yards past the benches, I'm back on the trailhead. I haven't seen Boots for about five minutes. In another five minutes, I'll finish the hike.

I walk down the hill, past the fire pit and pear trees. I walk up the hill to the back of the house. Boots is still not in sight. I step onto the back deck and look around for her. I call her again and tap my walking stick against the wood deck. When she doesn't appear, I head inside.

After ten minutes pass, I pick up the walking stick, go outside again and yell for Boots. I tap the walking stick against the deck floor. I go back outside every ten to fifteen minutes. It's now dusk, and I'm worried about Boots.

When I turn around once again to go back inside, Boots is watching me from the inside of the great room. By some miracle, she appeared out of thin air. She sits there looking at me with her bright green eyes and a cunning grin. I'm surprised and amazed at how she got there. As I look at Boots dressed in her white shirt and black tuxedo, I wonder, does she have some kind of magical power?

— William Clark —

16

The Doorknob Treatment

Cats are absolute individuals, with their own ideas
about everything, including the people they own.
~John Dingman

Melvin strolled onto my parents' property in the country and wouldn't leave. Even the dog, whose food he was stealing, couldn't chase him off.

My parents were dog people, not cat people, so how Melvin finagled his way into their hearts remains a mystery. Certainly, it was not his looks. He was a plain gray cat with short legs, short fur, a big head, and a stocky trunk.

When I came home from college, Melvin was not only living on the property but had laid claim to his own chair in the house. He would sit in one recliner while my father sat in the other, watching TV together. Mom was relegated to the sofa.

Melvin seemed to really like Dad, which was another mystery. Dad was not good with cats. He would take hold of a cat's head in his hand and slowly turn it back and forth like a doorknob. In the past, cats had reacted to this by biting Dad's hand and clawing his wrist and arm, leaving him scratched up and chuckling. Not Melvin. He allowed Dad to turn his head back and forth, and when Dad released him, he would shake his head a time or two and then stroll off with a look on his face like, "Hmm. Don't know what that was about, but it was pretty weird."

I am a cat lover and would scold Dad. "You shouldn't do that! Melvin's such a good cat. Why would you even think of doing that?"

"He seems to like it," Dad would insist. "He always comes back for more."

And Melvin did. Mom and I would pet him, but he still went back to Dad and received the doorknob treatment.

One weekend, I came home from college and was sitting on the sofa, watching TV with Dad, who sat in his recliner. Mom and Melvin were in the kitchen. Out of the corner of my eye, I saw Melvin enter the living room. Melvin strolled toward Dad, who was captivated by action on the TV screen and never looked down from it. Melvin hopped up onto the back of Dad's recliner and placed an arm on each side of Dad's head. He began rubbing them back and forth as if he were turning some gigantic doorknob.

Dad screamed, Melvin disappeared, and the recliner toppled over backward with 200-pound Dad still in it. It hit the hardwood floor with a loud boom, and Mom came running from the kitchen.

"What was that?" she gasped, a towel still in her hands from wiping dishes.

"Something just grabbed my head," Dad said, warily stroking his hair down and starting to lift himself up.

"It was Melvin," I said.

Dad stilled. "Where did he go?"

"I don't know," I said. "He could be under your chair."

The room grew silent, as we all thought of the implications of that.

"Don't move!" Mom commanded. She looked around the chair. Melvin was nowhere in sight. She lowered herself slowly to peer under the chair when a soft, scrabbling sound came from it.

Calmly, Melvin crawled out from under the recliner and strolled away from Dad leisurely with only one backward glance. It seemed to say, "How did you like that?"

Dad never turned a cat's head like a doorknob again.

— Ronica Stromberg —

17

Foster Moms

What greater gift than the love of a cat?
~Charles Dickens

"Can you foster a young kitten, Kathy? She was dropped off in a box at our back entrance, and she's in bad shape. I think she was beaten with a bat or something. She has one broken femur and loads of contusions."

Veterinarian Dr. Sally Hathford knew that I could no longer train dogs, as I was homebound with a severe back injury. "I think it would be good for you both as this little girl needs TLC, and you need a cuddle partner," concluded Dr. H.

Eight-week-old Phoebe was delivered the next day by a vet tech. He brought supplies, medications and a care list.

Phoebe was a sad sack, with her splinted leg and shaved patches held together with stitches and staples. She shied away from my hand and hissed a wee defense as I lifted her out of the carrier. A pretty, long-haired tuxedo cat with young eyes still blue, she melted my heart immediately.

"Poor little lady," I cooed. "I'm so sorry that someone hurt you. You're safe now, sweet, sweet girl."

Like many domestic cats, Phoebe needed only a short time to warm up to me. Initially, I spoon fed her to help us bond. Although I fashioned a bed of blankets next to my bedside, she preferred the warmth of my side.

I was amazed that she never had an accident, and she learned to use her litter box as if by instinct. On the advice of Dr. H, Phoebe could free feed, but she wasn't a glutton. I acquired a scratching post that she used regularly as she blossomed into adolescence. Vaccinated and spayed at the appropriate time, she was healing and thriving.

As my back began to heal and the depression I felt as the result of my disability lessened, I made a dear friend who is an avid shelter volunteer. Vicki spends time each week guiding timid, abused and feral cats to be the social creatures that they long to be. Adopted into forever homes when psychologically ready, these cats make loving pets and are adored by their new owners.

Through Vicki, I came to hear of a young litter without a mother that needed a foster home. I welcomed these three darlings into our domain, uncertain as to the now adult Phoebe's reaction. Wonder of wonders, Phoebe became the foster mother. I bottle-fed them until they could eat solid kitten chow, but Phoebe kept them clean, safe and nurtured as any fine mother would do. These three were tended to around the clock by Phoebe, and it was a tearful day when they moved on to their new homes.

Phoebe fostered a total of eleven kittens with me over the ensuing years. She was my first cat, and for this dog person, she was a stellar introduction to the wonders of felines.

— Kathleen A. Gemmell —

18

The Cat Behind the Toilet

When you touch a cat with your spirit,
in return they touch your soul with their heart.
~Author Unknown

"The cat is hiding behind the toilet, and I thought of you," Bill wrote in an e-mail to me. I wasn't too sure what to think of this. Bill was a veterinarian friend of mine, one of my professors in vet-tech school years ago. A caring person, he was also known for his dry wit.

"Why is he behind the toilet?" I wrote back.

"He's staying in my neighbor's bathroom," Bill replied. "She has a hundred dogs, and he's scared."

I queried Bill on various aspects of the cat, but he knew little. He put me in touch with his neighbor.

This case nagged at me. I had been thinking I wanted a younger cat to play with Nikki, my one-year-old cat, who annoyed the heck out of everyone. As if on cue, Nikki tore into the room and did a somersault over a toy. She was blind in one eye, but this never slowed her down.

The next morning, I went to meet the kitty hiding behind the toilet. The woman caring for him didn't know much beyond his name — Bolero. His owner was a schizophrenic, in hospice, and before this current placement he had been one of twenty cats and four dogs living with her. Cherry took me to see Bolero where he was hiding in her small bathroom. She picked up the stunning Siamese with deep blue-violet eyes and set him on a clothes hamper. I spoke softly to the frightened cat, gently stroking his head. I squatted down to his level to make myself seem more accessible to him.

The barking of her dogs could be heard outside the bathroom window. Occasionally, one would jump up and smack the window with its paws. "What do you think?" Cherry asked rather impatiently.

"I'll take him," I said quietly. This poor boy needed a break. I went out to my car to get the carrier.

When I returned to the bathroom, Bolero took one look at the travel box and flew up to the windowsill. Outside, the dogs went wild. I grabbed the beautiful boy by the scruff with one hand, supported his weight with the other, and set him in the carrier. He didn't try to escape or bite. Once home, I gave Bolero his own room and added a pot of oat grass, a catnip-laced scratching pad, and a pheromone diffuser to calm him and enrich his environment.

Nikki was delighted with this new roommate. Bolero had taken to hunkering down behind the futon, and Nikki would run into his room and crawl under the futon to greet him. She seemed to be saying, "Whatcha doing? Do you want to play?" Bolero may have been a bit alarmed by the one-eyed kitten with the jingling bell on her collar, but he never made a move to harm her.

Eventually, I got the scoop on my newest cat from Gabby, the former owner's caregiver. Bolero was eight years old, she said, and she told me a remarkable tale. One day, Bolero suddenly became obsessed with his owner's abdomen. He would nudge Rikki's abdomen, paw at it, and otherwise act strangely. Gabby took Rikki to the doctor, where it was discovered she had cancer in the area that Bolero was pawing.

Bolero had lived mostly outdoors, jumping in a bathroom window to eat. When Rikki went into hospice, all of her animals were placed except for Bolero. No one could catch him. The owner's family started renovations on the house to prepare it for rental, and Bolero was locked outside and dependent on the neighborhood kids to feed him. Eventually, a humane trap was set, and he was caught and taken to

Cherry's house, where he had been hiding in the bathroom. He had spent two months locked outside and two weeks behind the toilet. The poor thing was thoroughly traumatized.

I would sit on the futon and talk to Bolero, who hid in the corner behind me. I told him I understood that his last three months had been trying and frightful. I tried to reassure him he was safe. I even read to him to get him used to my voice and my presence. I gave him time and space to come out once he felt a margin of safety.

One night, Bolero had a surprise for me. He came out of his room at 3:00 a.m. He stood in the hallway outside my bedroom and yowled as only a Siamese can. There was a mournful quality to his voice. I spoke with Gabby a few days later and learned that Bolero's owner, Rikki, had died the very night he came out and cried.

It took months for Bolero to finally emerge from his room. He moved to my bedroom and climbed onto the foot of my bed at night when I slept. After a couple of months, he slowly crept up closer to me once the lights were out. Because of his cancer-detecting potential, I'll admit to being a bit paranoid. Did he know something I didn't? When he buried his head under my arm, I feared I had lymphoma. When he head-butted me, I worried about a brain tumor.

Six months later, Bolero ran out an open door. For two weeks, he refused to come back in. Occasionally, I would spot him in the evening in the neighbor's yard and would throw him treats. He ate them, but I couldn't lure him back in. I worried he was reverting to feral. Nikki would go out and hang with the hapless Siamese, and eventually she led him back into the house. He settled down after that, spending a good part of the day on my bed with my twenty-one-year-old, Twinkie.

When Twinkie was diagnosed with bladder cancer, Bolero shadowed her all over the house. I offered tempting food to Twinkie, which Bolero wouldn't touch, and he would attack any other cat who tried to go near it. He sat protectively beside her day and night. This high-strung cat had a new job, and he excelled in his role. Bolero came into his own purpose.

Twinkie's death seemed to hit Bolero as hard as it did me. He curled up with me at night, offering comfort as well as needing it himself. I witnessed the different sides of him—the aloof, the protective, and the vulnerable. Our bond strengthened. This cat with a tumultuous past was opening up to me. My Siamese boy with the blue-violet eyes was going to be okay after all.

—Terilynn Mitchell—

19

Johnny Cat

*One reason we admire cats is for their proficiency in
one-upmanship. They always seem to come out on top,
no matter what they are doing, or pretend they do.*
~Barbara Webster

My daughter answered her phone on the first ring. "Hi, Mom! I'm just getting home from a long day at work. What's up?"

"Not much, just checking in," I replied.

"Oh, no!" she shrieked in my ear. "Johnny Cat is going crazy in the bathroom! Can you hear him pouncing on the door? I must have locked him in accidentally when I left this morning. Now I'm afraid to open the door. Everything is going to be covered with poop!"

Jacqui had rescued the tiny kitten about a year prior when she found him meowing on her front porch. Within a week, the adorable little tuxedo cat had made himself comfortable in his home out in the country.

Johnny has proven to be quite the character with a big personality. He's a clever cat, who displays amazing new antics every single day.

He thinks the dog's, the other cat's, and the human family members' food is his. Usually, he finds a way to gain access to their food, either by being very sneaky or by putting on his irresistible pouty face.

Johnny enjoys taking long walks along the trails on the acreage with Jacqui and the dog, jumping and twirling in the air much like a gymnast in his attempt to catch a butterfly.

He delights in antagonizing other animals, whether they are family pets or wild creatures. Even the chickens or visiting deer are not safe from his tricks.

The older cat is easily perturbed by Johnny and would rather be left alone, especially when napping. But Johnny is exceedingly clever. He waits patiently until Beemo is fast asleep and then snuggles up next to him slowly and quietly.

He is extremely vocal with purring and growling sounds, so it's easy to know where he is—except when he's hiding and ready to attack.

But Johnny Cat isn't always a prankster, which brings us back to the beginning of this story where I'm on the phone with Jacqui.

"I'm holding my breath, Jacqui. Open the door," I giggled.

Johnny Cat rushed out when she opened the bathroom door, and Jacqui was speechless for a moment.

I assumed she must have been overwhelmed by the mess in front of her until she shouted, "Mom, Johnny is the smartest cat ever! Can you believe he pooped in the toilet?"

—Connie Kaseweter Pullen—

20

Clairvoyant Cat Communications

I have studied many philosophers and many cats.
The wisdom of cats is infinitely superior.
~Hippolyte Taine

I had been tossing and turning all night, sleeping badly and dreaming intermittently until morning. One of the dreams that I could manage to remember was rather disturbing. I had dreamt that a cat was fervently trying to communicate, but I couldn't understand what she was trying to tell me.

I woke up with a start just as the weird dream was ending. I shook off the remnants of sleep and began to get ready for my day. I was trying to forget about the strange dream, but it continued to puzzle me. My husband and I always had plenty of cats around, because we made a point of giving stray and shelter cats a good home. We had never been able to say no to a cat in need, so we had lots of them underfoot at all times. It wasn't surprising that I was dreaming about them.

We had just moved to a new home, so our situation was exacerbated because we were keeping all of the cats indoors until they got used to the new environment. We planned to begin letting them out a little at a time once they became accustomed to their new surroundings. The cats preferred to stay outdoors in the balmy weather, and we couldn't wait to condition them to the new house and yard so they could spend most of their time outside. We had far too many cats underfoot at the best of times, and being cooped up together inside the house in the nice summer weather was driving cats and humans alike totally bonkers.

We opened the door to the third-floor terrace to let some of the warm breeze flow through the house, giving the cats a chance to get some fresh air and sun themselves on the large balcony while we went about organizing our things and moving around the furniture in our new place. The terrace was high enough off the ground that we didn't worry about them escaping.

That evening, exhausted from unpacking, I decided to try out the tub in the new house for the first time. I ran myself a hot bath and poured a chilled glass of wine. Then I settled into the tub with a good book. I was just starting to relax when a cat started whining in the hallway. I needed to escape for a while, so I ignored it and put on headphones while turning on some classical music. Minutes later, I noticed the bathroom door handle turning slowly, and then the door swung open, exposing a cat hanging from the handle on the other side. Yikes! They had already learned how to open the doors in this house. I just wasn't going to get any peace and quiet this evening.

It was Kika, our pensive, watchful cat, who had been whining in the hallway. We had found her years earlier as a starving stray who had saved her own life by crying loudly to alert us to her dire predicament. Normally, she only meowed when there was something to meow about. She rushed over and started jabbering incessantly at me. She was in a bit of a frenzy. Since she had never been a drama queen, I didn't know what to think. I tried to quiet her and shoo her out of the room without leaving the comfort of my warm bath.

It was not to be. Kika was not leaving me alone and increased the intensity of her chatter. Suddenly, I realized that it was just like the scene in my dream sequence the night before when a cat was trying in vain to communicate with me. What on earth did Kika want?

Reluctantly, I put on my robe and followed her out of the bathroom. She marched straight through the terrace door that we had opened earlier and walked to the edge of the balcony, where she stared down over the ledge. I peeked down over her head to see our black, senior cat, Squeakers, down below on the lawn. It seemed that she got tired of being cramped inside the house with the rest of us, so she took it into her own paws to leap from the third floor.

Fearing the worst, I rushed downstairs and out the door, scooping her up carefully as soon as I reached her. Miraculously, Squeakers didn't seem any worse for wear. In fact, she seemed exhilarated that she had leapt her way to freedom.

Cats really do have nine lives and always seem to land on their feet. Thank goodness that Kika had the wherewithal to keep insisting that I come to see what had happened to Squeakers. And thank heavens for the premonition of imminent danger brought out in the dream, warning me of the upcoming events.

—Donna L. Roberts—

Chapter 3

When the Cat Chooses You

21

In Sputnik's Orbit

Cats know how to obtain food without labor, shelter
without confinement, and love without penalties.
~Walter Lionel George

Rhonda glanced up from my computer and saw the cat, who was chilling on my living-room floor the way cats like to chill on Friday evenings. Rhonda shrugged. The cat shrugged. They both went back to what they were doing.

Rhonda was my good pal and a professional graphic designer. I was a freelance writer who, in moments of procrastination, would tinker with my website and make a mess of things. I had asked Rhonda for too many favors already, and nobody likes a beggar, so this time I'd offered to pay her.

But such transactions can get awkward between friends. Rhonda wouldn't take my money.

"Just barbecue some bratwursts and buy some beer," she had said. "I'll come over on Friday."

So now, here we were. Rhonda was in my home office, cleaning up my digital mess. I was in the kitchen, rummaging through my black hole of a drawer on a quest to locate my missing barbecue tongs. Meanwhile, I had left open the sliding glass door.

I had just located my rogue set of tongs and was wrestling them out from under a spatula and a potato masher when Rhonda called from the other room: "Hey, Dave! When did you get a cat?"

I spun around and saw the cat, flopped out and purring as if he owned the place. A simple thought ran through my brain: *There's a strange animal in my home who has absolutely no concern for what he does to my carpet.*

Now, you and I both know the cat did not enter my condo with the specific intent of peeing on the floor. He came in following a different instinct. Cats have sharp senses of hearing. He must have heard me cracking open a bottle of brown ale.

He rolled over and batted his eyelashes at me in a thirsty way.

Well, I don't know about you, but I'm tired of cats always coming to my door begging for beer. Beer is bad for cats. It gives them overactive bladders, which is problematic when they're hanging out on your living-room carpet.

So, I was not about to give this cat a beer. Instead, I did what any animal lover would do. I yelled, "Get out of here, cat! Nobody likes a beggar!" Then I charged toward him with tongs in hand.

Running toward a strange animal is frightening. You never know if they'll run away from you or attempt to bite you on certain unmentionable body parts. But this cat fled out the sliding glass door and onto the cement slab that spanned the back of the building.

I followed, adrenaline surging. The cat stopped and stared me down.

"Okay, I'm out," the expression on his face said. "You're not really going to use those tongs on me, are you?"

He was a scrawny little guy with no collar or tail. He blinked at me and murmured a soft meow.

"Stop that!" I commanded.

He meowed again.

"You're not getting any beer!" I scolded.

"Okay, okay," his expression seemed to say. "I'm more of an IPA kind of cat anyway. Brown ales aren't my thing. But how about a snack?"

Now, I know what you're thinking: *Don't ever, ever feed stray animals, or they'll never leave you alone.* I've known this since I was a child. But this cat was using powerful mind control on me. Cats do that.

I broke down. The bratwursts weren't ready yet, so I offered some roast beef from my fridge.

I was now his slave for life.

Eventually, I grilled up the brats, and Rhonda and I sat down for dinner at the picnic table on my patio. The cat surveilled us from a few feet away, digesting his roast-beef appetizer and waiting for more.

"I think he's a stray," Rhonda said. "We should give him a name."

"How about Dave?" I suggested. I've always thought it would be cool to have a cat with the same name as me, but Rhonda thought that might get confusing when people called.

"We'll call him Sputnik!" she said. "He seems to like orbiting your table."

She was right. Sputnik was maintaining a safe distance, but he was circling, waiting for his main course. I offered him a small plate of bratwurst nibbles. He eyed me suspiciously at first, but then he wolfed them down.

An evening chill rolled in, and Rhonda and I went inside. Sputnik spent the next three hours trying to pry open my sliding glass door.

In the week that followed, he came for dinner every night. He was an intelligent feline whose sense of smell was as strong as his hearing. He learned quickly to identify the scent of lighter fluid, and he'd show up meowing before I even had the coals lit.

Over time, Sputnik the Satellite Cat brought me into his orbit and adopted me to be his human. He and I learned important lessons from each other.

He taught me never to leave my screen door open again, and that any cat of basic intelligence could see right through my ridiculous tong-attack charade. I taught him to stay away from my living-room carpet when his bladder was full.

He trained me to bring him dinner each night, followed by a neck and belly massage before bedtime. And I trained him to let me pamper him and do whatever he wants, at all times.

— Dave Fox —

22

The Cat Who Wasn't There

*If we treated everyone we meet with the same affection
we bestow upon our favorite cat, they, too, would purr.*
~Martin Buxbaum

t was a chilly, gray Southern California morning just before
Christmas. I was driving downtown, thinking not of trees and
turkey and trimmings, but of all the things my friends and I
had accomplished for The Cat People, our newly formed cat
rescue non-profit. We'd elected a president (me), hired a lawyer,
incorporated, filed papers with the IRS, held a fundraiser, opened a
bank account, and moved out of our interim office in a small house,
which was coincidentally just on my left. We'd...

Screech!

The driver of a red Toyota RAV4 ahead of me slammed on his
brakes, fishtailed, and came to a stop. I screeched to a halt right behind
him, wondering, "What the heck?" As I sat in my car, puzzled, a gray
tabby cat staggered out from under the RAV4 and then ran limping
into the yard of one of the houses on our left.

"You jerk!" I yelled at the driver ahead of me. "You hit her!"

I watched in disbelief as the driver of the RAV sped away. Angry
and sickened, I pulled my car over to the curb and parked. Taking a
carrier from the back seat of my car, I hurried after the cat. She'd been
limping; she couldn't have gone far. I'd probably find her in the first

flowerbed I came to.

An hour later, I'd knocked on doors, peered under cars, prowled through back yards, crawled under hedges, and called, "Here, kitty, kitty," a hundred times. I found nothing — not a glimpse, hair, whisker or meow. The cat had disappeared.

Christmas passed, and the new year arrived, The Cat People rented a combined shop/office, and got busy with fundraisers, rescue priorities, and foster homes, but I couldn't stop thinking about Kitty. What had happened to her?

Several weeks later, I was at the bank when I ran into our former landlord, Ernest Montoya.

"Say, when you guys moved out, you left your cat behind!" he said. I was insulted. The subtext of what he was saying was: "A fine lot of rescuers you folks are. You abandoned a cat on my premises."

"No, we didn't," I told him. "We took our office cat, Rosalie, with us when we left. She was the only cat we had there." *And besides, we would never leave a cat behind,* I thought. *That's not what we do. We rescue cats; we don't abandon them.*

"Look," he said, clearly exasperated. "There is a cat in that house. I see it in the window sometimes when I drive by. The house is empty now, and I'm going to have some renovations done, so I'd appreciate you removing your cat. I'll leave a key under the back doormat."

"But — " I tried to say.

"Just get the cat out of there," he said.

He's imagining things, I thought. Still, on my way home, I went by the house and looked carefully through the windows. Nothing. So, either Mr. Montoya was losing his marbles, or the cat was a ghost. But I guessed we'd better go through the motions. Fetching a humane trap from our storage unit, I drove back to Mr. Montoya's house, found the key under the mat, and went inside. The house smelled cold and musty. I searched in every room, closet, under-sink storage area, cupboard and broom closet, but there was no cat to be seen. Sighing, I opened a can of cat tuna, placed it in the back of the trap, put it in the middle of the empty kitchen, and left. I'd check in the morning, I told myself.

The next morning, it was raining, and I grumbled as I parked behind Mr. Montoya's house and hurried up the sidewalk to the back door. "This was a total waste of time," I muttered to myself. Wiping my feet on the back doormat, I unlocked the door. There in the kitchen, in our humane trap, was… a cat. It was a very scared, skeletally thin, incredibly filthy, dark gray tabby. Could it be the tabby I'd seen two months earlier that had been hit by the car?

"Kitty?" I called to her incredulously. But the sound of my voice made her frantic. "Shh, shh," I said. Gently, I draped my coat over the trap to soothe her. I guessed that after she'd been hit, she'd fled to the back yard of one of the nearby houses, found Mr. Montoya's back door open, and run inside and hidden. But where?

Determined to solve this mystery, I knelt down beside the trap. There, on the floor, were little piles of something that looked like black dust. Soot. Could Kitty have hidden in the chimney? I hurried to the living-room fireplace and looked up the chimney. Sure enough, about two feet off the floor, I saw a little ledge just big enough for a cat. Clever Kitty. She'd found a hiding place. But with nothing to eat for two months, and only water from the toilet to drink, it was a miracle she was alive.

I took the skinny, dirty cat to our vet, who was fortunately able to see us right away.

"She might be feral," I warned him, putting the trap on the exam table.

He peered at her carefully. "No, I think she's just a scared pussy-cat," he said, opening the trap and holding out a cat vitamin. I braced myself, expecting Kitty to bounce off the walls of the exam room, but she walked out placidly, sniffed the vitamin, nibbled it, and head-butted the vet. Whew.

Kitty, who turned out to be male, was soon neutered, and when he was under anesthesia, the vet repaired his hernia and removed a broken tooth. The clinic's staff gave him a bath and, after a bit of drying and fluffing, Kitty was revealed to be a truly handsome, golden-eyed, medium-gray tabby. But his poor, gimpy leg could not be fixed. Nerve damage had caused the muscles to atrophy.

So Kitty came to run our gift shop, and at a board meeting one night, we named him Ernie, for Ernest Montoya, and Haberdasher (a dealer in clothing and notions) because his job was to run our gift shop with its T-shirts and other logo apparel. But Ernie had talents we did not suspect. He loved being a foster dad to kittens; playing sponge-ball soccer with his buddy, Officer Steve; having his picture taken; giving head-butts and purrs; sitting on paperwork; and showing each new shopper where the treat jar was located.

Ernie Haberdasher lived with us at The Cat People's gift shop for twelve years. When he died from kidney failure, a volunteer at the shop wrote in our newsletter, "You were destined to be a lover boy, Ernie. What else? After all, you came 'home' to us from the vet on February 14th."

—Linda J. Wright—

23

A Tale of Meatloaf

How you behave toward cats here below
determines your status in heaven.
~Robert A. Heinlein

She didn't seem to have a home, this sweet-faced, sweet-tempered Tortoiseshell, wandering my city neighborhood of three-story apartment houses. Her random mix of autumnal colors was edged with black, prompting a neighbor to say she looked like a burnt meatloaf. The unfortunate name stuck.

A woman down the block said she'd adopt Meatloaf but couldn't ever seem to find the cat when she went looking. So I was elated the day Meatloaf found me and followed me straight to the woman's door and went inside. Meatloaf had found her new home!

Except that she hadn't.

It turns out that the man in the third-floor apartment next to me found where she had gone and accused the woman of stealing his cat. Irate, he led Meatloaf back to her home.

Except that he didn't.

Not long afterward, a truck pulled up, and the man moved away. But he left Meatloaf behind to wander the neighborhood once again, this time truly homeless. And pregnant.

The kind woman didn't want her heart broken a second time for the same cat. And I had a huge Maine Coon who loved only me and would not stand for interlopers. So my downstairs neighbors and I fed Meatloaf. We kept a wary eye on her growing belly and looked for possible homes.

Unfortunately, not many people are interested in taking in an abandoned, pregnant cat, regardless of how friendly and sweet-faced she may be.

I lived in the attic apartment at number 139. It was sweltering in summer, but heated by my downstairs neighbors in the winter. It had two big kitchen windows that faced east, right onto the roof of the house next door. One day that spring, I heard a series of insistent meows. I checked my Maine Coon, but he was sleeping, dreaming of world domination, undoubtedly. The meows sounded close, though, so I looked out my window, intending to see down into the yard. Instead, I found myself eye-to-eye with Meatloaf. She was perched on the roof next door, four stories up! The only person she could possibly have been talking to was me.

Instantly, I was terrified she was somehow trapped on the roof and would go into labor any minute. A steeply sloped roof is no place for kittens — or their mother, for that matter. I raced downstairs into the yard and circled the neighbor's house, looking for a means of rescue. And there, descending the fire escape and obviously quite pleased with herself, was Meatloaf.

Once she'd discovered the stairs and the roof next door, I saw her there regularly. She'd climb up and watch my Maine Coon and me through the windows, often narrating a tale she was intent on sharing. I never stopped worrying about her, but she seemed to be comfortable with her plan, as mysterious as it was to me.

As she grew rounder, I told her that she had to let me know when she was going into labor. There were a lot of cats, stray and not, in the neighborhood, and I wanted her and her babies to be safe. I hoped she understood.

The night of my company's annual fundraising gala, I arrived home after midnight and found I couldn't park in my own garage. Inside, I found a semi-circle of cats, all focused on one spot in the corner. I didn't recognize a single cat holding vigil, but somehow each of them had made its way to my garage on this night to witness one thing: Meatloaf in labor.

The strange cats scattered when I approached, and there she was, all heaving breaths and quivering, autumn-colored belly. I crouched, a feat never easy in heels, with my gown sweeping across dirt and old leaves.

"Let's go upstairs," I told her. "I have a safe place on the screened porch for us to have kittens together."

And we did.

I midwifed five impossibly perfect, tiny babies in that long, amazing night. They grew and gained eyesight and agility. I stopped watching television. Instead, I went out onto the porch for entertainment, watching Meatloaf's adventuresome assortment of kittens.

When the babies were old enough, my downstairs neighbors and I searched for new homes for the kittens — and we actually found them!

Except that we didn't, not entirely.

I kept one of the kittens, a gray-and-black tiger. He was the one who dragged himself over to me when all his siblings fell asleep in a pile after nursing. He curled up and slept in my hand. How could I not keep him after that show of devotion?

His baffling and intriguing kitten ways distracted my possessive Maine Coon enough that Meatloaf managed to slip into my apartment and stay there. She was already in my heart, anyway. She'd scaled city mountains to be with me and had arranged for a Greek chorus to dramatically inform me of her labor. She'd trusted me to share the astonishment of birth and had entrusted me with her tiny brood. How could she not be in my heart after that?

In hindsight, I think she may have told me from the roof that she'd already vetted and chosen me. I just hadn't understood her tale at the time.

Actually, I think it happened exactly as she had planned it all along.

— Christine Grecsek —

24

Not Without My Mama

Cats are endless opportunities for revelation.
~Leslie Kapp

Thirty-eight. That was how many stray cats I had been feeding on the street where I lived. I loved them all, but I did have a favorite. A gigantic yellow cat with blue eyes had captured my heart. I named him Butterball. Often, Butterball would try to jump in my car when I arrived home or come inside my house. I wished that I could bring him inside, but it was not allowed where I lived.

One by one, I trapped the cats, had them neutered or spayed, and released them again. This cut down on the new batches of kittens, but still, week after week, I fed the large group of cats. Mostly feral, none of them wanted to be touched. They would eat in a hurry and leave, but not Butterball. He would stick around for head scratches, purring loudly. I noticed that he was always in the company of a small Calico cat. Though not as friendly, she was touchable.

One day, my dreams came true, and I bought my own house. The cats, especially Butterball, watched anxiously as I started moving my things to my new home. I began to be away longer as I set up the new place, but I never forgot to go back and feed them every night. Butterball would jump in my car and try to get in extra cuddles. Sometimes, I found him amongst the boxes in the back when I came out with another load.

As I packed up the very last load and set out the cats' nightly dinner, I paused before leaving. The nights were starting to get cold, and soon winter would be upon us. Upstate New York winters can be brutal. Butterball seemed to know I was leaving for good. I gazed into his blue eyes and told him, "I will come back for you." He turned away as if he didn't believe me.

The next day, I returned with a group of friends. We set out a bunch of humane traps and caught the strays one by one. We transported them to a no-kill shelter. All except Butterball… I intended to take him to my new home. He steered clear of the traps, so I set out some food for him and left. The next day, I came back for him without a trap. I knew he would jump right into my car. But when I spotted him, he was hiding by a patch of bushes. I called for him, and he wandered over and jumped into my car, just as I thought. But when I tried to close the door, he jumped out.

"Come on now, Butterball. I came back for you as I promised. You are coming to our new home, a real inside home." He walked off toward the bushes, and I followed, determined to catch him. When he reached the bushes, the little Calico he was always with came out to join him. They both sat and looked at me. She must have hidden when we were trapping the others. I understood the situation. Butterball was not going anywhere without Callie. They were a package deal. Gently, I reached down and picked up the Calico. Butterball followed. I settled her into my car, and Butterball jumped in.

They explored their new home gratefully, sharing the cat bed I had bought. I posted pictures of my new cats online. I was surprised when I read one of the comments from my former neighbor. It said, "I am so glad that you took in the big cat. I remember when he was born. I see you took his mama, too."

— Jessica Reed —

25

How to Acquire a Cat Without Really Trying

Cats choose us; we don't own them.
~Kristin Cast

I am a traveling music teacher, giving lessons in several schools in northern Indiana and southwest Michigan. One day, I entered one of my schools to find a teacher holding a beautiful tuxedo cat with white whiskers. Apparently, the cat kept entering the school and they kept putting it back outside. I gave the cat a pet and went on with my day.

I didn't know it, but when they put the cat back outside again, it crawled up into the warm engine compartment of my car. I came out after a few hours and drove about thirty-five miles to a local university to teach for another few hours. The car sat at the university for about four hours, and then I went on to the next location, another forty miles away. This time, I traveled on the highway, 65–70 miles per hour for about forty-five minutes. After the car sat at that location for a couple of hours, I drove another fifteen miles home. At this point, it had been about twelve hours and I'd driven nearly 100 miles since my first stop that morning.

When I'd been home for about an hour, my husband and I heard "Meow" coming from the garage. We opened the door and in walked the black-and-white cat from the first school! He wasn't hurt, just a little dirty, and he wanted to be picked up. Needless to say, he'd found his forever home.

Very quickly, he became the ruler of the house, and my greeter and assistant in my home music studio. He meows to alert me when the students arrive, sniffs and inspects all shoes and cases, and often sleeps by the music stand while they play. He sets nervous new students at ease by providing a little entertaining distraction as we get acquainted.

I never thought much about having a pet until I was "adopted," but Mr. Personality won my husband and me over in a heartbeat, and now we couldn't imagine our home without him.

— Debra I. —

26

Demands Attention

Who hath a better friend than a cat?
~William Hardwin

I didn't intend to adopt a cat. I'm not even a cat person. But for some reason, I kept driving by the Humane Society. It sparked my curiosity, and soon I was looking at adoptable animals on their website. Then I told myself, *You might as well stop in one of these days because you have the time, and it could be fun, right?* One visit turned into several, and then suddenly I'd fallen in love.

I was sitting on the floor of an open cat room. I'm not the type to go up to cats and pet them. I wanted to give them the chance to feel comfortable and come to me. Suddenly, a dark gray cat with brilliant green eyes walked over, rubbed her cheek on my knee, and plopped herself in my lap.

And that is how I met Jade. She was sure that she was going to win me over. I snapped a few pictures of her snuggling up against me, and then I pulled up her bio on the Humane Society website on my phone. They described her as "a sweet, seven-year-old lady that demands attention with pervasive cheek rubs and an affectionate spirit." I wasn't surprised, since I had seen this spirit firsthand within a few minutes. However, I was surprised to learn that she had already been at the shelter for several months. The staff explained that no one had really expressed interest in her.

Her papers said she would be eight soon, and I wondered if her age was why she hadn't been adopted. I didn't want to rush into any decisions, and I still wanted to visit the other cat room down the hall. But Jade chirped argumentatively when I tried to stand up. She had a stronghold on my lap and wasn't letting me go. Through some gentle negotiation, I finally convinced her to let me stand up. Then, as I walked toward the door, she weaved in and out of my legs, meowing continuously. She didn't want me to leave.

Nevertheless, I played with and petted some of the cats in the other room, but my mind was on Jade the whole time. She had squeezed her way into both my lap and my heart. Still, I was incredibly nervous and indecisive about adopting. We had dogs growing up, but this would be my first time as a young adult being the one solely responsible for an animal. What if I wasn't a good caretaker? What if something happened? Would she be better with someone else?

It was a lot of pressure. But deep down, I knew she had already chosen me.

Cautiously, I told the staff, "I think I've fallen in love with one of the older cats." My application was already approved, so the decision was now mine. I let myself sleep on it, but all day I kept going back to look at the pictures and videos I had taken of Jade during our short visit together.

So, I went back to the Humane Society, completed the paperwork, and paid the adoption fee. On what was deemed Jade's eighth birthday, I pulled up to the Humane Society and went in to take my new baby home. While the staff finished some final logistics, they said I could go sit with her in the cat room. All the other cats were still in their cages since it wasn't visiting hours yet, so it was just Jade and me on the floor. I said hello, and she began rubbing her cheek on my legs, wanting to be petted. I was still nervous about adopting, and Jade seemed nervous, too. I think she sensed a change coming. But deep down, I think we knew we had made the right decision.

Soon, the staff was ready, so we gently put Jade in a crate and walked out to my car. As we secured the carrier in the passenger seat so I would be able to see her on the short drive home, the staff member who'd accompanied me gave Jade one last look. "Have a great life," she said to Jade. Suddenly, tears filled my eyes. We closed the car door, and it was time to go home.

Almost a year later, Jade sleeps soundly on her favorite blanket on my bed as I write this. If she were awake, she would be purring in my lap or climbing on my desk, making it hard to type, so I'll let her sleep. Though she has grown accustomed to her new home and life, Jade still "demands attention with... an affectionate spirit." She often curls up next to me at night to sleep, sometimes even under the blanket. She enjoys playing with balls and a toy banana stuffed with catnip. And it's still hard to walk across my apartment without her weaving around my legs, worrying that I'm leaving.

As soon as she hears my keys signaling that I'm back home, she runs to the door to greet me, and then rolls over for some belly rubs like a dog. She is definitely a nervous cat — nervous that I won't come back. But I always assure her that, though I have to leave sometimes, I will come back home to my Jade. She's mine, and I am hers.

I cannot imagine my life without Jade. She has brought so much joy to my life, and she has inspired me to try to only adopt senior animals. Sure, kittens need their forever homes too, but they are easier to place, and there's a special place in my heart for older cats.

I've heard it said that senior animals love deeper, and I think that's true. I know from Jade's cheek rubs and kneading my legs that she seems extra grateful to have been adopted. I get why people adopt younger animals. They want to watch them grow and their personalities develop. Most importantly, they want to have more years with them. But I was drawn immediately to an older cat for good reasons, too. Her personality was well-developed, so I knew what I was getting when interacting with her. And she didn't have kitten energy, so we could spend weekends lounging and napping together, with the right amount of occasional play.

As an older cat, Jade loves intensely. Though I'm likely to get fewer years with her, these years will continue to be filled with that love.

— Morgan Rondinelli —

27

In a Black Cat's Path

It's really the cat's house — we just pay the mortgage.
~Author Unknown

He was scrawny, had mange and open sores, and looked to be ten to twelve years old. He had a chipped tooth and a deafeningly loud meow. He threw himself against our bodies as soon as we stepped outside.

Snow was piled up almost a foot, and the temperature was below freezing. My husband and I were doing what we could for neighborhood animals that were too wild to come inside. We left fresh water and food out several times a day for wildlife and stray cats. We even set up a box outside with a heating pad inside for a stray ginger kitty who didn't let us hold her but still hung around.

So when I looked out the window one night and saw eyes staring at my window from deep inside the box, I assumed the eyes belonged to the little orange cat — until a skinny, black male cat stepped out of the box long enough to grab a bite to eat.

I'm sure he thought he'd died and gone to heaven. On his first visit to our covered patio, he found food, water, and a box with a heated blanket inside. He also found humans who happened to be crazy about cats.

I went outside to introduce myself to him, and I was stunned by how rough his skin looked. He had cuts on his lower back, large patches of hair missing and very scaly skin. I kept an eye on him for several days, keeping a heated blanket turned on for him and making sure he didn't want for food or water. I told my husband that I would be surprised if he made it through the winter considering his condition and what I'd assumed was his advanced age.

The joke was on me.

This black kitty was still around when the thaw came, and he loved us more than ever. He was still underweight, but I could no longer see ribs. And as his hair began to fill in and his wound started to heal, I began to realize that he wasn't as old as I'd assumed.

But, holy cow, did he love us. He followed our car down the driveway when we left, and he jumped in the car as soon as we pulled up and opened our doors.

As much as I loved him back, I doubted our inside cat (another black cat, this one a girl, Janie) would tolerate a new addition. She had always panicked when I'd tried to give her a furry sibling before, so we decided that as much as we loved the new guy, he would have to stay outside — until he got very, very sick.

Being the sweet boy that he was, he wouldn't fight back when other stray male cats attacked, and our little friend showed up one day with a bad sore on his back. It oozed and looked bad, and I told myself on Friday night that if it still looked bad the next day, I'd find a weekend vet to take him to.

At 6:30 the next morning, I opened the back door to feed him. For the first time in the weeks that we'd known him, he wasn't on the patio. I went looking for him and found him curled up under a shrub in my front yard, quietly preparing to die.

Not on my watch, kid.

I rushed him to a vet, who informed me that he was feverish and about to die. I spent $600 on surgery and medicine, and the stray black cat became *our* black cat, Edgar (Eddie when he feels casual), named after Edgar Allan Poe.

He had to wear a cone for a few weeks after his surgery, and our girl cat had no idea what sort of black sunflower she was dealing with when we introduced them for the first time.

The first few days were spent with my boy in a cone of shame, bumping off of walls and corners. (He couldn't navigate well with his cone.) Our princess crept after him from a distance like Gollum, hissing when he got too close but otherwise handling herself with aplomb.

Fast forward to now, almost five years later. The cat I thought was old was found to be barely older than our other cat. He now weighs around fifteen pounds and lives like a king. We learned quickly that he knows how to play fetch, and when we sing to him, he caterwauls and sings back. He begs for bacon and ham and demands attention constantly. He knocks on our closet door to get our attention while we're sleeping, or he knocks everything off our dresser when the closet trick doesn't work.

And he has still taught us some things:

1. Opportunity is sometimes right around the corner. I think about how he must have felt, sick and starving in a foot of snow, when he decided to approach our patio, probably one of the last stops before he would have starved to death. And like Paradise before him, there shone our supply of food, water and heated comfort. I'm so glad he didn't give up.

2. Sometimes, we have to let people help us. He couldn't heal his wounds on his own. Only medicine and a vet could. We have to let people do things for us that we can't manage ourselves.

3. People — and cats — can surprise us. I didn't think there was even the slightest chance that our diva cat was going to accept another inside cat. But she finally did decide to accept a scrawny, howling boy with a cone on his head and a drainage tube hanging out of his backside.

Now, if you'll excuse me, I have to wrap up this story. Eddie thinks it's time for dinner, but he doesn't want the dry food sitting out. And the wet food he tried an hour ago isn't his favorite, so now I need to find exactly what the king wants.

He's got it good.

But we've got it even better.

— Emily Dill —

28

Tummy Tickles

*People who love cats have some
of the biggest hearts around.*
~Susan Easterly

Newly divorced, I drove away from my old home with little more than the clothes on my back and a fluffy cat snuggled under my arm. My cat Princess wouldn't have had it any other way. We'd been through thick and thin together, so we were off on our own again.

Princess loved being with me, and we were inseparable. Her soft, thick fur just invited being caressed. However, she guarded her highly sensitive tummy with her life. As much as I would have loved giving her snow-white, fuzzy belly a rub, it wasn't going to happen anytime soon. She hid it so well from me that I rarely even had a peek at it.

I've lived with a lot of animals throughout my life, mostly dogs and cats adopted from the local animal shelters. All of the dogs loved having their tummies rubbed, while many of the cats were indifferent. Cats are known to be very protective of their stomachs, mainly because it leaves them completely exposed to danger if uncovered. The hair follicles on a cat's belly are also hypersensitive, so they can be overstimulated.

My friend Molly loves to tickle kitty tummies, so she would repeatedly try to rub my cat's belly, considering it a personal challenge. This only made Princess even more protective of her delicate stomach. Soon, she wanted nothing more to do with Molly and hid whenever she came to visit.

Eventually, I recovered enough mentally from my divorce to consider dating again and was invited out to dinner. My date arrived a little early, so I invited him in while I finished getting ready. I was pleased to overhear him talking to Princess as I grabbed my purse and headed for the door. By the time I got there, they were having a regular conversation as he crouched down at her level, with Princess rubbing her head on his trousers.

Our dinner date went marvelously, so we arranged for another the following week. Though delighted with everything so far, I wanted to take things slowly. When my date arrived even earlier than the last time, he explained that he was also a cat aficionado who would gladly spend time with Princess while I got ready for our evening out. By the time I was ready to go, Princess was looking lovingly into his clear blue eyes as she snuggled on his lap. While I was taking things slowly, Princess had other ideas. I'm ashamed to admit that I was getting a little jealous of her unabashed flirting.

Dinner date number three took place at my date's house. We were getting to know each other pretty well by now, so I was comfortable going there. Happily, Princess was invited too, and the three of us had a wonderful meal together. My new friend was a charming host and excellent cook, making a delectable feast for us to enjoy. Princess loved her dinner and the extra attention she was getting. She spent the rest of the evening sniffing around the rooms and rolling around on the carpets, making herself at home. I was beginning to get confused about who was dating whom.

Our next dinner together was at my place, and my guest arrived bringing chocolates and flowers for me along with treats and toys for Princess. My apartment was tiny, so I could easily chat from the kitchen as we enjoyed a glass of wine, while he wandered over to give Princess some attention in the living room. I took our hot dinner out of the oven and was heading to the dining table with it when I saw a sight that made me gasp.

Princess was sprawled out on the couch with her fuzzy belly straight up in the air for the first time ever, getting a gentle tummy rub from our new friend. Her face expressed pure bliss. I placed our dinner on the table before I dropped it and walked over in disbelief. I had never had a close look at Princess's beautiful tummy, while here was a new person in our lives giving her a stomach massage. It was unbelievable.

Needless to say, our relationship progressed much more quickly after that. Clearly, Princess had given this man her ultimate stamp of approval by trusting him with her precious tummy. Thanks to her bold moves and female feline intuition, we soon became a family of three.

— Donna L. Roberts —

29

Enter Love

A meow massages the heart.
~Stuart McMillan

I wasn't looking to adopt a cat for myself. It was my mother's birthday, and my sister and I had agreed that Mom needed a cat. Yes, she needed the soft warmth of a kitty, but she also needed to be reminded of her fierce independence and inner beauty.

Several years before, our lives had taken an abrupt and traumatic turn. At the time, we thought it was for the worst. My parents got divorced, and my mother remarried a charming man who turned out to be less than charming behind closed doors. Regrettably, we had already moved across the country with him, leaving our support network behind.

Now, we stood in the cat shelter searching for the kitty we had seen online. My heart sank as I recognised one of the kitties curled up into a tight, fluffy ball, her tail acting as a barrier to the outside world. I had secretly fallen in love with her picture, but I was not in a position to take on another responsibility. I was a single mom to an autistic baby, and I already had a little dog. That was enough for now, until I was on my feet again.

I sighed, turning away from the quarantine cage (my little friend had a cold) and started toward the front of the room. "I think I've found one, C.C.!" my sister called from near the door where she stood holding my nine-month-old son.

"I'm coming!" I called, noting my son was getting restless and beginning to fuss. My stomach lurched in alarm. When Johnny started fussing, I had to leave or face being kicked out. Very few people tolerated his spine-tingling screeches. We had to find a cat quickly. My sister would never forgive me if we didn't get our mom's present. "I'm coming!" I called again, my frantic eyes focused on the figures ahead.

A dark blob coming from behind me drew my attention away for a split-second. I felt a scream catch in my throat as a large black shadow leapt over my shoulder and into my arms. My eyes widened as the largest cat I had ever seen wrapped her giant black paws around my neck and pressed her startling green eyes to my forehead. Her deep, rich purrs began instantly soothing away the stress that had been bunching my neck and shoulders together.

The black cat rubbed her silky face down my cheek, stopping at my chin to lick and nibble it. I stood in awed silence, breathless. Her paws tightened around my neck, drawing me into a comforting hug.

"She's never done that before," the shelter volunteer said in surprise. "She seems to be saying, 'I've been waiting for you.'"

I looked down at the beautiful, fluffy black cat, my heart pounding with the realisation that something big had just happened. "She's very happy and sociable," I agreed, unwilling to presume anything.

The volunteer shook her head. "No, this isn't how she usually acts. Normally, she's aloof and distant."

I laughed as I allowed her to nibble the end of my nose. "This kitty, aloof?"

"She's been waiting for you," the volunteer said firmly. "You must take her home. Tonight."

I smiled into the cat's emerald eyes. "I would love to, but I can't."

"I'll waive the fee," the volunteer stated. "Just give her a good home, which I know you'll do. She's clearly saying that she's yours."

"But I don't have transport," I began. "Although I would love to take her home immediately. She's exactly what I've always wanted in a kitty, even down to her long, angora-like fur."

"There's no doubt she's yours," the volunteer said with a knowing smile. "You can use one of our transport carriers."

"Okay," I agreed, holding the kitty closer to me, my mind and heart not believing my ears.

My sister and I decided to make a special outing at another time and allow Mom to choose her own cat. Now, it was time to take this little kitten home to join my family.

I was concerned about how my dog, Angel, and Johnny would respond to the newcomer. But Lakshmi demonstrated right away that she belonged with us.

The first time Johnny began screaming, Lakshmi startled me by jumping up on Johnny's bed, purring loudly. Pressing her face against his forehead, she lay down close to him, pressing her long body against his. To my astonishment, Johnny calmed. Later that evening, as I was preparing his bottle, he started fussing. Again, Lakshmi lay down next to him, pressing herself against his body, purring loudly. I was horrified to see Johnny pulling her fur, screaming all the while. Lakshmi just purred, blinking her vibrant green eyes lovingly. When I tried to make Johnny release her fur, she glared warningly at me and wouldn't allow me to interfere.

From that time on, whenever Johnny began to have a meltdown, Lakshmi and Angel would come and act as a soothing weight for him. As my son grew into adolescence, Lakshmi and Angel have been there to support me in his raising and care. Constantly, they remind me to act and react from a place of love and acceptance. No matter how horribly Johnny acts, Lakshmi always acts in love. She is a fierce protectress, growling warning when an intruder is near.

Raising an autistic child alone can be a lonely, daunting journey, but with the help of Lakshmi and Angel, I've kept my sanity and remembered love.

— Cynthia Carter-Trent —

30

A Proper Introduction

You can't stay in your corner of the Forest
waiting for others to come to you.
You have to go to them sometimes.
~A.A. Milne, Winnie-the-Pooh

Scooter was the first pet Jack and I shared as a married couple. He was a gorgeous tuxedo with an aloof personality. We picked him out at the ASPCA in Manhattan the first year we were married. At that time, we both worked in the city and lived in a tiny railroad-style apartment on the top floor of a five-floor walkup on the East Side.

Within two years, we realized that city life was not for us, and so one day we packed up our few possessions and moved into a one-bedroom in the suburbs of Connecticut. A mansion compared to our city dwelling.

Moving to Connecticut meant that we would have to commute back into Manhattan. The trip in and out of the city would take three hours daily. This meant that our baby boy would be alone for more time then we felt comfortable. What should we do?

We decided that Scooter needed a friend. So off to the local shelter we went in search of the perfect companion for our dear boy. We would look for a female cat, hoping that Scooter might feel less threatened by a female.

Entering the shelter was quite overwhelming. There were long rows of cages — dogs in their kennels and cats stacked on top of one another — and so many sounds and smells commanding our attention.

There were probably thirty cats at the shelter that day. So how to decide? One by one a volunteer brought different cats for us to meet. Most looked understandably terrified as we tried to pet or hold them. When we were presented with a small gray cat with black stripes I knew we had found her. She melted into my arms as soon as she was handed to me. Within seconds she was purring and rubbing her head against my arm. I looked at Jack and he looked at me and nodded. This bundle would be coming home with us. We would have to wait twenty-four hours so they could do a background check. Feeling bittersweet as they posted an "Adopted" sign on her cage, we left her behind but were excited to prepare for the next day.

Books and articles we had read suggested that when you bring home a new cat you should not touch or hold it. You should bring her in and let your resident cat approach her and feel her out. From what we understood, Scooter should accept her into the family and then introduce her to us. We were determined to follow the instructions so as to have the perfect introduction.

We decided to name her Yaicha, after a Pousette-Dart Band song we loved. She was so small and so sweet. She made us smile. We were trusting she would have the same effect on Scooter.

We picked her up Saturday morning so that we would have the entire weekend to acclimate the two of them before we left for work on Monday. We were careful not to touch her as we bundled her in a towel that did not have our scent on it. Carefully we put her in a lined box and brought her home.

Quietly we entered the apartment and placed the box in the middle of the living room floor. Then we sat on the couch anticipating a Disney-like reception: new big brother to baby. "Scooter," we called. "Kitty, Kitty, Kitty."

We could hear Scooter in the bedroom. He was on our bed. Then, *thump* — as he jumped from the bed. We could hear his light *patter-patter* across the bedroom until we saw his gorgeous green eyes looking at us.

"Hey Scoots. Come here and see what we have for you." He was approaching us when he heard a slight meow come from the box. He turned and looked at the foreign object that had started to slightly move. He looked back at us again but then started in the direction of the box. Jack and I both let out a slight giggle as he walked towards Yaicha. He stopped, gave the box a quick sniff and then continued past to his water bowl.

Jack and I looked at each other. What just happened? How could he have no interest? Aren't cats supposed to be curious?

After a few loud sips he left the bowl, walked right past the box again and then sat not one yard from Yaicha to clean himself. We watched him preen for ten minutes, then decided it was time to intervene. As I kept Scooter's attention, Jack went over and gingerly tipped the box and out tumbled the little ball of fur. Jack joined me on the couch and we watched what we hoped would be a seamless introduction.

Once Yaicha got her bearings, she started to investigate her new surroundings: carpet, toys, and Scooter. She seemed delighted to have another cat so close to her and proceeded to nuzzle against him.

Scooter, on the other hand, was horrified. What was this? He turned abruptly, hissed at Yaicha, and then swatted her. He turned to head back to the bedroom but not before throwing us a most pointed glare that displayed his complete disdain.

This back and forth went on all day. Sunday morning we arose and saw that conditions remained the same. Scooter was asleep in our room and Yaicha in a little bed in the living room.

I put out some food for the two. Scooter heard the food landing in his bowl and ran to eat. Yaicha went to eat too, but when Scooter hissed at her she backed off. It broke my heart. This little motherless kitten wanted to be loved and Scooter was denying her that right.

The day went on the same. Yaicha would approach and Scooter would reject her, throwing her a swat or hiss. That night I finally had enough.

"Scooter," I scolded. "How could you be so selfish? So mean? This little girl deserves a family too." With him well lectured, I picked up

Yaicha and snuggled her against me. I gave her kisses and scratched her behind her ear until her purring could be heard in the bedroom.

Jack emerged from the other room, smiling at me. "So what happened to no human intervention?"

"I couldn't help it. Scooter was being so selfish."

With that declaration, Jack took her from me and the three of us sat on the couch together. Scooter was only mildly interested.

As night fell and we readied for bed, I went to turn off the living room lights and to check on the cats. I was disturbed to not find Yaicha in her bed. Scooter was lying quietly in his blanket-lined bed.

I went into the bedroom to look for her. Jack was already in bed reading. "What are you looking for?" he asked as I lifted the blankets for a better view under the bed.

"Yaicha," I said. "She isn't in her bed."

Jack got out of bed and went into the other room. After a few minutes, I heard him say, "I found her. You'll never guess."

He brought me past her bed and over to Scooter, who was half-hidden under his blanket. I stared at him as he lifted his head with an annoyed teenager glare that screamed, *WHAT?* Then I noticed a little movement under the blanket, and a little sleepy, gray head appeared. I heard a purring noise but wasn't quite sure from which feline it came. Then I felt a big purr come from me as I realized, that maybe what Scooter really needed was for Yaicha to have our scent on her. That by us showing him we loved and accepted her, he could love her as well. That was the best introduction of all.

—Jeanne Blandford—

What a Character!

31

Zen Master

I have lived with several Zen masters —
all of them cats.
~Eckhart Tolle

The tip of his tail sways gently. Eyes stare without seeing as his body relaxes into the cushion and the lids sink slowly like a sunset. It might appear to be a bored cat falling asleep because he can't think of anything better to do, but Snickers has entered into Zen meditation. He purrs, not an ordinary my-tummy-is-full purr, but his version of the mystic "Om." He is beyond trivialities in transcendental peace.

When the front door slams in the quiet, Snickers does not start in alarm like most cats. He does not even raise his head. One eye eases open, gazes at the disturbance in the oneness, recognizes that it is my wife, Carol, and then closes. Should a vacuum roar in the next room, he will not climb the curtains or dive under the bed, but walk away calmly from the barbaric beast.

Snickers disdains toys because he understands the emptiness of material things. My wife, who does not believe Snickers practices Zen, buys him furry mice on strings that she drags past him, mice that squeak, and mice filled with catnip. She believes if she finds the right toy, Snickers will pounce on it, tumble over and bat it into the air, and then hold it with front paws while his rear paws kick it. She wants him to have fun. "Cats are supposed to play," she mutters. "He doesn't do anything all day long!"

"He's meditating," I say.

"Yeah, right."

Snickers sniffs at today's new toy—a wind-up mouse—and turns it over with one paw to make sure it is no more than it appears. Then he glances up at Carol with disappointed, liquid eyes, the eyes of a Buddha with whiskers. When she winds the spring, the mechanical mouse zips across the floor and bumps into him. After it burrows into his hind leg and buzzes relentlessly for the third time, he rises so it can rattle past until it hits a wall, spins around, tears off in another direction and finally winds down. He watches it sputter to a stop, glances at us, and then at the silent machine. If a cat could shrug and speak, he would say, "Really?"

But I don't want to give the wrong impression. Snickers is not one of those skinny, self-denying swamis. He's more like the fat Buddha statues with roly-poly bellies one sees in Chinese restaurants. He eats the meals he likes with relish and licks himself lovingly afterward until his fur is shiny. It resembles the grooming other cats give themselves, but he performs it as if it were yoga. "This is philosophy in action," I say.

I feel that we misnamed him. It's embarrassing because Snickers acts nothing like his frivolous name. He ought to have been called Ling Pao or Mustapha, something exotic and mysterious. But he does not seem to mind. I imagine him saying, "What is a name? Is it me? I think not. Call me what you wish. I am not chained to any name." I hate to admit it, but he does sometimes act a little superior.

Like all of the nineteen cats we've had over the years, he was a stray. One morning, as I was building a porch for our house, I turned around and there he sat as if transported through the air, staring up at me with large eyes. "Well, hello there, buddy," I said. "Where did you come from—the Starship Enterprise?" He blinked and did not deny it. He hung around the porch for a few days, ignoring my hammering, accepting our food and contemplating the situation. A week later, he simply followed me into the house and never left. He's been here years, although if I didn't connect his arrival with building the porch, I'd have said he seems to have been with us forever.

Last night, a gray mouse—not one of my wife's toys, but a breathing one — appeared in our living room. It emerged from behind the television. On the couch, Snickers perked up, ears pricked forward, eyes dilated. I was almost surprised as much by his reaction as by the appearance of the mouse.

Snickers slithered to the floor, a sneaky move I'd never seen him make. Belly to the ground, he crept a few steps, and then paused, rigid, intense like other cats would stalk prey. The mouse sat up on its haunches, sniffed and twitched its whiskers, with its tiny front paws held to its chest. Snickers crept another two steps, now within three feet of the mouse.

My wife gripped my hand, and I gripped back. We certainly did not want a mouse in our house, nor did we want to witness a bloodbath. But what froze us from doing anything was the possibility that this might be the moment that cracked Snickers' serenity. Was he about to become a cat? His tail waggled, and his rear end quivered. The mouse crept closer to him and sat up again. They were scarcely more than a paw swipe apart. Although it's difficult to tell with a mouse, his beady black eyes seemed to stare into Snickers' eyes.

Then Snickers relaxed. He settled into the rug, and the tail slowed its waggling, even as the locked gaze continued. "Oh, this is unbelievable!" I said. I went to the closet, got an empty tennis-ball container and walked over to the loving pair. I tiptoed, but there was no need. Neither took any notice of me. I bent and lowered the plastic container over the mouse. "Can't you be a cat for once?" I said.

Snickers turned his head as if to ask, "What are you doing? Don't you see we reached an understanding here?" The mouse was circling around inside the plastic can and put up its feet. There was an aura of betrayal in the room.

"Oh, you're not putting that on me!" I said. "This is collaboration with the enemy."

"Are you all right?" my wife asked. "What do you mean by 'collaboration'? Who are you talking to?"

I slipped a piece of cardboard under the open end of the can so the mouse had to hop on it, and then I turned over the tennis-ball container and headed to the door. "What are you doing?" she asked.

"I'm going to take the mouse to the park," I said, "before this one invites all of his friends over for meditation sessions. Somebody here has to be the cat."

— Garrett Bauman —

Othello, The Amazing Black Cat

All cats like being the focus of attention.
~Peter Gray

I n September 2015, my partner David and I rescued a starving black cat that wandered into our garden. After spending a month trying unsuccessfully to find out if he had a home, we decided to adopt him. We called him Othello.

Years ago, we used to enter our Maine Coon cats in cat shows. At the beginning of 2016, I began to wonder if we could show Othello. He was only an ordinary little moggy, all black except for a tiny white patch on his chest and a similar patch on his tummy. But non-pedigrees, or "Household Pets" as they're called in cat-show terminology, are judged on presentation and temperament. Othello looked really good now; he had put on weight, and his black fur shone. He didn't seem to mind being groomed, and we thought he might cope with being given a bath, which is essential for a show cat. Best of all, he was a friendly, confident cat, who didn't seem to mind new places and meeting people.

He was about eight years old according to our vet, which was a bit old for shows, but we decided to give it a go. We entered him in a small show fairly close to home, but decided that if he seemed upset or unhappy, we'd withdraw him and take him home.

Othello took to it as though he'd been going to shows all his life. He sat on the table and purred at the judge. He seemed to be enjoying himself. In her report, the judge said he was a "delightful little fellow." And he won his class, gaining his first Master Cat certificate. He would need three of these to gain a Master Cat title, so we took him to another show a couple of months later. This time, it was a double show, two shows in one location, which meant two chances to win. We would have been delighted if he'd won one of them, but we were utterly amazed when he won his class at both shows. That was three wins. Othello was a Master Cat!

From then on, it would get much tougher for him to win. Instead of just competing against cats in his colour class, he would be up against all the other Master Cats for the Grand Master Cat certificates. "He won't get any further," we said. "After all, he's only an ordinary black cat." But to our genuine surprise, he won three more shows and became a Grand Master Cat!

Meanwhile, he was getting quite a following at shows and on social media. Everyone loves rags-to-riches stories, and people loved this friendly little black cat that had been rescued from likely death. At shows, people asked to see him and wanted to stroke him. And the judges seemed to love him. Eventually, we gave him his own Facebook page, and he started acquiring more and more "likes," often from people we'd never heard of. Clearly, there was something special about him.

However, again we said to each other that he wouldn't get any further at shows. He'd now be against all the other Grand Master Cats, and he'd need five wins for the next title of Imperial Grand Master Cat. How could he possibly do that? Amazingly, by the end of the year, he had managed it. In fact, he became an Imperial Grand Master Cat less than a year after we first started showing him. This would be pretty good for any cat, but it was incredible for one who was a starving street cat just over a year earlier. We couldn't quite believe it.

We were going to enter him for the newly created Olympian classes, where he would compete against all the other Imperial Grand Master Cats, but then we began to realise that Othello wasn't quite himself. His shiny black fur was getting dull, and he was losing weight. We were concerned that he might be ill, so we took him to the vet and had some tests done. Othello had hyperthyroidism, or an overactive thyroid gland. We now had a choice: keep him on medication for the rest of his life or try a newer treatment — radioactive iodine (I131), which is a complete cure.

We decided to go for the I131 and booked Othello into one of the few centres in the UK that performed this treatment. We had to leave Othello at the centre for a few days, and once again he proved what a special little cat he was. The staff clearly loved him, describing him as a "bonkers" cat who talked a lot and wanted people near him all the time. When we collected him, he was relaxed and seemed to think he'd just had a holiday! Best of all, his thyroid levels were down to normal. The treatment had worked, and he was cured!

Numerous people had followed Othello's treatment on social media. By now, he had even more followers than he had as a show cat. We decided he would just live happily at home from then on since he was officially about twelve years old. However, it seemed that he might be much older. A year or so later, he developed mild kidney disease. He got progressively worse quite rapidly, and a few weeks ago we had to let him go.

Othello will never be forgotten, either by us, his show buddies or his social-media followers. He wasn't quite as famous as Grumpy Cat, who died just a few weeks before him, but he had become a very well-known cat who appealed to all sorts of people. His Facebook page is still up, and he still gets new followers, though we don't quite know why. He truly was an amazing little black cat.

— Helen Krasner —

33

Paying for My Sins

Animals know more than we think and
think a great deal more than we know.
~Irene Pepperberg

I learned the hard way that a cat can hold a grudge.

Years ago, I was the proud companion to two Siamese cats, Samantha and Missy. My husband Jim and I owned a trailer park several miles out of the city, and the cats, while having free rein to wander around the park during the day, were always safely indoors after dinner.

They were typical Siamese, affectionate and aloof at the same time, totally aware of their royal blood but willing to dole out their favours when merited. Missy was a laid-back cat, but Samantha was an independent soul, certain enough of herself to chase a German Shepherd from our yard to his own on a regular basis.

One week, I discovered a cat could also have some less desirable qualities, like the ability to hold a grudge. I took a short holiday to visit my mother, leaving Jim and the cats to fend for themselves. On the day I was packing to return home, I received an unsettling call from Jim. "I hate to tell you this," he said, "but I thought I'd better warn you. I haven't seen either of the cats since the day you left."

I didn't give him a very pleasant reply, but he went on to say, "I think they're all right, though. I put out food every day, and every time I check the dishes in the morning, it's gone. But they won't come when I call."

The explanation didn't make me any less fearful. With the number of raccoons and other wildlife roaming the country, any animal could be eating the cat food. And that thought took me to an even worse one.

When I arrived home, I ran into the house and dropped my suitcases on the living-room floor. I called out to see if, by some miracle, the cats had returned. Jim gave me a sad shake of his head. Then, in a flash, I felt warm fur twisting around my ankles and soft purring chirps of contentment from Samantha and Missy.

I was ready to pounce on them with delight but was stopped cold by Samantha. She stared directly into my eyes. Then, with a flourish, she turned her back, raised her tail like a flag and disappeared into the kitchen. When I followed her there, she left the room. For three days, that cat wouldn't come when I called, look me in the face, or allow any affection.

It wasn't due to a sudden personality disorder. When my friend Teri came over for coffee, Samantha greeted her with joyous abandon, waltzing around her legs in ecstasy. "Wow!" said Teri. "She's never been this affectionate with me before." Teri sat down; Samantha jumped on her knee. Teri left; Samantha disappeared into one of her hidey-holes.

It was like that with every other person who crossed our threshold. It didn't matter who — a neighbour, tradesperson, or someone selling funeral plots — they all got extra-special treatment, rubs, purrs and delighted expressions. As each person left, Samantha would turn to me and repeat her gesture from the day I arrived home.

Eventually, she mellowed, and I was back in her good graces. I learned my lesson, though. If I ever went away on a holiday again, the cats were going to have to come with me.

— Sharon McGregor —

34

To Catch a Mouse

After scolding one's cat one looks into its face
and is seized by the ugly suspicion
that it understood every word.
And has filed it for reference.
~Charlotte Gray

"**M**elissa, this is gross!" my husband exclaimed as he looked at the remains of a lizard our cat had left in our living room.

"Well, John," I answered, "at least we know Sam can deal with any mice who may find their way in here."

John shook his head. "No! That's not happening."

I glanced over at our furry Samwise stretched out at my feet. Content that we had found his latest exploit, our long-haired silvery gray cat had rolled over onto his back and fixed his eyes on me, begging for a belly rub.

"I wouldn't be so sure. He just might surprise you," I said, bending down to scratch the furry tummy. Having grown up in the country, this cat fit my standards for a mouser. Samwise's body was so long that he could recline his head on my shoulder while his feet lay near my hip and his tail hung just above my knees as I carried him around the condo. His shoulders were nice and wide, and while he wasn't necessarily fat, his stocky girth showed that he had grown into his quarter-sized paws. Yet even after I pointed out all these natural attributes, my husband still insisted that Sam had too much of the gentle disposition of his hobbit namesake to make an effective mouser.

So I shrugged my shoulders and went to retrieve a napkin to dispose of our kitty's latest "gift."

A few days later, when all traces of the lizard had been removed from the carpet, Samwise and I were alone for a quiet evening while John worked the late shift at the hospital. Deciding to wait up, I turned on my laptop, plopped down on the carpet, and opened the file of a fantasy story I had been working on.

Losing myself in my faraway medieval world, I barely noticed when Samwise walked by my laptop. I reached for my mouse, heard a thunk, and felt my hand close around absolutely nothing! Zapped back to reality, I turned to my right and found the gadget had completely disappeared. Next came a frantic thud of paws intermixed with a strange clanking sound. I looked up to see Samwise running away with a cord clutched between his teeth as he dragged my computer's mouse behind him!

I laughed as the conversation with my husband rushed to mind. This may not have been how I had imagined it would happen, but technically speaking, Samwise was a mouser.

— Melissa Abraham —

35

Cat in a Tree

Firemen never know what they will encounter
on each call but proceed with the same level
of commitment and service.
~Byron Pulsifer

I have a friend who's a veterinarian. She likes to say that cats never really get stuck in trees. They just like to mess with their humans. "Did you ever see a tree full of little skeletons?" she asks. I used to laugh when she said that. But not anymore.

I have two cats. Seeker is a long-haired Calico Munchkin. (I'd never heard of Munchkins before I adopted her from a foster home.) She's half the size of a normal adult cat — everybody mistakes her for a kitten — and so short she can't jump on the table in one bound. She has to jump from a chair. But she climbs trees like she's half-squirrel.

Blossom is larger and older, but she lacks authority. She came to the house a year after Seeker and has always wondered why she's not the boss. She's a two-tone meatloaf Manx in gray and white. She has an extra toe on each foot and firmly believes that means she has the dexterity to type. (She's helping me now.) She can jump to the table easily, a skill she uses frequently to embarrass Seeker.

Since her short legs left her at a permanent disadvantage for jumping on tables, Seeker would often issue a counterchallenge to Blossom, running up and down tree trunks for Blossom to see. If Blossom couldn't see, Seeker would settle on a branch like a leopard, waiting for prey. As soon as Blossom stepped out, Seeker would swoop down the trunk and Blossom would jump back a foot and shriek.

Eventually, Seeker's taunts were too much for Blossom. One day, she went up the tree after the little cat. The "up" part turned out to be easy.

Seeker rushed in to tell us about it, waving her tail like a semaphore flag. I followed her outside, and there was Blossom up the tree. At first, I didn't see the problem. Blossom was just sitting there. I shrugged and went back to making dinner.

An hour later, Seeker figured it was dinnertime and came right in. But Blossom — who usually takes dinner very seriously — did not. Very odd. I went to the foot of the tree and called. She mewed, but she didn't come down. Unlike many cats, she usually comes when called. That was odd and I started to worry.

We were in and out of the house all evening, putting bowls of food out to tempt her. We tried calling, whistling, clapping, and waving her favorite toys. We got out the ladder, but it wasn't tall enough. It started to rain. Blossom hates the rain and being wet. Her crying got louder.

My vet friend is wrong. Blossom was stuck. Maybe most cats can get down by themselves. Maybe cats need a tail for proper balance when climbing, which my tailless Manx didn't have. But whatever the reason, my cat couldn't get down. She was trying. We saw her turning around and around. We watched her grapple with the branch and the trunk. She simply could not do it. And there was nothing we could do, either.

Come midnight, we had to give up. We couldn't even see her anymore. It rained all night. First thing in the morning, I went out. Blossom had stopped crying, but she started up again when she saw me. I tried all the same tricks — calling, clapping, whistling, offering food — to no avail. She cried and cried.

I couldn't stand it anymore. I went back inside where I couldn't hear the crying. I pulled up Google and typed in "how to get a cat out of tree." I was surprised to learn that there really are companies that will come and get your cat out of a tree. But they're expensive. Very expensive. I actually called one. They were sympathetic and polite. But expensive.

Still, if I'd had the money, I would have paid it. I'd have grumbled about it, but I'd have paid it. But I was between paychecks and just didn't have it.

I stared at my laptop. Should I try to find a cheaper company? Then I saw the pictures. There's always a line of tiny photos marked "images" at the top of the page when you search Google. This particular line of images contained a cartoon showing a fireman rescuing a cat from a tree. We've all seen pictures like that. Comic books and old TV shows are full of them. Small-town firefighters are famous for rescuing kittens stuck in trees. It's a symbol of how helpful they are.

But did it ever really happen? Recently? In any town larger than Mayberry? I'd certainly never heard of anyone calling the fire department for anything but a fire.

But I was desperate. I stuck my head outside. The rain had stopped, but I could still hear Blossom crying. She'd been up there for seventeen hours. She had to be getting hungry. So I called the Fire Department.

"Do you rescue cats?" I asked.

There was a long pause before a young man answered, "Are you kidding me?" I assured him I wasn't kidding. In fact, I poured my heart out. He probably thought I was going to cry. Soon, a fire truck rolled up the street (with no siren), and four brawny young men rushed out with a really tall ladder.

One of them was a "cat expert." (He'd had a cat once when he was a kid.) He looked like a samurai, all done up in a leather vest, heavy gloves and funny helmet. Just as well. Blossom bites. The cat expert grabbed a large carryall and swarmed up the ladder one-handed. Blossom did not see the carryall as an instrument of rescue. Seconds later, the carryall came flying down.

The fireman gave up on persuading Blossom to cooperate. He grabbed her and hugged her to his chest. (Hey, he was dressed for it!) She snarled all the way down. But on the ground, she put on a great air of nonchalance and strolled off to check out her food dish. I thanked her rescuers with considerably more enthusiasm. They wouldn't take tips, but a few days later I took them a homemade cheesecake. Heroism should be commended.

What is the moral of this story? I don't know if it counts as a moral, but I learned two things. First, cats really can get stuck in trees. Don't let anyone (even a vet) tell you otherwise.

And second? Firefighters are our friends. They really are there to help!

— Michaele Jordan —

36

Harley the Cat

It is in the nature of cats to do a certain amount
of unescorted roaming.
~Adlai Stevenson

We called him Harley. My wife picked the name because she said that when he purred, it sounded like a Harley-Davidson motorbike idling.

It was a cold morning in spring when he adopted us. Tracy had left an upstairs window open to allow a gust or two of fresh spring air to circulate through the house. Even though we lived in the inner metropolitan area of London, which, in those days, was known for its thick pea-soup smog, we were largely immune from the pollution as we lived up on the high ground of Hampstead where fresh air survived.

This did not protect us from the cold, so we tended to keep the windows closed throughout winter and open them again in springtime.

We'd had enough fresh air, so Tracy went to close the window.

"Rob! I need some help here." Her plaintive call for help drifted down the stairs. I duly responded and arrived to find my beloved staring with an exasperated expression at a large tomcat sitting on our windowsill. How he got there remains a mystery to this day. I tried to catch him, but he was too fast and elusive for me. Short of pushing him off the window ledge, there was no way we were going to evict him forcibly.

Finally, we tempted him inside with some chopped-up meat scraps.

After his meal, he followed us downstairs and made himself comfortable on my armchair. It was me who had to relocate.

We became Harley's humans for two years. His was not a continuous tenure. He would disappear for nights at a time, only to reappear on that windowsill when it suited him.

Then I was promoted — to Singapore. That entailed packing up everything, including finding a home for Harley. When we canvassed our neighbors to adopt our cat, they claimed that Buster was *their* cat. Then the neighbors on the other side claimed Clyde was *their* cat, and so it went on through the district.

Eventually, we said a tearful goodbye to Harley, Buster, Clyde, etc., with the good feeling that he had plenty of humans to look after him when we were gone.

— Les Davies —

37

Chicken Soup for the Soul

When Tuxedo Let Go

*Anyone who tells you fatherhood is the greatest thing
that can happen to you, they are understating it.*
~Mike Myers

Springtime is kitten time in Southern California, and especially in our back yard. One year, lured by the lush bushes and trees on our property, we ended up with a bumper crop of strays — three mothers, three fathers, and ten kittens!

Since we didn't know where they came from, my husband Don and I decided to allow them to stay, raising the little ones until they were old enough for good homes. That meant teaching them to eat dry food, use the litter box, play games, respond to petting, and all the other skills they would need to "graduate" out to the big world.

Two of the mothers decided to have their families inside our house. For the next six weeks, they made themselves at home in a constantly changing series of nests — linen and clothes closets, my husband's pajama drawer, inside the sofa, and more. They took over the entire house!

Since these inside guests were always around us, they were tamed quickly. Eventually, both pairs of mothers and fathers and their adorable offspring all found loving homes — to our own cats' immense relief!

But that still left the outdoor family. The father, called Tuxedo because of his dignified black-and-white "outfit," belonged to a home a couple of streets away. But at least three times every day, this very proud and doting dad made the trip from his house to ours to check on his little family.

Nosy-Rosy, the mother, was bright, assertive, and very attentive. Her main problem was that she always came to our house to eat, but kept her two little ones hidden in our back yard. Finally, after much coaxing, we were able to get her and one of her kittens off to new homes, too.

That left one little ball of white fluff alone out in our bushes, afraid to leave her nest or let us befriend her, desperately wanting her mother and sibling back. As this tiny "powder puff" continued to refuse to touch either the food or water we set out for her near her hiding place, we began to despair for her life.

So did her father. Even though he was quite distraught over the disappearance of his mate and one offspring, Tuxedo still returned three times a day to check on his remaining jewel. He worried about the best way to help her, at first trying to lead her out of our yard and across the street to his own home. She wouldn't follow him, though.

Finally, not knowing what else to do, he brought the kitten up to our back door, where I'd left some dry cat food and water. He showed her how to eat and drink. All that night and the next day, the kitten sat there and ate and ate. But she still wouldn't have anything to do with us.

Then the next night about 3:00 a.m., I heard a strange noise outside my bedroom window and got up to peek. Tuxedo was showing his little daughter how to use our cat door and urging her to go through it — even though he had never been in our house and wasn't about to start now. Next thing I knew, she'd slipped inside.

After that, we no longer had to look for a good home for Powder Puff. She had one — ours! After that fateful night, she became part of our family, adored being petted, and stole our hearts. And, of course, we were thrilled with her. Imagine a "powder puff" that purred!

It was all because of the selfless love and patience of her father. Indeed, a year later, Tuxedo still came over every day — at exactly 5:00 a.m. and 8:00 p.m. — to call for his daughter. He watched her play and eat, kissed her, and then returned home each time, satisfied he'd done the best he could for her because of his never-wavering love.

It was a love so strong that he was willing to let his beloved child be loved by others, too — a lesson my husband and I also had to learn as our own children grew up and we faced an "empty nest."

Love, but let go.

Thank you, Tuxedo!

— Bonnie Compton Hanson —

38

Cory T. Cat's Special Ornaments

Who among us hasn't envied a cat's ability to ignore
the cares of daily life and to relax completely?
~Karen Brademeyer

He sat alone in his cage. Another day. Another meal. How had he ended up in a small cage surrounded by loud, strange cats and nice but strange people called volunteers?

Meanwhile, I sat alone 600 miles away, looking at my computer. It was time to move again. I didn't know much about Buffalo, New York, but I knew there would be snow, lots of it. After seven years in Washington, D.C., without a pet, I longed for one. I missed cuddling with my previous cats, Samantha and Sassafras. Samantha passed while I was in Kentucky, and Sassafras passed in California. The D.C. job had too much travel to be fair to a pet, but the new position wouldn't have as much travel, so it was time. I looked on the Buffalo animal shelter's website to see who needed me.

Knowing the stories about how black cats were mistreated, I stated that I would be happy with a black adult cat. There was one available, said the kind lady volunteer on the phone. However, the kind lady told me about another cat that had been with the shelter for six months. He was getting anxious, and the volunteer was afraid that he would soon become unadoptable. Would I consider a gray tabby cat instead?

So, on my first Friday in Buffalo, I drove to pick up the gray tabby cat.

Named Cory by the volunteers, he was overweight at sixteen pounds from the months of confinement. He also didn't like all the cats and noise around him and he had withdrawn. When I looked in on him, he turned his back on me. I said, "Dude, it's you and me. I'm all you got, so you better learn to like me." He looked back over his shoulder and stared at me. And that is how Cory the Cat adopted me.

I paid for him and took him home. He walked out of the carrier, sniffed around for a bit, and then settled down on my best couch, the one covered with beautiful Italian linen. I looked at the two cat beds that I had just purchased and questioned if they would ever be used. They wouldn't. At bedtime, I told Cory T. Cat, "It's time for bed." He looked at me, got down off the couch, and walked to the bedroom. He jumped on the bed, where he slept that night and many more on my right shoulder, purring pleasantly in my ear.

His first weekend in the new loft was exciting. As I unloaded moving boxes, he played hide-and-seek with the mounds of wrapping paper, and jumped in and out of the boxes. He enjoyed living in the loft. The twelve-foot windows gave him great "cat television" as he watched the birds flying around him. The long hallway was his soccer field; he ran jingle balls up and down its length. The living area with the couches, footstools, and tables served as a great obstacle course when he played with flying toys. In no time at all, he was down to twelve pounds, a weight he has kept since.

At Christmas, I put up a small tree on the breakfast table. Cory T. Cat immediately assumed the tree was for him, so I chose wooden ornaments. Twelve of the ornaments I placed on the tree were olive wood ones that I picked up in Bethlehem many years before. Cory became obsessed with two of these — one showing the Baby Jesus, and one showing the Holy Family in the familiar manger scene. No matter how many times I put them on the tree, he would pull them off, roll over them, love them with his face, and then lie on them. He never bothered any other ornaments or the garland or lights, but he would not leave those two ornaments on the tree. So, I left them loose under the tree. Every evening, he would roll on them and then lie on them and sleep.

Our companionship grew. We played together, watched television together, watched the snow and sights from the window together, and got to know each other. He "helped" me read my books and type on my laptop. When the Buffalo winters were at their worst and all the birds were gone for the season, I would play YouTube videos of birds on my laptop for him. He would enjoy them while I read books and waited for spring.

Two years later, I received word that I was moving again, this time to Honolulu. I was worried about the move for Cory T. Cat. He hated loud noises and being crated up in his carrier to go for his regular nail clippings. How would he survive a long plane trip? Also, there was a four-month quarantine before he could join me. How would he do in foster care after having been abandoned once before? Would he think I was abandoning him?

I moved to Honolulu in November. Cory T. Cat joined me in February. After twelve hours in a crate, he walked out as if he hadn't just flown all the way across the country and halfway across the Pacific Ocean. He wandered around and found the bed. I joined him there, and he quickly settled down on my right shoulder and started purring as if no time had passed at all.

The Honolulu condo is very different from the New York loft. Along with bedroom windows, complete with a cat tree to watch the birds and the neighbors, and kitchen windows complete with a counter for soaking up the sun and watching the children play in the pool below, there is a screened-in lanai. It looks over palm trees where doves and other birds sit and "talk" with Cory T. Cat, who "talks" back to them. Cory T. Cat is kept busy socializing with the birds, children, and neighbors.

This Christmas, I took out my decorations and set up a small tree on the kitchen counter for Cory T. Cat. As I rediscovered my olive wood ornaments, I wondered if Cory T. Cat would remember them. As a test, I put them on the back of the tree and then pushed the back of the tree against the window.

When Cory T. Cat got up from his nap, he walked over to the

tree and sniffed it. Almost immediately, he started head-butting the tree away from the window until he could get behind the tree. Once there, he found his two favorite ornaments — Baby Jesus and the Holy Family manger scene. He pulled them off the tree and nudged them around until they were at the front of the tree. Then he rolled over them again and again. Soon, he had settled down for a nap on them. Cory T. Cat may now be a Hawaiian cat, one who loves watching kids in the pool and talking with birds on his lanai, but he has never forgotten his special ornaments on his tree that signals his Christmas season.

— Sheila Embry —

Feline Fetish

*I have noticed that what cats most appreciate
in a human being is not the ability to produce food,
which they take for granted — but his or her
entertainment value.*
~Geoffrey Household

There's no doubt about it: In a previous life, Lavie must have been a famous diva. This little bundle of creamy, furry fluff honestly believes the world is here to adore her. And when Lavie stares at someone with her beautiful green eyes, she is utterly irresistible. One swoosh of her tail, and Lavie has put them under her spell.

She's partial to men, and since I'm female, she uses and abuses me. But she is crazy in love with Paul and Toby (our adult sons and her owners), who pamper her and treat her like the princess Lavie believes she is. I have never seen a cat who philanders so shamelessly and knows how to get her way with the men, even when she's naughty.

Our sons have their offices and bedrooms in the upstairs part of our cabin. When it's time for bed, Lavie and her brother Claus sleep upstairs in a large kennel so they can snooze close to their humans, but not get into trouble or hurt themselves during the night.

At one time, Paul had a habit of doing push-ups before turning in for the night. Normally, he'd put the cats in their kennel while he worked out on the floor, but one night he did his exercises while the cats were still out.

And we could see it in Lavie's eyes…. She definitely had a push-up fetish. The cat went wild. She ran to Paul, swished her tail in his face and kissed him. She purred. She meowed, flirting shamelessly while her human tried to continue his workout. With each up-and-down repetition, she'd slink around, and Paul would end up cackling so hard he couldn't finish his routine. All he could do was surrender to Lavie's affections and lie on the floor laughing hysterically.

After that, any time that Paul tried his push-ups while the cats were out of their kennel, Lavie turned into an amorous, out-of-control feline.

As time passed, Paul got out of the habit of doing push-ups.

Over the years, the cats were pretty good about coming upstairs to bed when their humans called, though Lavie usually required a fuss made over her first. But occasionally she would outright refuse to budge and had to be carried up.

One night, an extremely stubborn Lavie sat at the bottom of the stairs despite my sons' efforts to coax her. Finally, Toby said to Paul, "Why don't you drop and do your push-ups? That should get her up here."

It had been quite a while since Lavie's last push-up fix. Would she remember? It was worth a try.

Paul dropped to the floor and started his push-ups. Within seconds, Lavie came flying up the stairs. Drunk with ecstasy, she swirled under his chin, meowing and kissing him like old times. It was hilarious. Amid Paul's laughter, he showered her with love and affection before putting her away in her kennel for the night.

Now it's a cinch to get Lavie to come upstairs and get ready for bed. Lavie might feel smug knowing she has her humans under her spell, but there's no denying that when it comes to Paul and push-ups, he has the little coquette beat — hands down.

— Jill Burns —

Elvira Ever Changing

A cat will do what it wants when it wants,
and there's not a thing you can do about it.
~Frank Perkins

"I s the black cat yours?" a woman asked me as I was weeding between the roses in my front garden. "Your cat is terrorizing my dog!"

The woman tightly held a leash attached to a large German Shepherd, a rather imposing one with massive paws.

"Yes," I responded. I gave her large dog another once over. "How could my cat terrorize your dog? He must outweigh our cat ten times over."

The woman's eyes narrowed as she stared into mine. "Your cat lurks."

"Lurks?"

"Your cat hides behind bushes and when I walk my dog, it jumps out at my dog and scares him to death."

I quickly put a hand over my mouth to hide my grin. "Um, I'm really sorry," I finally managed to say without laughing. "She's feral and doesn't have the best manners. She grew up in the canyons fighting predators to stay alive."

The woman raised her chin in an authoritative manner and stared at me down her long nose. "I don't care where she came from; make her stop threatening my dog."

At this point I stood up and faced the woman. "Are you serious?" I asked her. "The cat is wild. I can no sooner make her stop bothering your dog than I can change the weather. Besides, your dog could crush Elvira with one swipe of his paw. How could my cat possibly be threatening your dog?"

"Well, she just is, and you need to do something about it!" she snapped at me.

Trying to be neighborly, yet knowing I had no control over my feral cat I suggested that she walk her dog on the other side of the street. That didn't go over well at all. She tightened the leash on her dog and stomped off, passing my neighbor who was walking her three small dogs toward my house.

"Was she complaining about Elvira?" Joy asked.

I nodded and repeated the conversation. Joy said that the woman had complained about Elvira to her as well. Then I learned something new about our feral girl. Although I was aware that Elvira disappeared after dinner, coming home late at night, and I knew that she often climbed up onto the roof to sunbathe during the day, I didn't know that she would flatten her body against the dark shingles, waiting until a dog walked in front of our house. Then she would hunch up like a classic Halloween black cat and let out a frightening hiss. Unleashed dogs would take off and the leashed ones would bolt, dragging their owners up the street. I burst out laughing.

"It's really funny to watch," Joy said. "Elvira has no fear; she's such a cool cat."

When we were moving to a condo in another part of town one of the neighbors asked us to leave Elvira behind and said they would care for her. I knew that those neighbors were fond of her, but really, they wanted us to leave behind our cat? I told them that while I appreciated their fondness for our feral girl, I could not possibly leave her behind. She chose us to be her family.

On moving day, I worried. Elvira had never known any home but the canyon and our house. I worried about whether she could adjust to a whole new environment. When I let her out for her normal outdoor activities, I wondered if she would come back. Had she seen the moving truck and determined that we were abandoning her? I needn't have worried. When we returned to our old home a few hours later, after visiting the new one, we opened the back door and Elvira shot into the house. She was crying at a high pitch and frantically running around us, as distressed as we'd ever seen her.

We kneeled down to her level and rubbed behind her ears. "We weren't going to leave you behind," I told her. My husband put her in the cat carrier. She didn't fuss; she let her body go limp and settled inside. As far as we knew, this was the first time she had ever been in a cat carrier.

Upon arriving at the condo, she began exploring and getting her bearings. We told her that there would be no more going outdoors because of all the coyotes in the canyon that surrounded us on three sides. Although she had survived in the canyon around our old house, she didn't know this one. Our new neighbors told us that outdoor cats disappeared in this neighborhood. Elvira sat and listened, as though she understood. We figured that the first time we opened a door she would make a run for it. To the contrary, she never did. She seemed to understand that she was now an indoor cat.

It's been eleven years since Elvira found us and joined our family. At first, I thought she would always be wild and skittish. These days, not so much. She's become a total bed hog, as talkative as a Siamese, and hangs with us just for the sake of togetherness. When we moved to another state in 2018, she rode in the moving truck as though it was something she did every day. She sat in the passenger seat peering out at the broad landscape in silence. It was as though she knew that we were all in this together. And we were.

Once we settled into our new home, a small neighborhood dog appeared at our home. He was a sad little mess. Our neighbor didn't want the dog and asked us to take him. We did, even though we weren't sure if Elvira would accept him. Afterall, her forte was terrorizing big dogs. What would she make of a dog smaller than herself?

The first time we let him into the house Elvira sniffed him, turned around, raised and showed him her tail. What did that mean? Was it some feline to canine signal? We soon found out. She was the alpha. Once he tried to challenge her; it took only one swipe of her large paw to reinforce her position. He never tried to cross her again. Of course, it helped that she outweighed him by several pounds. She terrified him. I don't think she would actually try to harm him. She knew he was rescued from homelessness just like she was.

In the early years, I viewed her as simply a cat who needed a home. Over the years she has proven to us that she is much more than that. We learned that given patience, unconditional love, and compassion, anyone can adapt, even a feral cat who once got her kicks by frightening big dogs.

—Jeffree Wyn Itrich—

Chapter 5

Cat Therapy

41

Healing Kitty

If there were to be a universal sound depicting peace,
I would surely vote for the purr.
~Barbara L. Diamond

t began as a barely noticeable pain across my forehead, just a headache. When I woke up the following morning, it was still lingering in the background as I went about my day. Like an annoying mosquito buzzing around my head, it continued the next day and the next for a full week. I took a day off to rest. Maybe I was doing too much and needed a short break.

When I lay down, I could hear my heart pounding in my head. I could hear my children playing in the basement. I could hear the electric click of the TV when they turned it off. When they turned a doorknob, I braced myself for the impending thud of a door.

After another week, I went to the doctor's office. Why was the office so bright? Why did the lights hum and buzz? Why did the doctor talk so loudly? After tests documented that nothing abnormal was happening inside my head and pills did nothing to abate the pain, I was diagnosed with chronic migraine.

The world outside my home became a shouting, flashing nightmare of sound and light. When I walked, my head felt like a giant balloon floating up to the sky, tethered to my body by a thin string. With each step, my brain banged against my skull. Even sitting at a bench by the quiet lake made me nauseous as I watched the ripples on the water wave up and down, up and down.

I spent the days alone, hiding in my room. The sunlight was dimmed by the blinds. The children tiptoed by in whispers. I could not abide my husband at night in bed. His every small movement felt like an earthquake. His breathing sounded like the roaring of an Amtrak train hurtling down the tracks. I wrapped the safety of solitude around myself.

When I had to go out, I hid behind sunglasses and noise-cancelling headphones. The world continued around me, but I was trapped alone behind a glass wall of pain through which I could see only dimly. I felt removed, apart. I did not let the world touch me. The world hurt. Everyone and everything in it. I was alone.

I spent my days in the dark solitude of my room. I missed my family. I longed for the sweet touch of my children, but even when they were careful, they bumped the bed or spoke too loud.

Then they accidentally let one of our kittens into my room.

Our family had adopted a litter of four abandoned kittens two months before my headache began. I fell in love instantly with the two male kittens — one because of his orange stripes, and the other because of his loving demeanor. I kept the shy female kitten because my youngest daughter claimed her as her own. I was keeping the fourth, a small black female kitten, temporarily because I had been unsuccessful at finding her a new home. When I sat to play with the kittens, she refused to be held or petted. She jumped around, leaping to explore one new thing after another. She climbed up the door, the shower curtain, and my pant legs. I thought she might make a good barn cat. She was much too energetic to be kept inside.

But she was the cat who slinked past my door and into the confines of my hiding place. On soft kitten paws, she crept over the blankets heaped around me. Slowly, she tested each step. The bed barely moved. I became vaguely aware of her. One eyelid fluttered half-open so I could see her through my eyelashes. I wanted to call to someone and ask them to take her out, but I didn't want to raise my voice. Tensed, I watched her glide up to the pillows gently. I felt her curl her small, soft body around my head. I was anxious about her being there. If she rocked the bed or began to purr, I was afraid it would hurt.

But the warmth of her presence nestled against my pounding head eased some of the pain. I relaxed, and she began to purr. I could feel it and hear it, and it didn't hurt at all. Her soft vibrations seemed to pull at the squeezing pressure locked around my temples. My only fear was that she would stop. Her purr took away my pain. Slowly, gently, with each rhythmic vibration, I felt my headache dissipate until I slipped into a peaceful sleep.

In the days afterward, when the pain grew unbearable, I would lie down for my kitty-nap. She would come, always uncalled, dashing in my room just before I closed the door. With healing ministrations, she wrapped her small, warm body around my head and purred and purred until I fell asleep. She was the only thing that stopped the pain — not the doctor's pills or my husband's ice packs.

One day, I experienced a sharp throbbing in a specific place on my head. My kitten, for she was mine now, placed her tiny paw directly on the spot. Like the trained hand of a massage therapist, she proceeded to knead as she purred. She pulled the pain out of me. I awoke refreshed, the pain gone.

Months have gone by, and my migraines are a memory, but I wouldn't think of giving away Healing Kitty. Whenever someone in the house is sick or injured, she is there. My daughter sprained her knee. Healing Kitty jumped gently onto the sofa and curled herself up softly on the injured joint. My two youngest had the flu and lay on the sofa head-to-toe. Healing Kitty settled herself between them while they slept.

How my energetic kitten became a gentle nurse is a mystery. How she healed me with her loving touch is magic.

— Carrie Cannon —

42

Calvin's Best Friend

When a cat chooses to be friendly,
it's a big deal because a cat is picky.
~Mike Deupree

Calvin walked into the family room and stopped, lifted up his nose and sniffed. His tail twitched. Something smelled different.

On the couch lay my dog Tucker, his head encircled by a plastic veterinary cone large enough to pick up signals from space. He had just come home from the vet, where he had been treated for a split toenail. The sensitive quick was exposed — a very painful condition, particularly in the middle of winter when below-freezing temperatures exacerbated his discomfort. Tucker would lick his wound incessantly and thus had to wear the dreaded Cone of Shame.

Calvin must have noticed the unfamiliar scent of the dog's injury and perhaps the aroma of vet that clung to his scruffy fur. He approached Tucker slowly, his body stretched and low to the ground. The dog opened his eyes and barely seemed to register the kitty's approach. Emboldened, Calvin crept closer and then leapt up onto the couch. He padded softly over to Tucker and cautiously sniffed the edge of the cone.

Tucker sighed, repositioned himself, and closed his eyes, which was a bit unusual considering his shaky relationship with our four cats. Tucker loved to snuggle real close with my other two dogs, as well as the humans who inhabit our home, but he was a bit wary of the kitties. If any of his feline housemates walked into our bedroom, the dog would purposefully get up from his preferred spot on our bed, jump to the floor and army-crawl his way underneath, squeezing himself into the darkness and away from the cats.

If I were to guess, this precaution was related to the Ambush the Dog game our Tortie cat Athena played when the mood struck her. Positioning herself on the corner of the family-room coffee table, she would wait for Tucker to walk by on his way to drop a slobbery ball in one of the humans' laps; the dog was a bit ball obsessed. If he got close enough, the cat would deliver a formidable hiss/swat combination, teaching Tucker to be wary of the resident cats.

The cats also learned to give Tucker a wide berth. He was an effervescent presence in our house, always in motion: nosy, loud and bouncy. When he ran after his ball inside the house, he didn't stop to see if there was a cat in the way, which sometimes resulted in near collisions and puffed-up, indignant kitties muttering about the rudeness of Terriers.

So, for the most part, while cats and dogs lived together in our home, they left each other alone.

But a coned Tucker was a chastened Tucker. A sad Tucker. A quiet Tucker.

Up on the couch, Calvin stretched out his neck further, curving his head around the cone's edge. The movement was so subtle that the dog didn't seem to notice. Calvin leaned in and gently inspected the dog's eyebrows, nose and mouth.

I stood close by, just a tad concerned that Tucker might be a little unnerved at a cat in his space — about as in his space as one can get. Being restricted by a cone was bad enough, but to have someone — in particular, a feline someone — stick his face in there with him? Even a calm, accepting dog might have had an issue with that, let alone a pup who looked at cats and saw the sharp and pointy bits instead of the warm and furry ones.

But Calvin moved slowly, deliberately, ever so gentle. Then he slid out his bubblegum-pink tongue and gave Tucker's head a lick. Tucker opened his eyes again — and then closed them with a sigh. This was the permission Calvin was looking for, and he began grooming Tucker's head — inside the cone — in earnest.

It was a sweet moment between two individuals — of different species — who had mostly avoided each other until then.

And that moment changed things between Calvin and Tucker. The dog recovered, and within a week or so, the cone came off. While the other cats maintained their distance, Calvin would seek out Tucker. At first, Tucker was a bit suspicious, not quite sure whether to trust this particular cat. But Calvin worked his charms on the dog. He'd lie next to him, then inch a little closer, and then lay his head on Tucker's paw. The dog's eyes would widen at first and then soften as Calvin's purrs of contentment breached the language barrier between canine and feline.

When I opened the door to our bedroom in the mornings, Calvin would march in, meowing his greeting and looking for Tucker. Sometimes, Tucker would leap up onto the bed, and Calvin would read his body language and intention so fast that he'd jump up, too, with both dog and cat landing at the same time.

Now Tucker stayed on the bed instead of hiding underneath. And Calvin would parade around him, purring and rubbing him, and eventually snuggling up next to him. He was respectful of the dog, understanding intuitively that there were certain lines he shouldn't cross — like climbing on Tucker's back. But often I'd see Calvin put his small paw on top of the dog's foot or sometimes lay his head on Tucker's leg.

Being a ball-chasing, squirrel/chipmunk/groundhog-hunting, non-stop Terrier, Tucker wound up getting injured and had to wear a cone multiple times during his life. We all learned to give him a wide berth when he was coned since it didn't always prevent him from being his bouncy, in-your-face self. He was not quite aware of the width of the cone, which meant we humans would often get startled by a jab in our calves. Calvin's sibling, Elsa Clair, would skitter out of his way when she saw a coned Tucker coming, possibly afraid she'd be scooped up by the huge plastic collar.

But Calvin loved his friend, no matter what he was wearing. And every time Tucker was sentenced to the cone, Calvin would find a way to show he cared. He'd seek out Tucker to lie next to him, keeping him company. He'd purr at him and groom him.

The two had a special relationship that grew throughout Tucker's life. Calvin stood by him as the dog battled an aggressive cancer and offered comfort to his companion right up until the end. After Tucker died, Calvin found ways to connect with my other two dogs, and they now let him rub them, but it's not quite the same. I know my cat still misses his buddy and holds a special place in his heart for the Terrier who became his friend.

— Susan C. Willett —

43

Nurse Cats

*If purring could be encapsulated,
it'd be the most powerful anti-depressant
on the pharmaceutical market.*
~Alexis F. Hope

My first thought was that my bed was vibrating and one side of it was much warmer than the other. I opened my eyes and found my cat Bobbie causing this strange phenomenon.

My second thought was *Ow! This hurts!*

My brain was foggy, but I remembered vaguely that I spent the night in the ER with a kidney stone. Now it was probably afternoon.

The doctors sent me home because I had already passed the stone. There might be some pain, they said, so they loaded me up with painkillers and some anti-nausea medication, and I ended up in my own bed.

Bobbie stared up at me from where he was plastered against my side — my right side, where the pain was. He moved to come up and stare at my face, and immediately I missed the warmth he had given me. It had dulled the pain.

Some pain? Yeah, right. Understatement of the century.

A face popped in the door. "Oh, you're awake. Time for your medicine." My ex-husband was the one lucky enough to be called to bring me home and he was sticking around to take care of our kids — and me.

My ginger tiger Howard followed him in the door and jumped up on the bed. He walked carefully across the blankets and gave Bobbie a hard stare. Bobbie left, his shift apparently over while Howard settled his sixteen pounds of attitude right next to me. I was so happy a feline heating pad was back; it really did make a difference.

My ex motioned toward Howard. "He came and got me. I had on my headphones, so I didn't hear a thing." He gave Howard a pat on the head and got swatted for it, claws out. Howard is not the friendliest of cats and apparently being on duty makes him even nastier.

Taking my meds and downing some water — the only thing I could keep down on Day 1 — I looked at my furry pal, one of my Nurse Cats.

If I closed my eyes, I could almost picture them with those white folded hats that nurses used to wear. Bobbie would look adorable, being a masked black-and-white kitty of very fine taste and manners. But Howard? That'd be like putting a tiny nurse's hat on The Rock.

Whenever I am sick, or my kids are, it seems the cats know before we do. They start following us around, staring intently. They share silent cat comments with each other, and one of them is always with the person who is sick. It's like they are saying, "I'll take 11:00 p.m. to 7:00 a.m. and you can cover the morning."

I've heard of dogs who can sense seizures, low blood sugar and other health issues, so I guess it isn't too hard to imagine a cat having the same talent. Maybe we smell different to them when we're sick. Maybe they can sense pain or blood pressure changes or something. In this case, I made it easy for them. They could hear me moaning until the medication kicked in.

I'd given birth to a baby weighing over ten pounds the normal way, no sweat, but passing a tiny stone put me completely out of commission. For days my Nurse Cats tracked my every move. They probably even took my vital signs when I wasn't looking.

Trips to the bathroom? One of them was there to make sure I didn't fall.

Need meds or water? Howard got a human to help.

Crying? Yes, there was some crying, and that was Bobbie's moment to shine. He'd touch my cheek with his nose — his way of asking to be petted. It is impossible for me to cry for long when petting a cat because it is just so soothing. They know this about me.

They know lots about me, apparently, including the fact that I don't like to be alone when I'm sick. Day and night, they kept me company, one or both of them. They didn't budge an inch unless I needed them to.

Time passed slowly, but by the third day I was mostly pain-free. I could sit up in my favorite chair, and Howard would take naps in my lap to keep me warm while Bobbie kept an eye on me from the couch. Life was getting back to normal.

I give tons of credit to my Nurse Cats, Bobbie and Howard. They couldn't take away my pain, but they made it much easier to bear and certainly helped keep me happy while I was healing.

— Shawn Marie —

44

Sufi and Groucho

*The cat, it is well to remember, remains
the friend of man because it pleases him
to do so and not because he must.*
~Carl Van Vechten

've never considered myself a cat person. In fact, I always considered cats to be somewhat arrogant creatures, but my opinion and life were changed with a trip to the mall. My wife and I were strolling by the pet store when we noticed a veterinarian we knew inside and decided to say hello. He was tending to a tiny white kitten that had just arrived from a breeder. His expression told us something was wrong.

"I'm afraid this poor thing isn't going to make it if it stays here," he said in almost a whisper. The kitten's sad blue eyes looked like she had been crying, staining her fur. Her nose was runny, and her breathing seemed labored. I'm not sure what the agreement was between our friend the veterinarian and the pet store, but there was definitely tension in the air.

Normally, I would have said "no" to buying a kitten at a store instead of adopting at a shelter, but this was different; this was a rescue. The main thing was to get this kitten home where it would receive the tender love and care it desperately needed and we could provide.

Days passed, and Sufi (we named her after watching a rerun of *The Jewel of the Nile*) slowly grew stronger. I've heard it said that "love is the best medicine" and, if true, Sufi was receiving a double dose.

After a week of round-the-clock care, my wife had to leave on a business trip, entrusting me with sole care of our charge. I must admit, I was worried. Was I up to this task? What if Sufi took a turn for the worse or the unthinkable happened? She was seldom out of my arms and never out of sight over the next few days. At night, I slept on the couch while she slept in a well-padded box next to it. I chose the couch because it was lower, and I could be closer to her than I would have been on a bed. Sleeping lightly, I often reached down to make sure she was breathing. I never expected it, but Sufi and I were forming a lasting bond during this time.

Much to my relief, when my wife returned, Sufi's health was improving, but she still wasn't out of the woods. There would be more half-slept nights ahead. Miraculously, Sufi beat the odds and made a complete recovery. Also, unbeknownst to me, another miracle had already begun to take place.

"Groucho," as I was nicknamed, was undergoing a transformation. This bundle of fur was softening my heart, causing an anti-social, hardened-by-life person to slowly begin opening up. It was almost as if she had me under a magical spell. I often napped with Sufi curled upon my chest. Perhaps her gentle, loving personality was being transferred to me during these special times together. I know my naps were never more relaxing. My wife even asked jokingly, "Who are you, and where is the grouch?"

I wouldn't officially classify Sufi as an emotional support animal, although perhaps she was. I believe I actually suffered separation anxiety whenever I was away for any length of time. I can't believe I'm admitting this; "Groucho" would never have expressed himself in such a manner.

Sufi was also an intuitive creature and a great judge of character. My wife had built a successful photography business with me as her equipment caddie. Before accepting a client, she interviewed them. Sufi enjoyed having visitors. Her usual greeting consisted of a visual appraisal followed by a gentle brushing of their leg, indicating they were kindred spirits. We learned by experience that if she shied away from someone, it was best to refer them to one of our competitors. The one time we didn't, it turned out to be the wedding from hell.

Sufi's contributions earned her a partnership in the business, sharing profits in the form of treats and catnip. Because of her beauty and gentleness, she often posed with like-minded souls, creating beautiful, touching portraits.

Sufi was truly a blessing during her nineteen years of life. I believe it was divine intervention that brought us to the mall that fateful day. She was a wonderful companion. Her gentleness, joy in simple pleasures, and unconditional love inspired me to become a better person, friendlier and more outgoing. Family and friends call my transformation a miracle, and I suppose they're right. Thanks to Sufi, the miracle worker, I'm happier than I could have ever imagined.

—J. Truluck—

45

Sweet Talk

*Our perfect companions never
have fewer than four feet.*
~Colette

At the age when most toddlers can speak small sentences and use about 200 words, my curly-haired fireball, three-year-old Kimber, knew only fifty small words.

She expressed herself in different ways. Wonderful ways! She pointed, climbed, gestured, cried, and even learned baby sign language. But Kimber did not use words if she could help it.

Kimber was tested, and we discovered she had speech delay. Later, we learned this was due to processing and executive function disorders. Those deficiencies made it very difficult for her to learn new sounds, letters, and pronunciations. To make matters worse, Kimber was smart enough to recognize that she didn't say words the same way as everyone else. If she couldn't say words right, she didn't want to say them at all. And she hated to be corrected, so she didn't use words. Ever.

Weeks and months of treatment did very little to help her progress. This therapist held up flash cards. That therapist brought treats. Another therapist repeated fun phrases, all to no avail. We couldn't seem to find the perfect person to help. Kimber was not interested in using words for anyone or for any reason.

That changed one hot summer day while we hid from the Arizona sun by visiting a friend. My friend had a litter of kittens ready to give to good homes. Most of the kittens hid in the closet when my curious toddler came poking around, but one little ball of gray fluff did not flee.

The sweet puff of fur approached Kimber on his kitty tiptoes. Stretching his tiny back, he purred his way across the carpet and rubbed my daughter's little ankles. When Kimber reached for the kitten and picked it up incorrectly, I panicked. "No, Kimmie, he'll scratch you!"

But he didn't. The patient little critter purred even louder as I taught Kimber how to hold him against her shoulder and pet him nicely. He purred when Kimber put him down and played with blocks beside him. He purred when she scooped him up again to go outside together. He batted her curls. She stroked his fluffy tail. That creature followed my little girl during the entire lengthy visit.

When it was time to leave, my friend winked wisely at me. "Looks like the cat chose your daughter," she said. "You're going to have to take it home."

"No way," I responded. "My husband hates cats. He won't budge on this."

"Well, take him home to visit for the day. You can bring the kitty back tomorrow."

Since Kimber had the kitten over her shoulder and its Velcro paws were attached to her shirt, I agreed. Kitty came home with us, letting his kitten motor run all the way to our house.

That night, I had to leave for a meeting. My husband, Howard, came home later than I expected, so I ran out the door as he was coming in. I forgot to mention the kitten. He found it while I was out. When I got home late that night, oh boy, did he have something to say.

"You got a cat? I thought we agreed never to do that."

"Don't worry, I can take him back whenever," I consoled. "It was just such a nice little thing and great with Kimber, so I brought it home to visit. My friend said she'll take it back tomorrow."

With a groan, Howard let it be. He huffed into our room, and I went to tuck in our kids.

When I entered Kimber's room, I thought a fan was running. But no! Kitty was lying on Kimber's tummy, purring away louder than the A/C buzzing outside. And Kimber was doing the most amazing thing.

She was talking!

"Good kitty. Lay down. Go sleep, kitty," Kimber said, petting the cat. "Good night, kitty."

She giggled and smiled, lovingly putting the kitten to sleep with words. Her own words. Words no one had to tell her to say. Words she wanted to use. For a kitten.

My eyes filled with tears as I witnessed the miracle. That charming cat inspired her to overcome her own self-doubt and use the words she knew! I sat in wonder, listening to her calm and reassure her new little pet.

Once Kimber fell asleep, the kitten roamed into my bedroom and turned up the purring as it circled my husband's ankles. Howard picked it up, and Kitty immediately snuggled my husband's neck, letting his purr come to full volume.

"Honey, you're not going to believe this," I said. "Kimber was talking to him!"

"What do you mean?" Howard asked.

"She was trying to get him to fall asleep with her. It was so sweet!"

He looked at me with a strange expression and stared at Kitty. Seeing my husband's walls purred down, I baited him. "But I told you I'll take him back tomorrow, so she will have to say goodbye."

"Yeah, I guess." Howard petted Kitty until they both fell asleep.

The following morning, Howard was preparing for work, and Kitty would not let him alone. He followed Howard into the kitchen. Once I joined them, I noticed fresh tuna in Kitty's food bowl and a dish of milk beside his water.

As Howard got ready to leave, he kissed me goodbye and picked up Kitty for one more cuddle. Kitty snuggled Howard's cheek, purring with all the strength an eighteen-ounce ball of fur can produce.

I smiled. "Call me crazy, Howard, but it doesn't look like you hate this cat at all. I noticed you fed it some tuna and milk. If I didn't know any better, I would say you liked it."

Howard petted Kitty and set him on the floor. "Well, he's not so bad for a cat."

At that moment, Kimber woke up and toddled out of her room.

She scooped up Kitty, kissing his furry face. "Kitty, come here. It's time to play!"

Kimber used her words for her cat.

Seven words in a row from Kimber's lips were all my husband needed to hear. Kitty never went back to my friend. He won his place in our home with a sweet disposition and love for a toddler. He was the purrr-fect pet to help Kimber.

Who would have guessed a kitten could do what speech therapists could not? Through his unconditional love and acceptance, Kimber overcame her fear of saying things wrong. She used words to help Kitty understand. And Kitty didn't have to say anything at all.

— Kate E. Anderson —

46

Sammy the Supercat

Cats are designated friends.
~Norman Corwin

We're really lucky to have a superhero in our family. He can't fly, he doesn't wear a cape, and he has no immediate plans to save the world. Instead, he's four years old, furry and pretty average to look at — he's no rare breed or pedigree. He's certainly not the smartest feline on the block. But he does have one very special role — he is my son's best friend, therapist, stress-reliever, and all-round supercat.

My son, Alfie, is on the autism spectrum. The world doesn't make sense to him, and every day brings fresh challenges and new struggles. Autism is a lifelong condition that cannot be "cured." As a spectrum disorder, it affects people in different ways. Common challenges can include repetitive behaviours, resistance to change, intense interests in often unusual subjects, social interaction and communication problems, and difficulties in sensory processing such as over- or under-sensitivity to sounds, lights or touch.

Life can be tough for Alfie, and following his diagnosis in 2014, we wondered what the future would hold for him. Would he know how to make friends? Would he be teased for being different? How would he cope at school?

I read about autism, and then I read some more. I spent months trying to get a glimpse into the world as Alfie was experiencing it. There was a recurring theme in many of the resources I was reading — that animals can have a profound impact on children with autism.

Sammy and his brother Boj joined our family as kittens in the autumn of 2014. They were from the same litter and the only two kittens who hadn't found a home, so we took to them immediately as the "underdogs." Alfie and Sammy's first meeting was heart-warming. As Alfie reached out with a tentative hand to stroke Sammy for the first time, little did we realise that the bond created in those few brief seconds was set to last a lifetime.

Sammy was a shy cat from the get-go. His brother Boj preferred to take centre stage and seek out special attention. But Sammy was perfectly at ease in Alfie's company. We only had to walk within five feet of him for him to scamper, but he would actively seek out Alfie, preferring special time with him and him alone, as opposed to attention from the rest of us.

If Alfie couldn't communicate with the rest of us, then Sammy was equally aloof and non-communicative. But together they bonded in a most inexplicable way — sharing a love of solitude, routine and mutual cuddling sessions.

Sammy had a sixth sense for Alfie's moods. Sensing a meltdown was on the horizon, Sammy would pre-empt Alfie's much-needed "time-out" by heading up to his bedroom and waiting there for him — making himself available for some sensory therapy via cuddles and strokes. Many times, once the storm of the meltdown had passed, I walked into Alfie's room to find Sammy rubbing his head against Alfie's in order to provide some comfort.

Many kids on the autism spectrum struggle to maintain a two-way conversation, particularly if — like Alfie — they have fairly narrow interests and topics they want to talk about. Sammy is the best type of sounding board for Alfie because he's happy to chat dinosaurs and sharks all day long without complaint! Sammy is a very undemanding friend for Alfie because all he really wants is love and affection — and Alfie is happy to provide that in bucketfuls.

Every night, Sammy will follow Alfie upstairs to his bedroom and get into bed with him until he falls asleep. Sleep is known to be an issue for many kids on the spectrum, but Sammy's presence at that crucial settling-down time has really improved Alfie's ability to drift off. They are both picky eaters and can only eat if they know what to expect. Alfie likes the same foods presented the same way, day in, day out. Sammy likes the same bowl and will not tolerate his food being moved anywhere else. He just won't eat if that's the case!

Both are very sensitive to sounds. Boj, Sammy's brother, couldn't care less about the washing machine, vacuum, or lawnmower, but Sammy will be the first to run off and tuck himself away in a safe place (normally the sanctuary of Alfie's room), with Alfie not far behind him.

Sammy really comes into his own for Alfie's sensory stimulation, though. Just being able to touch and stroke Sammy is an instant mood-lifter for Alfie, who is calmed by his soft fur. When we can see Alfie's anxieties starting to surface, the first thing we'll say is "Go and find Sammy for a cuddle." Often, that is enough for Alfie to find his happy place again.

Many kids with autism struggle with imaginative play due to the rigidity in their thought processes, but Sammy has opened the door to creativity for Alfie. One of Alfie's favourite pastimes is creating little stories about Sammy's adventures in and out of the house, and he is often seen with pen in hand drawing Sammy's latest escapade. Sammy has even been the inspiration for a poem, and he has unlocked a talent in Alfie that we never thought possible.

The depth of their relationship has enabled Alfie to understand the wider world, and he has taken a keen interest in the plight of endangered big cats and Cats Protection, a feline welfare charity. So great is his commitment to these causes that for his seventh birthday, he asked to sponsor a snow leopard and donated his birthday money to Cats Protection, rather than spend it on toys.

Sammy is priceless to us. He is Alfie's best friend, saviour and motivator. Alfie said to me last week that whenever he finds something tough, Sammy pops into his head and says, "You can do it, Alfie!" Alfie lives for Sammy, and the feeling is mutual.

We couldn't ask for more from our amazing feline friend. I know

Alfie wishes Sammy could go to school with him, although I'm not sure his head-teacher would be thrilled with that idea. Our only hope when Sammy joined our family was that he would help Alfie connect with the world, even on just a basic level, but our special cat has helped our special boy in ways we hadn't even contemplated.

Sammy might not be able to save the world, but he's saved Alfie, so he'll always be Sammy the Supercat to us.

— Carrie Roope —

Tenderhearted Tickles

Just being there for someone can sometimes bring hope
when all seems hopeless.
~Dave G. Llewelyn

My cat puzzled me. I'd always taken good care of her. I kept her fed. Gave her plenty of love. So why, after all these years, did she want to run away? Time and again, she walked a quarter-mile down the road to my elderly parents' house. It didn't make sense. What was so special about their house?

At first, I thought she liked catching mice in their barn. But all our neighbors had barns. Mom would call, saying the same words I'd heard many times before.

"Tickles is here again."

It wasn't a big deal. I stopped by Mom and Dad's every day anyway. I only grew concerned when I realized Tickles was expecting. I didn't want her to have kittens at Mom's. Even worse, what if she gave birth somewhere along the way?

As it turned out, Tickles delivered her babies at home in a warm, cozy box. She was a good momma. But six weeks later, she was ready to go back. This time, five little fur balls followed close behind.

"Tickles brought her kitties over again," Mom said when I called to check in. Now instead of bringing Tickles home, I hauled five kittens back as well.

Eventually, her kitties grew tired of making the trip. Like rebellious teenagers, they ignored their momma's wishes. But that didn't stop Tickles. Her babies didn't need her, so off to Mom's she went. In time, all that walking started making her thin. Mom felt sorry for her.

"I think I should feed her," she said one day. "She keeps meowing at the back door." Mom's handouts only encouraged her to visit more often. When the temperatures dropped, Mom brought Tickles inside the house. That's when I lost my cat.

"Next time I come over, I'll bring some cat food," I told Mom one morning as I cleared her breakfast dishes.

Mom waved her wrinkled hand. "Oh, that's okay," she said. "She's not your cat anymore."

To be honest, I really didn't mind. With Dad's physical limitations and Mom's forgetfulness, Tickles was a simple way to brighten their day. I didn't know what the future held for my parents, but I knew one thing: They both loved that cat.

One afternoon, I dropped by, and the house was quiet. I tiptoed to the living room. When I reached the doorway, I couldn't help but smile at the peaceful scene. Sunlight streamed in through the large picture window. Dad snored softly in his favorite recliner. Mom rested on the couch with Tickles nestled close beside her.

Well, that explains it, I thought. I always knew God provided comfort in many different ways. Why not with a cat? Clearly, my parents needed this kitty more than I did.

In time, Mom and Dad required round-the-clock care. I'll never forget the day my siblings and I took them to the nursing home.

Before we left, Mom sat on her bed, watching me sort through her clothes. Tickles wandered into the room and rubbed against her leg. Mom looked up.

"If I go away, what about the cat?"

Knowing this question would come, I took a deep breath. "It's too bad you can't take her with you, but the nursing home doesn't allow pets. Tickles can visit, but she can't go with you." I kept my tone cheerful, as if talking to a toddler. "It's okay," I said. "I can take her. I'll take good care of Tickles."

Mom looked down at the floor, collecting her thoughts. "Okay," she said. "But don't let her outside. She'll think she needs to come home."

Tickles soon adjusted to life at our house again. My husband never cared much for cats — especially cats in the house — but he understood the situation. Tickles and Ed found a way to make it work — they ignored each other. That is, until Ed came home after his knee surgery.

I couldn't believe the sudden shift in their relationship. Before the surgery, Tickles wanted nothing to do with Ed. After the surgery, she jumped off my lap to go sit with him. While Ed recuperated, Tickles stayed by his side.

It's been two years since my parents went into the nursing home. Sadly, Mom's dementia has progressed to the point that she no longer speaks. She rarely smiles. Most family members are strangers to her. She's in her own little world, and with every visit it becomes more difficult to reach her.

During a recent visit at the nursing home, I noticed a picture of Tickles on Mom's bedside table. I held the picture out to Mom.

"Do you remember her, Mom? Do you remember Tickles?" Her eyes narrowed as she stared at the photo. Suddenly, she smiled. It was not just a little twitch on the corners of her mouth, but a wide, beautiful smile. She took the photo in her shaky hands and stared at it for a moment.

Something was stuck to the front of the glass. Mom picked at it, distracted. I took the frame, cleaned it off and handed it back. She smiled again, as if seeing it for the first time.

"Mom, do you want me to bring Tickles over to see you?" I detected a slight but undeniable nod. Now I was smiling. With a little help from Tickles, I had reached my mom.

— Janet Haynie —

Not Quite Purrfect

When I play with my cat, who knows if I am not
a pastime to her more than she is to me?
~Michel de Montaigne

When my husband died suddenly, followed by our aging dog, and then our old cat disappeared, I figured my pet-owning days were over. I was pushing eighty-five and woke up every morning saying, "Okay, Lord, what's going to hurt today?" I had reached the point of wondering if there was even any point to getting up.

Then my veterinarian's wife tipped me off that a litter of kittens was on its way to the animal shelter. My brain was obviously not in gear. Before the day was over, a three-month-old kitty had moved into my home and heart. I've rescued cats my entire life, but no kittens in the past twenty-five years. What was I thinking?

I named her Purrfect, and there was no turning back after one snuggle. Little did I realize how life-changing this little fur ball was destined to be.

During the few years of living alone without a husband, dog or free-ranging old cat, I had gotten in the habit of reclining for hours in my lazy-girl chair. Now, with the arrival of Purrfect, I figured naively she would be content to recline for hours in my lap as I watched sappy old movies. So much for that fantasy. Purrfect spent her first three days exploring the house and approving the location of the litter box, food bowl and water source.

I remember clearly reading the newspaper on day three and feeling my sneaker laces being untied. Perhaps as an attention-getting ploy, Purrfect had managed to untie both shoes and was looking up at me as if to say, "Well?" I wadded up a piece of paper and pitched it across the living room. She not only raced after it, but picked it up in her mouth and brought it back. It was such a cute surprise that I applauded and pitched it again. And again… stupidly clapping in delight.

When you live alone, you can get away with stupid. During that first game of "Paper Chase" I counted eleven completed retrievals before she got bored and started looking around for a new game. It was like living with a toddler.

She spotted the walker I keep on hand to use as a wheelbarrow. My doctor doesn't want me carrying heavy stuff. Purrfect hopped up on the seat of the walker and flashed me the look that says, "Well?" I hauled myself reluctantly out of the recliner, curious to see what she would do. As I pushed the walker, she stayed put, sitting tall and proud. For fifteen minutes, we traveled in and out of every room on the main floor of this house, including the garage. If I slowed down, she stood up and put her front paws on the rail of the walker. I was reminded of that romantic moment in the movie *Titanic* when the young lovers stand on the bow of the ship. It occurred to me that I was getting an unusual amount of exercise without even leaving the house. When she finally hopped off and looked up at me, I applauded. What rational person behaves like this? Other than Paper Chase and Ride the Walker, here are a few more games still going on.

Hide, Seek and Meow: Since she is young and I'm home a lot, she considers me her entire world. She will never be allowed outside due to lurking predators. Although she loves to cuddle, she has to be darn tired first. If I leave a room, she follows — thus began the game of Hide, Seek and Meow. This house has many hiding places, so I wait for her attention to wander, and then I hide. When she can't see me, she starts meowing, which is my cue to meow back. (You are now thinking I have finally lost it, and it's time for the Funny Farm.) This game continues until she finds me, which makes her so deliriously happy that she runs like a crazed critter all over the house, giving me time to hide again. This game goes on until one of us gets tired… usually me.

Spin Class: My husband's office chair sits next to mine at the computer because I often need a friend's help solving PC problems. When Purrfect started sitting on that chair, I reached over and gave it a slow spin. She loved it, dug in her claws and as much as said, "This game is lame. Can you make it go faster?" After a dozen spins, she will hop off and stagger around like a happy drunk. This activity is so dumb that it does not require applause.

Box Cat: Several months ago, I decided to start de-cluttering, which of course involves boxes… and no cat can resist a box. Picture three cardboard boxes plunked on my bedroom floor. Picture Purrfect sitting in a box looking at me as if to say, "Well?" I stopped sorting sweaters and pointed to the second box. Immediately, she ran and jumped into that box, so I applauded and she smiled. I pointed to the third box, and she hopped in that one. More applause and Purrfect smiles.

I am in and out of the bedroom frequently, and so is she, sitting in a box waiting for the game to begin. All I have to do is point to another box and applaud. Knowing my friends would not believe this, I tried getting a video with my phone. But first I got a black marker and numbered the boxes 1, 2 and 3, figuring it would be fun to tell folks my cat "knows her numbers." Finally, I got good video proof, but it's not easy to applaud while holding a cell phone. So far, she has not tired of any of these crazy games.

I do get to recline occasionally, but Purrfect sees it as an opportunity to get on the back of the chair and groom my hair. I love sending a selfie to friends showing my personal in-home hairdresser in action. People theorize that she either considers me a litter mate or there is catnip in my shampoo.

Purrfect has now been my kitty companion for eighteen months and shows no signs of slowing down. She has kept me young and on my toes. And she has certainly given me reasons to laugh when I thought my life had run out of laughter.

The only fly-in-the-ointment is perhaps the name I gave her. In a lifetime of being owned by cats, Purrfect does lack one ability so common in cats — she does not purr. She never has and probably never will. But she is perfect enough for me.

— Bobbie Lippman —

Mabel Made This Family

When someone leaves, it's because someone else
is about to arrive — I'll find love again.
~Paulo Coelho, The Zahir

Before Mabel, there was just me. I was thirty years old and single. The long-term relationship I had invested all my energy in for the last five years had broken down. My heart had a big crack in it, not entirely broken, but not in perfect working order, not capable of real trust. I felt cold on the inside, so I went to warm clubs and danced with sweaty people. I was lonely and sought company.

In this manner, I ended up with a heart that was not only still cracked but also tired. It was tiring to try to connect with people when I was trying to protect myself at the same time. If I went on a date with a handsome young man and he asked me reasonable questions about myself and my life, I would come up with evasive answers. I would hear myself trying not to let him know me. When, after two or three meetings of this nature, he didn't call again, I would sink into a new layer of my old sadness.

When my elderly neighbour passed away, I grieved for that loss, too. She had been like a grandmother to me. A magical sort of little old lady, she'd also been a cat breeder. One or another of her five Abyssinian cats would climb across me and leap onto her shoulder while we chatted, while the other four sat contentedly on shelves and windowsills, grooming their sleek, sandy-coloured coats or cocking their large ears at noises from the garden. When I heard that she had died I needed some comfort, so I went to visit my friend Alex.

I didn't know how many cats to expect to meet when I went to see Alex. There was always Lucy, her gorgeous Tortoiseshell, but there were also others. Alex worked for a charity that rehomed feral cats. The cats would be rescued from the city streets, neutered and either re-released or brought to Alex for socialisation. Some of these cats had never been touched by a human before. Upon arriving in her apartment, the cats would invariably hide under the bed, where they would stay for as long as it took for trust to grow between them and Alex. There was no one more patient than Alex.

That day, I said hello to Lucy on her armchair, and then Alex introduced me to the beautiful ginger kitten who jumped up onto the coffee table. She explained that he was just about to be adopted by a couple who were on their way over. He was a real scamp, full of life and energy. "The mother was brought in just before she had her kittens, so these guys have been an easy case," she said.

Then I saw the other one. She was sitting off to the side, watching me. She was mostly gray, but when I looked closer I could see patches of orange and white beneath the smoky coat. "That's Mabel. I thought her name was Marble because I read her papers wrong, but she looks like a marble, doesn't she? She's a Dilute Tortoiseshell." She picked her up and put her in my arms. The purr that started up was like a small engine, and I held her against my chest. I felt my shoulders relax as a smile spread across my face. I rubbed my cheek along her spine. She twisted her body to see me, and I looked into her sparkling green eyes. She blinked slowly and then held my gaze again. I didn't want the moment to end. But she was full of life, too, and she clambered up to my shoulder, just like my elderly neighbour's cats. She perched up there, her purr idling in my ear until the doorbell rang and she jumped down.

The young couple fell in love immediately with Mabel's ginger brother and coaxed him into the carry case they had brought with them. While Alex was explaining his food and preferences, clearly having a bit of trouble saying goodbye, Mabel reappeared. She sat on my feet. She stared up at me. She said to me quite clearly, *I am going home with you.*

A few days later, I was back at Alex's with my own carry case. This time, the parting was joyful. Alex would be able to keep in touch with Mabel. They would always know each other.

I took Mabel home and let her out in my bedroom. She explored every corner, climbed on every surface, pounced on the toy mouse I had bought her and patted at it playfully. She leapt onto the windowsill and swiveled her gray ears at the sounds from the garden. She seemed to be satisfied, and my cheeks ached because I was smiling so hard.

Then, as though she had done it a thousand times before, she lay down on my pillow. She stretched her front legs out past her whiskers and sighed. I lay down beside her, my arm around her soft, little body. Her purr started up, and I felt tears slide across my face. For the first time in a long time, I felt my love received and returned. Mabel's warmth was like hot tar, finding that old crack in my heart and sealing it up for good.

Within six months, I met Eddie. By summer, we were talking about the future. By autumn, he had proposed. After a really special weekend together, Eddie started packing reluctantly. He threw his bag on the floor, and when he turned to put in his dirty socks, Mabel was sitting inside the bag, staring up at him with her emerald eyes. Eddie laughed and called to me to come and see. I picked up Mabel, and the pair of us held her between us. "So, you like him?" I said to her. "Don't worry, he's not going anywhere."

We got married and moved in together. Mabel had just found a spot on our new windowsill when I became pregnant. Now she lies against my big, warm belly. I tell her that the baby will be here soon, and she blinks slowly and knowingly. My family has come into being because of Mabel. I let myself love her, and then I let myself love the man who became my husband. I am so grateful for this spirit, Mabel, who looks like a marble. She sat on my shoulder and my shoes, and mended my cracked heart.

—Jessica Parkinson—

50

The Cat Named Blessing

Human beings are drawn to cats because they are all
we are not — self-contained, elegant in everything
they do, relaxed, assured, glad of company,
yet still possessing secret lives.
~Pam Brown

There were elderly residents at the nursing home where I worked, but there were some young ones as well. They were there because of life-altering illnesses. One of them, Diane, was only fifty-six, but she had muscular dystrophy. Her mother had passed, and Diane needed the services the nursing home could provide her. Everyone loved her, nurses and residents alike. She was full of cheer and positivity, spending her days using her electric wheelchair to visit the patients in all four wings of the home.

When Diane heard of the new trend of having animals in nursing homes, she approached Ruth, the administrator. She wanted the home to adopt a kitten and train it to visit the residents.

Ruth asked the head office, and the request was granted. Ruth went to the animal shelter and brought back a white cat with blue eyes. She was a beauty. Everyone loved her as soon as they saw her. Diane named her Blessing because she would be a definite blessing to all who lived and worked there.

Blessing took on her job with gusto. She would make her rounds to all the patients, and the ones who were sick were first on her list.

After a few weeks on duty, Blessing did something unusual. She crawled onto the bed with Mr. Russo and refused to leave, putting up a fuss when the nurse grabbed her and put her out in the hall. She was back in Mr. Russo's room and on the bed in a flash.

Finally, the nurse was able to get her out of the room, but Blessing would not leave the door. She meowed loudly, almost like a scream. The fuss was so loud that they decided to let Blessing stay with Mr. Russo.

Through the night, Blessing stayed very quiet and lay on Mr. Russo's bed right near his chest. Mr. Russo had been ill for some time, and he passed on during the night. Only after he passed did Blessing return to her own bed.

The next day, Blessing was back on the job, visiting all the patients. Two weeks later, the fuss that had occurred in Mr. Russo's room was repeated in the room of Mrs. Adams. We left Blessing with Mrs. Adams, wondering if she would pass, too. Sure enough, around 7 p.m., Mrs. Adams passed on. Then Blessing went to her own bed.

Nothing else occurred for several weeks, but then Blessing caused a big commotion in another lady's room. Sure enough, the lady passed later that morning. Was Blessing aware that these people were in their final hours?

Life went on at the nursing home, and Blessing continued to predict the passing of residents. Then one day, Diane got very ill. She was sent to the hospital, and Blessing checked her room several times a day.

When Diane returned to the home, Blessing jumped on her bed after a few weeks, and the entire scenario was repeated. She stayed there for eighteen hours without moving from Diane's side. Shortly after 4 a.m., we saw Blessing heading for her bed. When we checked on Diane, she had indeed passed away.

Blessing lived at the nursing home for twelve years, but one day we noticed a lump on her hip. She was taken to the vet and diagnosed with a rare form of cancer. The vet advised that she be put to sleep to ease her pain.

We made an appointment for the next day and took Blessing home to make one more round of the patients. This time, she was carried.

That night, Blessing died in her own bed, a fitting end for this beautiful cat who had dedicated her life to the patients who lived there.

— Mary M. Alward —

Oh So Naughty

51

Cat with a Conscience

Even if you have just destroyed a Ming vase,
purr. Usually, all will be forgiven.
~Lenny Rubenstein

I'd moved everything to the new apartment on Friday because I could only afford to take one day off work. The last carload included a carrier with my very freaked-out black cat, Leonore, who had watched her things disappear one by one and was now living her worst nightmare: riding in a car. Her wailing, keening, and what I can only describe as moaning could be heard three states away.

I hoped the weekend would be enough time for her to explore the new place in my presence so she would feel at home by the time I left for work on Monday. But I was a little worried that she would need longer to adjust. It's common knowledge that cats need to explore every inch of a place before declaring it their own.

When I first brought her inside, she went right under the bed. But she came out after a few minutes, with dust on her whiskers, and started sniffing everything. She was happy to see that her favorite furniture had not disappeared and even happier to be done with the dreaded automobile ride.

Soon, she began chatting about everything from the placement of the television to the color of the bedspread. You see, Leonore was a talker. The mere presence of a human activated both her purr motor and her running commentary of meows. This was a cat who would look you straight in the eye, whether she'd ever met you or not, and initiate a ten-minute conversation.

Looking back, I think what she was usually talking about was laps. When were we going to produce a lap for her to sit in? Would it be now or five minutes from now? Sitting on a human lap was her greatest joy. When I met her for the first time at the shelter, she immediately jumped into my lap, purring loudly and making the adoption decision very easy. I felt special at the time, but now I'm pretty sure she would have gone off with anybody who appeared before her in a seated position.

So, despite her vociferous protestations during the car ride, it didn't take long for her to settle down on the bed while I organized my clothes and shoes. We had a nice weekend together, with me unpacking and her advising me on the placement of things. Still, when Monday morning rolled around, I left for work reluctantly, hoping she would be okay on her own.

When I returned home from work Monday evening, I opened the door to an apartment bathed in the light of the summer evening sun. And I was greeted by a cat who seemed panicked about something.

Yes, she was meowing (she was never not meowing), but instead of rubbing all over my legs like usual, she began walking through the front room, slowly but with determination. She kept turning around to look at me, and it was clear that she wanted to make sure I was following her. In this way, she led me through the front room and into the kitchen, where a grand mess awaited.

In her exploration while I was away, Leonore had jumped onto the sunny kitchen windowsill where I'd placed a house plant in a terra cotta pot. She misjudged the space and sent the pot hurtling to the ground. The pot shattered, scattering the dirt and shards onto every one of the white floor tiles. Leonore looked from the disaster scene to me and back several times (punctuating her movements with meows, of course).

When the pot crashed to the floor, the poor cat must have been scared half to death! But as she showed me the scene of the epic disaster, she didn't act scared or anxious.

She acted sorry.

Here was a cat not only confessing to a crime but asking for forgiveness. Clearly, she thought I would be angry at her.

Laughing, I picked her up and gave her hugs and head scratches, telling her that everything was okay. Before I even started sweeping up the crime scene, I sat down on my plush orange chair and made a lap for her. She understood that she was forgiven for the accident, and I understood that I had a very special cat, one with a conscience.

— Rachel Evangeline Barham —

52

Does Insurance Cover That?

A well-balanced person is one who finds
both sides of an issue laughable.
~Herbert Procknow

After unpacking my suitcase, I carried my dirty clothes to our lower-level laundry room. Walking through my son's bedroom on the way to the laundry, I had that peculiar feeling that something wasn't right.

I travel for business quite often, so I'm accustomed to a few surprises upon return, such as toppled plants, hairballs and cat-hair tumbleweeds chasing me around the house. There's always hair on the couch, which the cats aren't supposed to nap on. As the primary guardian of Colby and Lance, two adult male cats, I've come to appreciate and accept the quirky things they do when I'm gone.

I started a load of darks and returned to Andrew's room for another look around. It's a clean room when he's away at college, but today there were pieces of white chalky ceiling tile on the blue plaid bedspread. Looking up, I saw a two-foot by three-foot hole, exposing the upstairs floor joists. There were six complete ceiling tiles missing. I cleaned up the mess and went to bed wondering about the crime scene in my basement.

The following morning, after sending my seventeen-year-old

daughter, Alyssa, off to school, I ventured back to Andrew's room to investigate. Weird things often occur in our house. We blame Bobby, our ghost.

When my children and I bought the house, there was a pair of dirty white toddler sneakers outside the back door. We were told that the eccentric lady who lived and died in the house was adamant about Bobby. She believed that he lived in the attic and needed the shoes to go out to play.

It was spooky, but the legend endeared me to the house. I'm a collector of creepy odds and ends. Even creepier is that the attic was accessible through a turquoise stairway in the kitchen closet. To be honest, I didn't sweep the kitchen at night if alone. I'm not sure if it was the ghost or the color of the closet that frightened me more.

The day we took possession of the house, we decided to keep the shoes in the same place, just in case. We didn't want to take a chance on disturbing Bobby.

Now I dug under the sink, around the cleaners, air fresheners and dusting spray. I found my flashlight and was thrilled to see that the batteries were charged enough to use it.

I surveyed the exposed hole to see if there was a cause for the damage. I found a small copper pipe that led from left to right. Copper pipes contain water. It didn't feel wet, but a water leak was my conclusion.

I called my insurance agent. Within thirty minutes, he was in Andrew's room with me surveying the damage. (One can still get quick personal service in a small town in Iowa!)

Crumbled ceiling tiles in a basement bedroom doesn't sound like a big deal, but having researched online, I found that those tiles were no longer available. I'd have to replace the entire ceiling if I wanted a cohesive look. Anyone who has ever made home improvements knows that one small project can and probably will turn into a total remodel.

Mike, the insurance agent, agreed that it appeared to be a water leak. He told me the adjustor would visit within three days, and then he would be able to quote the payment I would receive. I was satisfied. I'd be compensated for a new ceiling.

But something still bothered me.

I asked my father to stop by after work and review the damage with me. We stood side by side on the rumpled bed and gazed up into the hole. I explained that the agent and I agreed it appeared to be water damage because of the copper pipe immediately above. But as Dad and I discussed it, I realized there were no watermarks on the wooden joists or on the broken ceiling tiles.

"Come over here with your flashlight. I think I found your problem," Dad laughed. Lance, our fluffy ginger, sat looking down curiously at us from the darkened space, licking his paws.

While Lance relaxed in his secret lair, Dad and I went into the laundry room and tracked the steps of the culprits to the scene of the caper.

It appeared they'd hopped onto a counter and traversed several cardboard boxes, delivering them to the ceiling of the adjacent room. A cool, dark cavern above Andrew's room, it was the perfect napping place in the summer.

Lance is a lightweight cat and probably wouldn't have fallen through. Colby, our seventeen-pound coral shorthair, is built like a mountain lion. We determined that when following Lance to his secret hideaway, he fell through the tile like an anvil. Their expressions must have been priceless as they plunged to the bed. Did they land on their feet? Did they each lose one of their lives in this misadventure?

Dad and I sat down to a cold beer and a good laugh. Suddenly, it occurred to me that I'd have to call my insurance agent and explain the situation. Would he think it was as funny as we did after he had visited my home, contacted an adjustor and submitted a claim for me?

I explained the situation, and he did think it was funny—extremely funny. He'd never heard anything like it, although he had heard plenty. When I asked sheepishly if my insurance would cover the damage, he laughed and said, "No, but it's a great story!"

I removed the boxes on the counter and blocked the entry to the dropped ceiling. Shortly after the episode, we replaced the missing ceiling tiles and painted the entire ceiling white. When all the same color, it wasn't noticeable that the texture pattern was slightly different.

We love our cats and feel fortunate that they let us live with them, but come on… Some places in the house should be off-limits!

—Debi Schmitz Noriega—

53

A Puzzling Choice

A cat is a puzzle for which there is no solution.
~Hazel Nicholson

Our house is home to three cats. One is a sweet-tempered, docile ginger tabby. One is a gray-and-white kitten, playful, silly, and endearing in the way all kittens are. The third is Puzzles... and Puzzles is a cat like no other.

She weighs a little less than eight pounds—a petite feline, truly—but her attitude belies her size. She terrifies human visitors with nothing more than the animosity of her gaze and a well-timed hiss. Once, extended family members were visiting, and I hadn't seen my niece in a while. I found her cowering in the bathroom. She was afraid to come out because Puzzles was perched like a gargoyle on the stair rail, watching... and waiting.

Another time, we went on a weeklong family vacation. Checking in with the cat sitter on our return, I learned that Puzzles had hissed and growled every day despite the cat sitter's best attempts to become friends. "I thought she'd learn to like me," said the cat sitter. "Or, at the very least, she'd tolerate me once she realized I was the one bringing her food. But no."

No, indeed. Somewhere along the way, without any inciting incident and despite being socialized gently ever since she was a kitten, Puzzles has decided to hate visitors. She's never hurt anyone, though. Hers is a psychological warfare, and it's safe to say that she's won every battle.

She's also a troublemaker. "Puzzles, what did you do?" is a common question in our house.

She is obsessed with rubber and silicone. I was unprepared for this. Do you realize how many kitchen items are made with one of these materials? The first time I saw a piece from a baby bottle on the floor, I figured it had fallen out of the dish drainer accidentally. When I found the next one chewed to bits, I realized my mistake. What followed was a months-long battle of wills as I attempted to find places for drying silicone straws, bottle pieces, and even the gasket for the blender that were beyond the reach of a determined and intelligent cat.

Suffice to say, I spent a lot of money on replacement parts. It is very difficult to outwit a cat with the above two characteristics.

She also loves opening drawers. She first taught herself to open cabinet doors in order to chew into a bag of cat treats I had "hidden" underneath the sink. (I'm a slow learner, but I now know it's almost impossible to hide things from Puzzles.) Once she realized her power, she started to test her limits. Occasionally, I will wander the house to find that every single dresser drawer has been pulled wide open. Recently, she's realized that there are upper cabinets. I heard a strange thumping sound one day and found her perched on top of the washing machine, trying to open the cabinet there.

She steals food. Let me start by saying that we adopted Puzzles when she was three months old, and she has lived on a steady diet of cat food and (occasional) cat treats ever since. We do not feed her people food. She has no reason to want people food. She is a well-fed and spoiled cat. Nevertheless, she has decided that she must have certain foods — sliced turkey, corn, tomatoes, and peas, to be precise. One time, she attacked a pineapple. Why? I don't know. All I know is that the humans of the house must maintain extreme vigilance to keep her from seizing her prize.

She climbs on the TV. Doesn't sound that impressive? Let me be more specific. She sits on top of the flat screen TV above our fireplace. It's an impressive leap that gives her very little to balance on, and once she's accomplished it, I can't reach her without a ladder.

You might be wondering — and I have been asked — why would

you pick a cat like that?

Well, the thing is, we didn't choose her. My husband, son, and I visited the local animal shelter one evening to adopt a cat, and I had only one requirement: no long-haired cats. An hour later, disappointed that none of the cats we'd asked to see had "clicked," I looked around the shelter one last time. That's when I noticed her: a kitten with long, fluffy, multicolored fur. She sat calmly in her cage, with all her attention focused on us. The rest of the cats were eating food, grooming, sleeping, or looking at each other. Only this long-haired kitten was making eye contact. When the volunteer took her out of the cage to meet with us, she went to my toddler immediately and began rubbing against his legs. "She likes me, Mom!" he squealed. She purred, which sealed the deal.

I had no intention of adopting her, but she chose us to be her people. Who can resist that? She may hate visitors, but she loves the family. When my husband works from home, she sits on his desk and meows occasionally to remind him to pet her. When the kids are here, she's usually in the middle of the action, watching over them. In the evenings, she takes turns visiting each of us, making sure we pet and admire her. And when it's time for my older son to go to bed, she does her best to herd him into the bedroom. Then she rests, cozy and comfortable at the end of his bed on a special fleece blanket he made just for her.

She may not be the sweetest or easiest feline to live with, but I feel lucky that she chose us. She's always entertaining, sweet (when she wants to be), intelligent, and loyal. Warning visitors to be cautious and keeping a watchful eye on our food and kitchen accessories seems a small price to pay for such a cat.

— Megan Nelson —

54

Lesson from Larry

Cats will outsmart dogs every time.
~John Grogan

I've wanted a cat for as long as I can remember. Now that I'm thirteen, I finally have one. His name is Larry.

Actually, my whole family, except for Dad, has wanted a cat for a long time. About a year ago, Dad finally gave in, and he and Mom went to the animal shelter. They brought home three-month-old Larry. My two younger sisters and I jumped for joy. At first, Larry trembled constantly because of our two large Labrador Retrievers. It wasn't long, though, before he taught us an important lesson.

The day was bitterly cold outside. Our family of five, along with our two dogs, was snuggled near the warm fireplace watching TV. The dogs, who weigh about ninety pounds each, were sleeping calmly together in their new dog bed after a long day of activity. Their eyes were closed, and they were snoring peacefully.

Larry had been keeping a watchful eye from atop his cat post. All at once, he jumped off his high perch. He bounced off the floor, raced over to where the dogs were sleeping and swatted them sharply, like a human swatting a fly. Larry was ready to fight, his claws out, his muscles tight. Larry wanted the new dog bed for himself, possibly because it was next to the warm fireplace, or maybe he just wanted to snuggle into the fluffy fur.

The second Larry attacked them, the dogs jumped up and yelped.

Both raced off their bed and out of Larry's way, their tails between their legs.

We couldn't help but laugh. What had just happened? Had our cat just kicked two ninety-pound dogs off their bed? Perfectly placed next to the warm fireplace, Larry fell asleep and had a wonderful nap. No one bothered him, not even the dogs.

We learned an important lesson from Larry that day, which we won't soon forget: Size doesn't matter. If you want something, go for it.

Thanks, Larry.

— Brook-Lynn Meijer, age 13 —

55

Convicted Feline

Tree decorating with cats. O Christmas tree,
O Christmas tree, your ornaments are history!
~Courtney VanSickle

"Ohhhh, Kobe, not again," I moaned as I walked into my living room after a long day of work. My sweet cat Kobe had once again unwound all the Christmas lights from the tree and laid them in straight lines across the carpet. He sat among the strands and gazed at me proudly. How Kobe was able to accomplish this feat, and why, remained a mystery.

"Kobe," I would sigh every time I re-strung the lights, "I love you, but you're making so much work for me!"

These petty offenses, though, were trivial compared to what became known to our family as Kobe's criminal "feline-y."

Kobe was a Christmas kitty. I had adopted the tiny white ball of fluff at the age of eight weeks from a shelter on December twenty-first several years earlier.

"He's the only survivor of the litter," the manager had informed me. "His siblings all died from a flea infestation in a house whose occupants should never have owned pets."

Named because he closely resembled the statuettes of the iconic Japanese white lucky cat, Kobe was the happiest and most affectionate kitten I had ever known. His purrs were so loud that a young neighbor nicknamed him "Motorhead."

Immediately on his arrival in my home, Kobe made his bed under the Christmas tree on top of the gifts. During his second Christmas season, my mischievous little cat began his years-long habit of climbing up the tree and disassembling the lights. He also found my prized ornaments especially delectable.

Despite his eccentricities, Kobe was a beautiful, loving and healthy cat. I adored him.

A few weeks before Christmas one year, my elderly Aunt Fiona called.

"I'm sending you a little something I made for your tree," Fiona said when she announced that she'd be flying in to spend Christmas with the family. Picturing a knitted ornament, I thanked her politely.

Aunt Fiona had left California many decades before, marrying a small-town doctor in the deep South. We all loved her and smiled at her fierce allegiance to proper Southern customs that were often at odds with our casual West Coast lifestyle of shorts and flip-flops.

When Fiona's gift arrived a few days later, I was flabbergasted. She had hand-stitched an exquisite Christmas tree skirt. On its base of white felt, my aunt had sewn the Twelve Days of Christmas out of thousands of brilliantly colored beads and sequins. Each of the days was separated from the next, with literally Six Geese a-Laying and Seven Swans a-Swimming among the various sections.

"Oh, Aunt Fiona, this is gorgeous," I gushed when I called to thank her. "It's truly a work of art that belongs in a museum! It must have taken you months to create."

"Well, honey, I'm glad you like it," she replied. "I made one for your sister, too. I look forward to seeing them under your trees when I get there."

Knowing Kobe's fondness for gnawing on anything Christmas, I stored the tree skirt in a closet until shortly before Aunt Fiona arrived.

The morning of December twenty-third, I placed the skirt carefully around the base of my Christmas tree and covered it all around with gifts, towels, wrapping paper, heavy boxes and chairs to keep it safe.

"Nice job, Nancy!" I congratulated myself on protecting Aunt Fiona's masterpiece.

"And Kobe," I warned him, "I need you to behave today because Aunt Fiona's coming to see us." I gave him a hug and headed out the door for my last day of work before Christmas.

Arriving home in a holiday mood at 6:00 p.m., I turned on a lamp and glanced over at my Christmas tree.

"Good boy, Kobe," I said, praising my mischievous kitty for leaving all the lights on the tree for a change.

But upon turning on the tree lights, I gasped.

"Oh, no! Aghhhhh!" I jumped back and shrieked in horror.

Kobe had somehow uncovered Aunt Fiona's tree skirt from its protective packages and devoured the Eight Maids a-Milking, Nine Ladies Dancing and Ten Lords a-Leaping — hundreds of sequins and beads, along with the thread. All that was left was a wide swath of empty and shredded white felt with a scant few stray beads. I should have known better.

"Kobe! How in the world did you do this?" I demanded of my little white beast. He looked up at me sweetly and purred.

I called my longtime veterinarian in a panic.

"Doctor, you're not going to believe what Kobe did this time!" I was nearly hyperventilating. I needed a doctor myself.

"Bring him in," she instructed. Dr. Anna was accustomed to my kitty's misadventures, including his appetite for odd items. On her examination table, she lightly squeezed up and down Kobe's belly and determined that he hadn't devoured anything of size.

"I'm giving him a laxative. Take him home, give him water and don't let him eat anything but cat food," she advised. "It should all come out naturally."

Returning to my house, I closed Kobe in a bedroom and frantically called my older sister Julie to tell her about my cat's latest misadventure.

"Aunt Fiona's going to be shocked," she scolded. "How could you let that happen?"

"I know it's all my fault," I replied as tears filled my eyes.

We talked about possible solutions considering Aunt Fiona's imminent arrival.

"You can show it to her and break her heart," Julie said.

"Or I can tell her beforehand and still break her heart," I replied.

We called a quick family meeting, and everyone decided in favor of kindness toward Aunt Fiona, due to her advanced age. I turned the tree skirt around so the damaged area faced the wall, but it was still visible. If Aunt Fiona noticed it, I would apologize profusely for Kobe's destruction.

On Christmas morning, my relatives rang the doorbell, and the festivities began.

I held my breath as Aunt Fiona inspected her creation.

"It looks just lovely under your tree, honey," she said.

"Thank you, Aunt Fiona. I will always treasure it," I answered truthfully.

For days, Kobe's litter box sparkled with multi-colored sequins and beads.

In the end, we never had to reveal that my impish kitty had chomped down three of Aunt Fiona's Twelve Days of Christmas. And I never again laid what remained of her magnificent Christmas tree skirt under my tree unless I was in the room to supervise.

As for my precious, precocious Kobe, he astonishingly lived a very long and happy life.

— Nancy Saint John —

56

The Houseguest

Down deep, we're all motivated by the same urges.
Cats have the courage to live by them.
~Jim Davis

We'd always looked forward to visits from my brother Ron and his family during the summer. They'd load up their four young daughters and head across the Canadian border to our home in Sandy, Oregon, for a two-week stay.

Although every visit has been memorable, one in particular comes to mind more frequently than the others — the summer they decided to bring along their newly adopted cat.

Panther was a large, mixed-breed feline with beautiful green eyes and a mischievous attitude to put it mildly.

Since my parents lived up the gravel road from us, my brother and sister-in-law slept in their upstairs spare bedroom, while their daughters usually chose to stay the night at our house with their cousins.

Although Mom and Dad hadn't owned a cat in years, they had been toying with the idea of adopting one; that plan fell to the wayside after spending time with Panther.

The feisty feline landed somewhere between a welcome distraction and an unbelievable nightmare — leaning heavily on the nightmare side. In fact, Mom honestly began to wonder if his antics were peculiar to Canadian-bred cats.

Panther took great pleasure in lurking around the corner, waiting for the perfect opportunity to leap out and startle Mom and Dad. He would also run in front of them in what appeared to be a deliberate attempt to trip them.

I'm not certain that Panther meant to scare the living daylights out of Mom when he gifted her with a lively little mouse, dropping it at her feet while she was preparing dinner. Perhaps he thought of it as an apology for his earlier pranks. But Mom wasn't buying it, and her shrieks frightened away both the cat and the mouse.

But the night Panther snuck out, climbed to the top of the roof of my parents' two-story house, and howled at the top of his lungs took the cake. Since my brother was out having a drink with my husband, my tenacious sister-in-law Carole tried for over an hour to coax the stubborn cat down without success. Afraid he'd wake up my sleeping parents (and, more importantly, the surrounding neighbors), she had to resort to more extreme measures.

Though terrified of heights, Carole's only option was to drag a tall, wooden ladder she found in the garage to the roof's edge where she lured the cat over with a treat. Grabbing him with one arm while hugging the ladder tightly with the other, she prayed nobody would mistake her for an intruder in the dark night and call the police or, heaven forbid, take action on their own.

That terrifying thought, however, soon proved to be the least of her worries.

Halfway down the ladder, the frightened animal leaped frantically from Carole's tight clutch, crashed through the huge screen on my parents' open bedroom window, and landed smack on top of my sleeping mom. *Splat!*

Carole, who was faced with calming my mother and the cat, claimed Mom's screams could be heard around the world!

For obvious reasons, the entire family spent the rest of their vacation sleeping at our house. We didn't mind the rowdy cat; in fact, he wasn't much of a challenge for our four energetic boys. Together, they provided just enough feistiness to keep us all on our toes.

The morning our guests prepared to leave was met with mixed emotions. We always hated to see them go, but there was little doubt in my mind as to how relieved Mom and Dad were about the prospect of being Panther-free for at least another year.

Not surprisingly, my parents never did end up with a cat of their own. Before Panther had even gotten home to Canada, Dad was checking out available dog adoptions.

— Connie Kaseweter Pullen —

57

Perfect Angels

*Dogs come when they're called; cats take a message
and get back to you later.*
~Mary Bly

I hated when our neighbors went away on vacation. They were great people and always brought us nice gifts when they returned, but I hated when they left because they always asked me to care for their two cats.

How hard could it be? That's exactly what I thought the first time they asked me to cat-sit. *Sure, I'd be happy to do that. I love animals.* They were indoor cats, so I simply had to feed them in the morning and make sure they had water. I'd clean the litter box, and that would be it until dinnertime when I would feed them again and check their water. No big deal, right? Wrong!

Our neighbors' cats didn't like it when their "parents" went away. And I don't think they liked me. I can't be sure about that because I never got close enough to them to pet them. Actually, I only ever saw one of the cats, and that was when he dashed out of the room when I came in. My neighbor told me she had two cats, but maybe one of them was imaginary. I never saw the second cat.

Here's how my cat-sitting adventures would go: My neighbors would leave, and I would start my cat-sitting duties. The first day wasn't bad at all. My guess is that the cats hadn't figured out that their parents had left yet. I would walk next door, open the front door and call to the cats, Bobo and Buddy, in the sweetest voice possible. "Here, kitty, kitty. Nice kitties. Do you want your dinner?" No answer. No sweet meows to acknowledge my presence. No hissing. Nothing. I would open the cans of cat food and dump the food into their bowls. I would make sure they had extra kibble and water, and then I would leave until the next morning.

I dreaded going over in the morning. By then, Bobo and Buddy had figured out that they had been left behind and I was taking care of them. Oh, the price I had to pay. As usual, I would walk over and open the front door. I would call sweetly as "the streaker" dashed out of the room and down the hall. Then I would look around the room and see the havoc that had taken place during the night.

Plants — and my neighbor had a lot of plants — would be overturned, and the dirt would be all over the floor. Books and pictures would be knocked off the shelves and strewn about. The two food dishes would have been batted out of the kitchen. Thank goodness they were always empty, so I didn't have to clean up the food. The water bowls would be overturned, with the water spilled everywhere. The litter box was another matter. The litter would be scattered all over, but it wasn't used. Instead, I would find "gifts" on the floor in all the rooms of the house. And I had to look for my gifts so they wouldn't stay there the whole time my neighbors were away and ruin the floors. I guess that was the cats' ultimate vengeance.

So, the clean-up would begin. It would take me over an hour to get things straightened up. I would grumble and mumble and swear at those damn cats the whole time I was picking up plants, sweeping up dirt, picking up books and pictures, mopping up water, sweeping up litter and picking up "gifts." Then I would refill the cat food and water bowls, and make sure there was enough litter in the litter box. I'm not sure why I bothered since the cats didn't use the litter box.

After my morning duties were finished, I would go home. All day long, I would be dreading my return trip at dinnertime. It would be a repeat performance of what I had found in the morning — more messes, dirt and "gifts" for me to deal with. Damn cats!

They knew exactly what they were doing. It was retribution for their parents leaving them. I tried to tell my neighbors what went on when they were away, but they had a hard time believing me. Their sweet kitties would never do that! They never had to deal with the vindictive behavior that I received. Not once. No plants overturned, no books or pictures knocked off the shelves, and especially no strewn litter or unwanted gifts! Just picture-perfect kitties.

My neighbors finally moved away and took the cats with them. I did miss my neighbors, but I didn't miss having to care for the cats — if there were actually two of them!

— Barbara LoMonaco —

58

Attack Cat

Cats are only human; they have their faults.
~Kingsley Amis

Miss Skitters moved in for the kill. "Mom," I warned. "She's not playing."

"Yes, she is," my mom answered, peeking at Miss Skitters from around the corner of the kitchen. This was not going to end well.

"She's really not playing!" I insisted, watching as my cat stalked my mother.

Then it happened. Miss Skitters leaped and wrapped all four legs around Mom's right leg. Mom let out a shout and shook her leg to get rid of the biting, scratching, hissing and growling beast. Miss Skitters clamped down harder. Mom panicked. I raced forward and tugged until the cat's claws ripped away from Mom's jeans.

My husband and I always instructed friends and relatives not to touch our gray-and-white cat. The warning generally went unheeded. Why? She was extremely cute and appeared harmless. But looks, as they say, can be deceiving.

Take the time our good friends came to visit. This was their first time meeting our cat. Our friend walked toward Miss Skitters and crouched down. He stretched out a hand to our feisty feline.

"I wouldn't do that if I were you," my husband warned.

"All animals like me," he replied. He proceeded to wiggle his fingers.

"Here, kitty, kitty," the soon-to-be-victim called out.

"Honey, maybe you shouldn't do that," suggested his wife.

Miss Skitters' eyes glared at him from beneath the couch. Her throat rumbled. Still, he reached forward. A glint of Miss Skitters' lightning-fast claws flashed — or should I say, slashed? Our wide-eyed friend became the recipient of Miss Skitters' wrath — a six-inch gash on his arm. My aunt once made that same mistake and received the same parting gift.

Perhaps better than anyone, my sister understood my cat's capabilities. When my sister came for visits, she slept on our couch in the living room. One night, she awoke to Miss Skitters perched atop her chest, hissing and growling. Our cat's teeth hovered inches above her face.

Miss Skitters attacked out of fear — but also out of loyalty. Our cat acted as a protector. A knock at the door always brought Miss Skitters running. Once, when my husband was out of town for work, she became particularly aggressive. As I talked with a salesperson, door partially open, I used my right leg to keep my shrieking cat at bay. Ears flattened, Miss Skitters wanted to sink her fangs into this unwanted intruder's leg. The salesperson knew it and ended his sales pitch quickly.

And then there was the time we went on vacation. My friend stopped by our apartment to check on Miss Skitters and our other cat, Little Buddy. Little Buddy posed no threat. Miss Skitters, on the other hand, acted like a guard dog. Before leaving, my friend used the bathroom. On her way out, Miss Skitters appeared and blocked her path.

"It's okay, Skitters," my friend said soothingly to the growling sentinel.

For whatever reason, Miss Skitters allowed safe passage. My nephew wasn't as fortunate. On that day, everyone was outside. My eight-year-old nephew went inside to use the bathroom. Wondering what was taking him so long, I went inside and discovered him crying. He stood stock-still, afraid to leave the bathroom. Miss Skitters was putting on a fearsome display.

"Go on, Skitters," I commanded.

Reluctantly, she acquiesced and retreated, narrowed eyes still planted on my nephew.

Even at the end of her life, in extreme pain, Miss Skitters offered one final demonstration. She provided throat rumbling, shrieking, and spitting while lying on the vet's table. He administered a sedative before putting her to sleep.

"I'm glad you loved her," he said. "I don't know if anyone else would have."

The words sound harsh, but they weren't. Our kind-hearted vet simply spoke the truth. We were destined to be her people. Skitters was intended to be our cat — and she demonstrated her love for us fiercely.

— Lisa Mackinder —

59

Squeak

Cats don't like change without their consent.
~Roger A. Caras

L iterally everything that could have gone wrong in my one-bedroom flat had, culminating in a fevered rush to escape what seemed like a cursed home. There was the upstairs neighbor who started using a poorly made 3D printer that shrieked and groaned throughout the night like an unappeased ghost. There was the landlord's decision to tear up the flooring in the hallway, so that tenants had to step cautiously across large and worrisome holes. Yet it was a burst pipe in the ceiling and the surprise waterfall that flooded my entire apartment that finally inspired me to move to the first suitable new accommodation I could find.

In my haste, I packed up everything easily transportable, including my newest foster cat, and fled to what I hoped would be greener pastures.

Pushed into a cat carrier and whisked away from everything she knew, Chicory was not pleased and showed it by wailing loudly. Never one to hide her feelings, she allowed everyone we passed on the street to know that she was quite angry. She caterwauled miserably in the taxicab, yowled up the walkway of the new apartment building, and cried out passionately as I unlocked the front door of the new flat.

Having taken pains to arrange the furniture exactly as it had been in our old apartment, I opened the carrier door and let her out, hoping she might be fooled into thinking we were back home. Yet, once free,

Chic didn't stop her vocalizations. Switching from loud, angry calls to suspicious hissing, Chic threatened the sofa, lamps and coffee table before retreating to the bedroom to hide.

Chicory had been a rescue. Lost and starving on the street as a kitten, she had come to me hardened and fearful of humans. As with most feral cats, she made me work to earn her trust, and I worried that the move would destroy all the months of hard-won progress. Hoping she would let me know when she was less angry and afraid, I set out her food bowls and litter box and went to unpack.

For three days, I worked on settling in, catching glimpses of Chic only at mealtimes. I did my best to reassure her that we were in a better, more peaceful place, but she was having none of it. Accepting my petting with sulky looks and a few muttered hisses, she would slip back under the bed, waiting for the moment when she felt this new apartment was her own territory.

That moment came sooner than I expected.

At the end of our first week in the new flat, I was weary and looking forward to going to bed when I heard a strange little noise. It was a repeated, high-pitched sound that made me pause while I was arranging my books on the new bookshelves.

Listening intently for a few seconds, I had to admit that it was undeniably an insistent, continuous squeaking.

My heart sank. *I've got rats!* I thought, rubbing my hands over my face. *Oh, heaven help me. I've got rats.*

The curse of the bad apartment seemed to have followed me, and this time it was even worse. How in the world could I deal with a rat infestation? Having spent all my money in the move, there was nothing left for even the most basic of pest-control measures.

Disheartened, I tried to track down the sound, but when I finally followed the noise to the kitchen, it stopped, replaced by expectant silence. Even stranger, all of the plastic bags I had stowed under the kitchen sink were strewn across the floor. Hesitantly, I returned the bags to their cardboard storage box, and closed and latched the cabinet door, wondering if it was possible that I was losing my mind due to stress.

Exhausted, I got ready for bed and settled down, but in less than twenty minutes I was brought to full wakefulness by another round of squeaking.

Leaping from bed, I ran to the kitchen and flipped on the light, only to once again find complete silence and the plastic bags strewn across the tiles.

When I turned, I found Chicory blinking at me from beside the refrigerator, a sheepish look on her little gray face.

"Baby, do we have rats?" I asked her, recognizing panic in my voice. "Did you see little ratties, sweetie?"

Strangely, Chic came and wrapped herself around my ankles. Then, in a high, sweet voice that I hadn't heard since before we moved, she chirped, asking me for food. It was a sure sign that she was pleased with herself.

Hoping that Chicory the Mighty Hunter was on the case, I stroked her ears, gave her a midnight snack and went to bed more confused and upset than when I had gotten up.

The next day, I awoke to find once again that the plastic bags had been pulled out of their box and were heaped on the floor just under the kitchen sink. One or two had been dragged out to the hallway, but the rest had been formed into a small, neat pile, almost like a nest. There was no sign of rat droppings or any indication that rodents had gnawed at the food items on the shelves, but I could think of no other explanation for what was happening. It seemed that my living situation had gone from bad to worse, the apartment curse following me like a poltergeist.

That afternoon, I waited miserably for the sound of rodents while answering e-mails. When the inevitable squealing began, I stood up and took off my shoes, determined to catch the culprits in the act.

Rounding the corner to the kitchen on my tiptoes, I stopped in my tracks, mouth falling open in shock. Instead of rats, I found Chicory standing on top of a pile of plastic bags she had dragged out from under the sink, the cabinet door mysteriously unlatched and open behind her.

As I watched, she leaped into the air and landed on the bags, squealing in delight. Over and over, she pounced. Then with a deft strike of her paw, she swiped at a bag, squeaking joyfully as she knocked it aside. After a few moments of vicious assault, the bags were arranged to her liking, so Chic sat down to clean her tail, purring in obvious contentment.

A mixture of relief and delighted indignation swept through me. It seemed that rats were not the problem after all. Unable to stop myself from giggling, I called out to Chicory.

"So, what do you think?" I asked her, hand extended to stroke her chin. "Still mad at me?"

Looking up from her pile of plastic bags, Chic eyed me for a moment, as though uncertain. Then, rising to her feet, she sauntered over for a petting.

— Alex Lester —

60

Stuck in a Tree

You can judge a man's true character by the way
he treats his fellow animals.
~Paul McCartney

"Oliver's stuck in a tree and can't get down!" my son Spencer cried frantically. "Call the Fire Department! Call the Fire Department!"

Trying to act composed, I responded that Oliver had climbed the tree and would climb down when he was ready. Oliver, a friendly gray-and-white male cat, loves chasing birds and squirrels. He's always running off, but is never more than a holler away. The first time Ollie escaped from the house, we were worried. He returned unscathed and looking quite content as he sat on the window ledge waiting to come in. After that incident, Oliver makes a habit of coming and going several times a day, settling in at night.

Ollie often climbs a big tree trunk in the yard, using it as a scratching post, but it was unusual to see him venturing out on a tree branch a few stories high. He had spent three hours out on the limb when nine-year-old Spencer decided to take matters into his own hands. Without anyone's knowledge, he leaned a ladder against the tree and attempted to coax Oliver down.

"Spencer's stuck in a tree with Oliver, and they can't get down!" my other son Steven cried frantically. "Call the Fire Department! Call the Fire Department!" This was beginning to look like *Groundhog Day* as events began repeating themselves and getting more complicated each time.

I called the Fire Department and told them my son had climbed up to rescue our cat from the tree, and now they were both stuck.

"Well, don't send anyone else up, or you'll have your entire family sitting in a tree," he said jokingly. "We'll be right there!"

A fire truck arrived minutes later with the proper equipment: a rescue ladder and two men with gloved hands. They climbed the ladder lickety-split and did their job. My son came down step by step without a scratch. Our cat was tossed gently into a small net. It was an exciting double rescue that my family and neighbors won't soon forget.

The next time Oliver climbed up the tree, we ignored his meows. He got the message and always came down on his own.

I know the decision for my two boys to become firemen had nothing to do with this rescue, but it was a positive learning experience in their lives. Today, as they save people and animals from burning buildings and commit to their community, they exemplify the best role models for our younger generation.

Ten years ago, Spencer the fireman rescued two kittens from a burning building. Since Momma Cat was nowhere to be found, the kittens were adopted by our family. Fortunately, these two kittens are indoor cats and have neither had the opportunity to climb a tree nor be stuck in one. Of course if they did, I could get a friendly visit from my sons.

— Irene Maran —

Four-Legged Friends

One Special Friend

Prowling his own quiet backyard or asleep by the fire,
he is still only a whisker away from the wilds.
~Jean Burden

I grew up with animals, so when I was away at college and lonely I decided to get a cat. I searched and searched, finally finding a family that was looking for a home for their Maine Coon, a huge, fluffy, polydactyl cat.

Asumo and I adjusted to each other pretty quickly. It was a smooth transition, except that his first family made him eat vegan, so some adjustment to his diet was needed. Given his hunting skills, I'm pretty sure he was never fully vegan anyway.

This cat was amazing. I would go on walks through the woods, and he would follow behind. He would be waiting for me when I got home from classes. There was never a moment when he wasn't there for me.

Yes, we had some issues in our relationship. He insisted on bringing me presents and leaving them on my bed, sometimes alive. As much as I loved him sleeping with me, the gifts got him kicked out of my bedroom. He also had a thing for salads. I could never make a salad without him jumping up and begging. He loved tomatoes and lettuce — probably a throwback from his vegan days.

But his most enduring trait was that he was never haughty or mean. He was a big, deep sea of calm. Nothing ruffled him. Big dogs would accost him, and he would just sit there. They would get the funniest look on their faces and just give up. I watched a bear walk by him and give him a wide berth. He would watch other neighborhood cats fight it out, but he never got involved.

Asumo did have one good friend — one that I wasn't happy about. I met the friend one summer night when I had left the kitchen door open. I heard Asumo eating in the kitchen, but when I went in I saw two animals eating from the cat dish: Asumo and a skunk. I froze and backed out of the room slowly. After the skunk finished eating, he walked outside and I was able to close the kitchen door.

That was a close one. But that wasn't the last time. Mr. Skunk was around so much that I eventually named him Bob and started keeping the cat food outside. He and Asumo would be found lounging together on my deck. For two years, they were pretty solid companions. I got used to coming home and having to wait for Bob to leave so I could get out of my car.

Bob stopped coming around one day, and Asumo truly mourned. Asumo didn't come home for days and continued to look for him for quite a while. Eventually, I got another cat to give him another companion, but that didn't work. He never made a friend again.

Asumo lived a good, long life with me. When he died at sixteen I buried him far back on my property underneath a huge rock formation. I thought it would be fitting as he liked to climb to the top and watch everything. And wouldn't you know it, a skunk family moved into that rock formation the next spring.

— Karleen Forwell —

Sibling Rivalry

*The reason cats climb is so that they can look down on
almost every other animal.*
~KC Buffington

Like many young couples, my husband and I were looking for something to nurture but weren't quite ready to start a family. Into our lives came Smoky and Sparky, gray and black littermates. They were aptly named since my husband was a fireman. It was so much fun having two kittens together. Their antics were hysterical, and we were never short of entertainment.

We got these two while we were in an apartment, but soon purchased our first home, a small bungalow. The cats were now able to play in the yard as well as the house. Not long after, we added Sheba to the mix, a rambunctious white German Shepherd. Sheba loved to chase the cats around the house and often singled out Smoky for her torment. Maybe she did it a little too often for the frisky young feline. Maybe she was a little too rough about it. Either way, Smoky must have been fed up, given what she did next.

One beautiful sunny day, I had thrown open all the windows and was enjoying the fresh air. The curtains waved softly in the breeze, birds were singing, and all was good. Working around the house, I suddenly heard incessant barking coming from one of the bedrooms. "What is that dog up to now?" I thought. "Is she torturing one of those cats again?"

I walked briskly into the bedroom, ready to scold her and get her away from whichever cat she had cornered. I was stopped short by the sight in the window. Smoky was on the outside, hanging onto the screen with all four legs sprawled out from her body. Initially, I thought she had gotten herself stuck trying to get in, and I was about to go outside to rescue her.

It only took a moment to understand what was really going on. Sheba had her front paws up on the windowsill and was barking furiously into Smoky's face. The cat remained suspended and motionless in the middle of the window for a couple of minutes. All the while, the dog was going nuts.

It occurred to me that she was doing this on purpose, knowing full well that the dog couldn't get to her. It was as if Smoky was taunting Sheba like a child chanting, "Nah, nah, nah, nah, nah! You can't get me!" I laughed out loud and cheered her on, now unconcerned that the screen might get wrecked from her claws. I'm convinced she hung there as long as she could take it. Then she extracted herself, dropped down and walked away. Point made.

I leaned close to the window and observed Smoky heading to the back yard. I'm pretty sure I detected a proud strut, not just a regular walk. I imagined her saying, "Humph, that'll teach you to mess with me!" After all, cats rule, dogs drool.

— Carolyn Barrett —

Gizmo to
the Rescue

*Nurturing is not complex. It's simply being tuned in
to the thing or person before you and offering small
gestures toward what it needs at that time.*
~Mary Anne Radmacher

When we walked into PetSmart, I had no intention of going home with a kitten. We were only there to shop for the dog; I never should've let my husband out of my sight. On my way to the checkout counter, with a bag of dog food in one hand and a box of treats in the other, I saw him wave at me from behind a cat-toy display. "Hey! Come look at this kitten."

"But I don't want another cat," I protested.

"Just come look. I'm not saying you have to take it home."

The local animal shelter had partnered with the store to help cats and kittens find their forever homes. I followed my husband to the windowed wall at the end of the cat-food aisle. The first kitten I noticed was a gray mackerel tabby with bright green eyes. She watched us intently as we approached and then stood on her back legs and pressed her front paws to the glass.

"See?" my husband said. "She likes me."

I touched the window, and the kitten patted at my hand, first with one paw, then the other. Her tiny mew from behind the glass was barely audible. I laughed as she peered at me from between her front paws — pink toes pressed against the glass. She reminded me of a kid peeking into a candy-store window.

"I'm not sure how Charlie would feel about having another cat in the house," I said.

Charlie is the blind cat we'd rescued the year before. He got along well with the dog, but I was apprehensive about taking home a kitten.

"But maybe Charlie needs a companion," my husband said.

"He has me," I said. "We'd better go." As we walked away, the tabby patted at the glass as if to say, "Wait. Where are you going? Take me with you."

We paid, left the store and got into the car. Before turning the key, my husband looked at me. "Are you sure you don't want her? She seems nice."

I nodded, and he pulled out of the parking lot. We drove in silence all the way through the city. I couldn't stop thinking about that sassy kitten. Did Charlie need a companion? He already had an anxiety disorder. Would a kitten create issues? Would the kitty get adopted or end up back at the shelter?

"I was just thinking…," I said aloud.

From the driver's seat, my husband smiled. "I'll turn around and go back," he said. Twenty minutes later, we were back at the store, filling out adoption papers and buying kitten chow.

At home, I set the cat crate on the kitchen floor, opened its door, and carried Charlie in to introduce him to his new sister. He picked up her scent before she ventured out and puffed up and hissed. His low growl changed pitch and elevated to a scream. The kitten retreated to the back of the carrier, and I closed the door, fearing a catfight would ensue. There was an intruder in Charlie's house, and he was not happy about it.

I knew it would take days, maybe even weeks, for the cats to accept one another. So, the next morning when they curled up together on the dog's bed, I was shocked. Almost instantly, Charlie decided the little intruder would be his friend. They've been inseparable ever since.

We named the kitty Gizmo, and she made herself at home quickly.

She learned her way around by climbing curtains, jumping onto counters, knocking over plants and ignoring the words, "Stop that!" More than once, she made me spill my coffee. I wasn't used to turning around in the kitchen and seeing a green-eyed gremlin staring at me from atop the refrigerator.

Months passed, and as she grew from kitten to cat, she mellowed out and found her place in the world as companion to her blind friend.

The same neurological issue that caused Charlie's blindness also made him prone to seizures and bouts of anxiety. We don't know what triggers the episodes, but when he has a bad day, he'll pace the house repeatedly and meow incessantly. He spins, pants and becomes so agitated that he can't sit still for more than a few seconds. That's when his little sister will come to the rescue.

Gizmo will follow Charlie, intercepting his pacing. She'll put a paw on his neck and lick his face and ears. Within minutes, the two of them will be playing together or snuggled up on a chair.

If Charlie has a seizure, he's exhausted for hours afterward. Gizmo is always there to comfort him, grooming his face and ears and sleeping at his side until he's feeling better.

Now grown up, fourteen-pound Gizmo doesn't care to be held and has no interest in cat toys. Her affection and playtime are reserved for Charlie. The two of them engage regularly in epic wrestling matches and love chasing each other up and down the hall—feet thumping like Clydesdales—usually at 3:00 a.m. When it's mealtime, she sits patiently, allowing her companion to eat before helping herself to the kibble. She is a considerate and loyal friend.

It is clear to us that Gizmo is Charlie's emotional-support animal. And because of her, we've been able to avoid treating his anxiety with medications. Until the day we brought that sassy kitten home, I had no idea what was missing from Charlie's life. I'm glad my husband wandered off that day in PetSmart, and I am grateful for the pink-toed tabby who plays such a significant role in our family.

—Ann Morrow—

Friendship Is the Best

There are friends, there is family, and then there are
friends that become family.
~Author Unknown

I read "Free Kittens" on the sign
At Geren's old feed store.
With fingers crossed I made my way
Straight through the large scuffed door.

There and then I spotted her
Amidst the playful cries;
The sweetest orange tabby cat —
Big ears and bright green eyes.

She'd really be quite perfect
For mother and for me;
A delightful furry bundle
Of boundless energy.

We chose to name her Pumpkin
Since it was late in the fall.
With harvests all around us,
It was the perfect call.

A clever little lass was she,
And oh so very bright;
Full of savvy elfin pranks
Like turning off the light.

With no tolerance for grandkids,
She kept them all at bay.
She wasn't fond of other pets,
Quickly hissing them away.

A self-appointed princess
who proudly claimed her reign.
No cats or dogs were brave enough
To challenge her domain.

But Pumpkin's ten long years of rule
and calling every play
Ended quite abruptly
When Ralph showed up one day.

The scruffy little Terrier
Was quick to settle in.
But Pumpkin was determined
To resist through thick and thin.

So when he had the nerve to jump
Upon her favorite chair,
And snooze there like he owned it,
It was more than she could bear.

She dashed into the bedroom
And hopped on Granny's bed.
But before she got a plan in place,
He was nudging at her head.

This wasn't going smoothly.
Ralph couldn't comprehend
the plain and simple fact at hand —
She didn't want a friend.

She clearly was the princess,
And this was her terrain.
The nerve of that mere common mutt
Was truly quite insane.

Still Ralph persisted weeks on end;
He couldn't let it lie.
She might never learn to pal around,
But he'd give it his best try.

When he tried to share his toys,
She'd snub him nonetheless.
Attempts to lie down next to her
Were met with no success.

But Ralph was slow and steady;
He never held a grudge.
And Pumpkin mellowed gradually,
And learned how to not judge.

Day by day the hissing slowed,
Since much to her surprise,
He wasn't near the awful threat
That she had first surmised.

Ralph taught her by example,
And Pumpkin soon caught on.
She knew that she would miss him
If tomorrow he were gone.

Now purring sounds are plentiful.
And we can all attest:
Regal bearing's admirable,
But friendship is the best!

—Connie Kaseweter Pullen—

65

War and Peace

Meow means "woof" in cat.
~George Carlin

A tough, tiger-striped tabby, Bogey isn't the sort of cat who takes to strangers. He never runs away or hides like most cats do when alarmed. Bogey's behavior is far more dog-like. He heads straight to the front door, determined to sniff out the facts on whether the person who rang the bell is friend or foe.

Given his personality, I worried about what would happen when I brought home a rescue pup named Winston. Would Bogey hiss and swipe at his new housemate? Determined to make the situation work, I introduced them slowly. Bogey eyed Winston with a wary gaze, his tail straight up and his hair puffed out so far that he looked enormous. Winston's tail wagged to a blur, and he dropped into play bow position, clearly showing he wanted to be friends. But Bogey glared at him with disdain and stalked away, not a bit interested in a canine companion.

This went on for days, with the addition of deep feline growls whenever Winston got too close. I sighed. Not only were my cat and dog apparently not destined to be chums, but Bogey had declared war. The best I could hope for would be tolerance. Even when feeding them, I kept their bowls a room's length apart. It wouldn't help matters to have either animal treading near the other's food.

A few weeks after Winston's arrival, I was preparing their dinners when the doorbell rang. I plopped the bowls on the floor and scurried to answer the door. Neither of them followed me. When it came to a choice between food or checking out a stranger, they agreed on one thing: Food came first.

After I signed for the package, I realized I hadn't separated the food bowls! I raced for the kitchen. There I found them finishing up their meal while giving each other the side-eye. Fearing a potential conflict was brewing, I stepped to the area where both bowls sat empty on the floor. My cat stayed still as a statue while Winston inched toward him… and then slurped his face. I held my breath, prepared to intervene, but nothing happened. No puffball of fur. No hissing. No swipe of the paw.

From that day forward, things changed. I caught Bogey and Winston lying side by side on the sofa. Some days they'd chase each other — for all the world like a couple of dogs playing tag. They delighted in wrestling their way across the carpet, obviously having a wonderful time. I'd never seen anything like it between a cat and a dog.

The kicker came on the day my son stopped by. He played with Winston by holding a toy just out of reach while Winston jumped for it, barking loudly. Soon, Bogey came on the run. He hissed at my son, apparently thinking Winston was getting a raw deal. Amused, my son let Winston have his toy. This settled Bogey down, who then leaped to a tabletop where he kept a watchful eye on the proceedings.

My cat had transformed from enemy to protector in a swift détente. I never would have guessed at such an outcome.

"You two are a pair," I told them after I stopped laughing.

Who knows? Maybe world peace is possible after all.

— Pat Wahler —

66

Yours, Mine and Ours

*I love cats because I love my home, and after a while
they become its visible soul.*
~Jean Cocteau

We were newlyweds, the second marriage for both of us. We were empty nesters except for our long-time pets. Katie was Jim's sixteen-year-old Westie, half-blind, mostly deaf and arthritic, but still full of personality. I brought two elderly cats into Katie's house. Maggie was fourteen years old, red-haired and feisty like her namesake, Margaret Thatcher. Wally was fifteen, a big, lumbering joker. He had long gray fur that looked like a science experiment with static electricity. Lovingly, we called him Wild Wally.

Jim and I could not let our elderly pets keep us apart, so we hoped that they would find a way to coexist. Luckily, after a few tense encounters, they formed a workable truce. The cats, Wally and Maggie, were still nimble enough to hold the high ground, while Katie the dog owned the floor.

Wild Wally kept a wary eye out for Katie, hugging the perimeter of a room with an eye on his escape route until he reached his elevated destination. Maggie was the smarter of the two cats. She would sit in the doorway of the room and assess Katie's status. Once she was sure the dog was sleeping, Maggie would stroll brazenly into the room.

Eventually, Maggie's scent woke Katie. She would jump to her feet, growling, nose to the ground, hunting for that pesky feline intruder. By then, Maggie was safely on my lap, purring contentedly. We are convinced her purring was the feline equivalent of laughter as she lorded it over the dog.

Jim and I had combined two households, and we finally realized we had to slim down our belongings. Our yard sale was held on a sunny and warm June day. I was filled with emotion as I watched so many of my possessions carted away. No one knew the memories that went with those appliances and furniture and bits of sports gear.

At the end of the long, hectic and emotional day, we were preparing to feed the pets. But Wally was missing. My cats had lived their long lives indoors and had no experience outside. Wally must have run out during the hubbub of the yard sale. We walked the neighborhood calling his name.

I walked alone after dark, crying as I continued the search. Our neighborhood is an isolated oasis of a few hundred homes in the middle of thousands of acres of farmland. The gentle breeze moving the trees created night noises that were frightening to a lifelong city dweller like me. The moonlight cast shadows, and spooky sights were around every corner. If I was frightened, what must Wally be feeling?

I returned home, determined to create a "Lost Cat" sign that would tug at the heartstrings of our neighbors and encourage them to help us. I sat on the floor and tearfully painted these words on poster board:

Wally is lost. Old, fat, fuzzy, gray
cat. Please call 123-555-1234.

My new husband stood over me with both sympathy and a smile on his face and said, "I'm glad you added the word 'cat.' Up to that point, you described every husband in Harbor Hills."

All I could do was sit back and laugh, crossing that well known line between tragedy and comedy.

Our concern for Wally ended at five the next morning when he knocked on the door and streaked by us on his way to the litter box.

The poor thing didn't even realize that he was allowed to use the great outdoors when "nature called."

I learned two things that day. First, that the cats could take care of themselves and find their way home if they got out again by accident. Second, that after being divorced and living as a single mom for almost thirty years, I had found the perfect husband.

Years have passed since that fateful day. As Jim and I built our life together, the individual items in the house lost their designation of "yours" and "mine." Everything here has become ours. Katie, Maggie and Wild Wally have passed away, but they left us with a treasure chest of happy memories. Now we have Maisie, our new Westie, who entertains the neighborhood and strikes fear in the hearts of the squirrels in Harbor Hills. And my life is still good, better than I ever dreamed.

— Cheryl Krouse —

67

Cat and Little Red Hen

The language of friendship is not words but meanings.
~Henry David Thoreau

At the end of summer, my brother-in-law brought me a feral cat that someone had dumped near his property. Cat was so wild that I was afraid to put my hand close for fear he'd bite me. I kept him in a cage for a week while feeding him and sitting next to the cage talking for several hours a day. Eventually, Cat stopped cowering at the back corner and worked up the courage to eat and drink while I sat nearby. Summer was ending and the evenings were cooler, so I moved Cat to the garden shed. There was a lot more space for Cat to move about.

At first, Cat stayed hidden behind boxes, and I wondered if Cat had somehow escaped. But the food I put out disappeared and the litter box needed to be emptied, so I knew Cat was being shy. The grandchildren visited the shed often, and Cat grew accustomed to them. Cat finally got brave enough to come out and peek at me when I opened the door with food. He even came to the food bowl when I gave him enough personal space.

One day, Cat looked at me and meowed shyly. It was a big step for us. I propped open the shed door and sat back. Cat put both front paws outside the door and felt the dirt. Cat looked left and right and made some tiny meow noises. Then Cat walked out into the big garden area before sprinting off to the barn.

Cat stayed out of sight for several days and did not come to the shed to eat. I thought he had found a different home until my husband saw him in the barn.

Winter set in and I worried about Cat until one morning when my husband caught sight of him leaving the chicken pen. Cat had found a warm, cozy spot to sleep.

One day, the chickens made their way to the back yard and I noticed Cat walking along with them! Cat stretched out on a garden bench in the sun and watched while the chickens went about pecking in the grass. As the chickens moved away, Cat moved with them.

More and more often, Cat joined the chickens while they fed around the homestead. Cat particularly liked walking with the one we called Little Red Hen. She was the runt of the chicks and had been abused by the others when they were born in the spring.

One day, I noticed Cat and Little Red Hen looking in my front door together. That's when I knew they had become the most unusual best buddies.

Soon, I realized they were looking out for each other. One afternoon, they were together in the front yard. Little Red Hen pecked something out of the grass, walked to the sidewalk and dropped it. She stood guard over the prize until Cat came. Dutifully, Cat ate the prize while the chicken watched.

It occurred to me that Cat might be hungry, so I took a handful of cat food to the spot where Little Red Hen had fed Cat. Cat heard me call and came back to the spot. He smelled the dry food I'd left but didn't eat. Instead, Cat walked to Little Red Hen, walked in a circle around her and gently allowed his tail to wrap around her before walking back to the food I'd left. Cat waited until Little Red Hen came over and ate the food. Amazing!

A few days ago, Cat came to the back door and meowed. I took that as a sign that he wanted to be fed and I made a little pile of cat food on the porch. Cat ate about half of the food and then looked toward the chicken pen and meowed. All the chickens came running and finished off the cat food. Unbelievable!

Today, one of my grandchildren and I were enjoying the warm weather on the back porch when the chickens and Cat came to see what we were doing. We spread some cat food out on the porch, and then we watched with glee as the chickens and Cat ate together.

—Jeannie Clemens—

68

Foe or Friend

The only way to have a friend is to be one.
~Ralph Waldo Emerson

A s I opened the car door, our new rescue dog Yukon, a Husky/Shepherd mix, jumped out before I could grab her collar. She ran straight toward our Calico cat Buddy, who arched her back and hissed ferociously.

Yukon tried to stop, but she slid a millimeter too close.

Buddy's front paws flashed forward.

Yukon yelped and jumped backward.

As the days passed, Yukon went out of her way to befriend Buddy. But even though the dog wagged her tail and approached slowly, Buddy's back arched, her tail fluffed, and she growled or spit. The best it got in the next eight years was begrudging tolerance. Buddy seemed to say, "You can live here if you must, but give me a wide berth."

As they aged, Yukon's arthritis made it hard for her to get around. Buddy moved more slowly but kept an eye on the dog. After the cat died, the dog kept right on "smiling" and wagging her tail. Her hobbling got so bad that we thought we might lose her, too. We talked about getting a new kitten.

A few days later, Yukon lay in the center of the pickup seat while my husband went into a friend's house to choose a kitten. He came out with a handful of Calico and sat her down on the seat. The tiny kitten looked around, marched over between Yukon's front paws, sat down, and looked up at the dog as if to say, "Here I am, you lucky dog."

Yukon stiffened. Her eyes got big. She lifted her snout as if trying to avoid the inevitable onslaught. Nothing happened. She turned her head, disbelieving. Then she looked back. The kitten started purring.

At home, the kitten rubbed against Yukon's legs. The dog didn't know what to make of the odd, little creature. But the kitten seemed intent on being friendly. The skinny, little kitten with the flagpole tail and oversized feet just kept loving the big, black, burly dog.

Within a few days, we had figured out that Mischief would be a fitting name for the kitten, and Yukon had figured out that Mischief had come to be her companion. Sometimes, the kitten would walk up to Yukon and swat her nose gently. Soon, Yukon recognized it as an invitation to play and she responded happily. If Mischief slept too long, Yukon would nudge the kitten and start the games herself.

Within a few weeks of Mischief's arrival, Yukon started bouncing around in ways we hadn't seen for two years. Perhaps love and respect had healed her ills. And Mischief earned rich dividends on her deposits of love. The two played together. They napped together. They wandered our three acres together. At night, Yukon curled up in her house. Mischief tucked herself between Yukon's legs, next to her heart.

I marveled at the friendship between the unlikely pair and was saddened about the friendship our earlier cat had missed. Whatever the reasons, she hadn't made room in her life for love, and she was the loser.

Mischief and Yukon's friendship continued to inspire me. One morning when I fed the two in their separate dishes, Mischief ignored her bowl and tramped toward Yukon's.

Uh-oh, I thought. As sweet as Yukon was, she'd whisper a tiny growl if we seemed to threaten her food when she was eating.

Yukon noted movement to her left. She glanced at the approaching Mischief. I could almost see Yukon thinking.

Mischief arrived at the bowl, meowed once at her canine companion, and started eating.

Yukon watched for a moment, and then lowered her head and ate alongside the kitten.

Mischief had gained Yukon's trust by choosing to give love and respect. Together, they reaped happy rewards as friends, not foes. Day in and day out, the big black dog and the little Calico kitten reveled in fearless friendship.

— Helen Heavirland —

69

Bons Amis

Friends are the family you choose.
~Jess C. Scott

I'm not sure that anyone ever expects to go to their local animal shelter and see the largest rabbit known to man. I certainly didn't. But sure enough, last spring I went for one of my regular volunteer shifts and was greeted by the afternoon supervisor with a hearty recommendation, "You've got to see what's in the 'Exotic' room today!"

I was used to seeing an occasional lizard or parakeet, but I was not prepared for the gigantic steel-gray rabbit that filled the cage in front of me. It was a solid two feet long, fat and full and round with long, silky ears. It sat quietly munching away on a little piece of hay while I gawked in disbelief. I think I said, "It's huge!" about fifteen times in a row until Chuck added finally, "Oh, it gets better. Look." Gently, he pushed a yardstick through the wire of the cage and raised the rabbit's midsection a few inches. Much to my surprise, a small gray kitten was nestled there.

"What in the world?" I asked, stunned to see another living animal of a completely different species hidden peacefully under a rabbit that was already shocking to behold.

"It's weird, huh?" Chuck laughed. "A guy from over in Town Acres called yesterday afternoon saying there was a huge rabbit in his back yard that had been sitting there for a full day, and it hadn't moved an inch. He thought it was injured, so Tommy and I went out to look at it. Now that's a French Lop, and she's definitely somebody's pet. No doubt about it. But she still didn't budge when we got close, and when we went to pick her up, that little guy was right underneath her — just like he is now. We've got some flyers up around the neighborhood, but so far nobody's come in. And when we tried to separate them, that kitten just about mewed its head off! It was like being separated from its mother."

"Animals are interesting, huh?" I said. "Wonder how those two got hooked up?"

"Well, it's a mystery for now," Chuck responded. It certainly was curious, and for the next three days, everyone at the shelter fondly referred to this unusual pair as The Gray Duo. I took several kids into the "Exotic" room to see the giant rabbit and her little feline friend, and we all enjoyed speculating about what had brought them together in the first place.

But to be honest, in the world of animal shelters, if no one has come in to inquire about their missing pet after three days — especially about an animal as unique as a French Lop rabbit — it begins to feel like there might be a reason she was found sitting in someone else's yard. I couldn't imagine a person not missing an enormous creature like her.

A few people who came in were interested in taking the kitten. After all, he was a beautiful gray color with sparkling light eyes. But every time he was pulled away from the mammoth hare, the painful mewing ensued. Not only did the cat clearly — and audibly — prefer to be with the rabbit, but every time he was taken out of the cage, the rabbit would freeze like a statue until he was returned to his nest under her belly. Then she would happily go back to munching her hay and twitching her nose. So for the sake of both animals, the shelter director felt it was best to keep them together.

But after four days no one had responded to the flyers or inquired after a lost pet. Just when we were beginning to think about how to separate the two animals, to make them more adoptable, Mrs. Lloyd walked in.

"My grandson, Tyler, called me about my rabbit. He thinks you've got her here." She unfolded one of the flyers from Town Acres. "I let

Jeanne-Louise sit out on my patio on nice days, but Tuesday afternoon, I came out to get her, and she was gone. I thought she'd been stolen — she's a French Lop, you know. Either stolen or squeezed herself through a slat in the gate, but that would have been a mighty tight fit! She'd been real interested in this old mother cat and her kittens that passed through my yard. One of the babies was just about Jeanne-Louise's same color, and I think she could sense that. I really do."

We walked Mrs. Lloyd back to the "Exotic" room, and she knew instantly that this was her rabbit. "Uh-huh. You bad thing," she scolded the gray giant. "What on earth got into you?"

"Well, Mrs. Lloyd, we think we may know the answer to that." And Chuck used his yardstick to raise the rabbit's belly.

Mrs. Lloyd looked shocked. "Why, that's the kitten I told you about. It most certainly is — look at those shiny eyes. Shame on you, Jeanne-Louise… But I guess everybody needs a companion, huh? Looks like I've got a French Lop and a kitten now. I think I'll call the cat Petit Chat. That's Little Cat in French. Yep, everybody must need a friend. I should remember that."

It turned out that I didn't live too far from Mrs. Lloyd, and she let me come over for a visit a few months later. It was very interesting to see Jeanne-Louise and Petit Chat outside on her patio that afternoon. Petit Chat was now much closer in size to his rabbit companion. They were completely at ease, sitting side by side gnawing carrots, their fur almost identical shades of silvery gray.

"They're really good friends," Mrs. Lloyd told me. "You wouldn't expect it, but Petit Chat doesn't even know he's a cat." And he climbed on top of Jeanne-Louise and fell asleep in the sun. We should all be so lucky to have a friend like that!

— Rebecca Edmisten —

70

How Many Cats?

One cat just leads to another.
~Ernest Hemingway

How many cats would you say is enough?
With which added cat does the going get tough?
What number of cats is simply too many?
Some would say "Five," while others say, "Any."
My old cat thinks one is the ultimate number.
That's her on the red cushion, deep in her slumber.
But Kukla and Frannie and Ollie and Roo
think having five cats is the right thing to do.
Annie may hate them, but they are sanguine.
Their sibling act is a well-oiled machine.
With one cat on my stomach and one on each knee,
don't expect an impartial opinion from me.
It's clear that my thinking is slightly off-kilter.
I simply don't have an intact kitty-filter.
I have enough stools and pillows and mats
to accommodate a few additional cats.
The problem is whether one human's enough
to serve as a mattress for five balls of fluff!

—Judy Dykstra-Brown—

Chapter

8

Tricks & Traits

71

Frankie vs. Blitzen

*The problem with cats is that they get the
exact same look on their face whether
they see a moth or an axe-murderer.*
~Paula Poundstone

Frankie the tabby cat was in boxes; he was in gift bags; he was underfoot, and he was chasing the bows and ribbons as I tried to wrap gifts. At least it kept him out of the Christmas tree. After one particularly frustrating session of being head-butted repeatedly by him as I tried to remove some of the thousands of cat hairs that now were Scotch-taped to what could best be described as a "fuzzy gift," I was thrilled when he became bored and headed outside.

Although Frankie is an indoor/outdoor cat, he has a poor track record with wildlife. He has tried hunting a time or two, but being a runt he tends to flounder if he actually catches something. Because of that, he now prefers to attack vegetation instead of actual wild critters.

Overall, Frankie led a sheltered life in a small yard with limited wildlife contact beyond a few squirrels and chipmunks. When we moved to a larger piece of property, however, Frankie met a new gang of squirrels who harassed him from the tree branches, several birds that enjoyed dive-bombing him, and a couple of chipmunks that taunted him.

Then there was the deer. Frankie was exploring new territory, the front yard, after confining himself to our new back yard for a month of orientation. The Great Deer Stampede of 2019 took less than fifteen seconds, but it will undoubtedly go down among the great "Did you see that?" moments in our lives.

While my wife and I were relaxing on our back porch, there came the sound of a very un-relaxing commotion somewhere just out of sight up the driveway. About that time, a huge fur ball came barreling down said driveway at top speed. *Surely, that can't be Frankie,* I thought. *He's only half that size and half that fast.*

But it *was* him, fluffed up to twice his normal size and moving so fast that his paws only touched the ground occasionally. For a moment, I wondered what could have frightened Frankie so badly.

"Deer!" my wife exclaimed.

"What, dear?" I answered. But she was talking about the real deer who'd just galloped into view, only a few feet behind Frankie and swiftly gaining on him.

In desperation, Frankie suddenly took a ninety-degree turn at full speed and did a semi-controlled slide across the slick floor of the carport adjacent to the driveway. Drifting out of the slide in a way that would make Richard Petty proud, he fishtailed toward the stairs leading to the back porch, cleared the entire flight in two bounds, hit the pet door in midair, and escaped into the safety of the house interior, all within a span of five seconds. Meanwhile, the deer — either having enough sense to avoid an out-of-control slide at high speed or perhaps just to escape what he must have assumed was a suicidal cat — continued running straight ahead and disappeared into the woods.

As always happened when Frankie was humiliated by wildlife, he retreated within the house to a hiding place only known to him. (Although we know generally where his hiding places are, we act like we don't know in the hope of buoying his self-esteem.) Later, when I went back to wrapping gifts, I found him asleep in a box decorated with reindeer that were prancing and laughing. Oh, if Frankie only knew the irony! But it made me think.

Due to her vantage point on the porch, my wife had by far the best view of the chase, and I have to wonder if she knows the difference between a white-tailed deer (our native species here in the southeast

U.S.) or a reindeer (which are native to colder climates, like Russia, Scandinavia, and the North Pole). It was obviously a member of the deer species, but which one? It was very windy that day, blocking the sound of the chase.

I only bring up that detail because of what happened later. While I was unraveling a tangle of sleigh bells from some intertwined multi-colored light strands, the bells gave an audible jingle. As if goosed by an elf, Frankie jumped straight up from the box, launched himself vertically in midair, bounced off a bookcase, and ricocheted across the room onto a table that he promptly slid off of, triggering a motion-activated quarter-scale figurine of Santa Claus to announce in a loud mechanical voice, "Ho! Ho! Ho!" Frankie hit the carpet, gaining instant traction, and launched himself into the adjoining room, not to be seen again for several hours. Eventually, Frankie came out of hiding (after we took the batteries out of Santa and hid the sleigh bells).

Of course, we know it was only a native white-tailed deer that chased him, just another species of local wildlife that, for whatever reason, couldn't see eye-to-eye with Frankie. There are no reindeer in Georgia — except, of course, once a year.

— Butch Holcombe —

72

The Cookie Snatcher

I'm not sure why I like cats so much. I mean,
they're really cute obviously. They are both
wild and domestic at the same time.
~Michael Showalter

He came out of nowhere, dashing into the store when my husband Bill opened the door. He was a lanky, gray-striped cat. The store was a Dutch market a few miles from our country home. The market had a simple portico running the length of it with a concrete floor and a variety of outdoor items for sale housed under the roof. The young cat slipped from some hiding spot on that cold January day and sprinted into the warmth of the market. Bill caught him just inside the store and set him back outside, closing the door quickly.

Within the store, facing the entrance, was a large, two-tiered stand filled with homemade bakery items: loaves of bread, bags of cookies, and ready-to-eat pies. We were looking at the baked goods when the door opened, another couple entered, and the cat darted back inside.

The cat shot past their legs, past us, and leaped onto the display stand.

The four of us stared, stunned, as the cat snatched a bag of oatmeal raisin cookies, spun around, jumped to the floor, and tore off a short distance. Hunched over the bag, he ripped it open with his teeth and began gobbling cookies. The other couple started laughing at the cat's antics, and we joined in, amused that he seemed to know exactly where the cookies were on the stand and which kind he wanted.

The storeowner came from somewhere in the back as we were still crowded near the front.

"Your cat is hungry," I said, nodding toward the cookie snatcher, who was emitting small growls as he devoured his "catch."

The storeowner made a disgruntled sound, replying that the cat wasn't his, but it had been hanging around the store for a while. I remembered then that I had seen the cat early in the fall, meandering around the covered porch, enjoying a brief rub and scratch from customers. I had thought he belonged to the storeowner.

It struck me then that this was no mischievous cat stealing cookies for fun. The cat was starving.

"Are you feeding him?" I asked uneasily.

The storeowner shook his head. My uneasiness increased. How long had the cat been without food? Water? He had shelter but little else it seemed.

The storeowner didn't want the cat, and he wasn't going to take care of it. "Why don't you take it?" he said.

No, my inside voice replied loud and clear. I had rescued cats for years, at one time caring for thirty strays, rescues, and dumps—all living in the cattery we had built in our barn. It was time-consuming and exhausting, both physically and emotionally. Getting attached and loving was easy. Letting go was difficult beyond words. My rescuing days were over.

But the cat was starving.

As I studied the cat, who remained intently focused on his cookies, biting and swallowing without even chewing, I could see that he was too skinny.

I looked at my husband. He looked at me. We had a ten-second conversation with our eyes. Then we both nodded.

"We don't have a carrier with us," I said.

Bill turned to the storeowner. "Do you have a cardboard box?"

The next few minutes were chaotic as Bill and I chased the cat around the store, trying to catch it. I think the poor cat thought he was going to be tossed back out into the cold, and he wanted no part of it.

At last, we cornered him. Bill placed the protesting cat inside the box, holding him, while I hastily folded the flaps shut.

After all that mayhem, we left the store without even purchasing what we had stopped to buy.

In the car, I held the cumbersome box on my lap. The cat was quiet and still on the ride home. I believe he knew he was safe; the struggle to survive had ended. I stuck my finger through one of the holes on the side of the box, and he nudged it with his head.

Our cattery was home to only one cat, Betty, alone since her feline companions had passed on one-by-one through the years. Although Betty appeared content to have the place to herself, I was often bothered by the idea of her spending so much time alone. I would have kept Betty in the house with our other cats except that our one female cat loathes Betty… but that's another story. At least Betty would now have the cookie snatcher to keep her company.

I put the cookie snatcher in a room separate from Betty's living area until I could get him to the vet. He showed no distress at being in a new home. He helped himself to the food and was soon lounging on the wide windowsill and curling up to sleep on the sofa.

At the vet clinic two days later, he was neutered, vaccinated, and given a clean bill of health. Then he was allowed in with Betty. I can't say that Betty was thrilled to have company, but I hoped they would bond and become friends with time.

It took several days of getting to know the cookie snatcher's personality beyond that of desperate, starving cat for me to properly name him Simon. With a continuous supply of food and water, Simon soon lost that hollow look. He remains lanky but is now solid. And sassy.

At the matronly age of seven, Betty's vote is still out on whether that rascally, two-year-old intruder should be allowed into her domain, but at least he has stopped chasing her around the room every day.

Simon's struggle to survive might be over, but his adventurous spirit remains. While we don't know where he came from originally, we often wonder if his sense of adventure led him astray in the first place.

He might have mellowed with Betty, but when he's outdoors, his wild side takes over. It's not unusual to see him romping with our Great Pyrenees, racing across the yard with abandonment, or scrambling up a tree after a squirrel. He even climbed onto the roof of the house one day. He lets us know often, with a nip or a swat, that while we might think he's tame, he's still a wild cat inside, one who wouldn't hesitate to snatch another bag of cookies if he got the chance.

— Teresa Hoy —

73

Cat Burglars

If a cat spoke, it would say things like,
"Hey, I don't see the problem here."
~Roy Blount, Jr.

Teddy and Tessa joined my cat family after a failed adoption. "They're only six months old and so cute! Their new owners moved away. Please, please take them," the cat rescuer begged. The cat rescuer happened to be my daughter, so I agreed. I never could resist her impassioned pleas. This was a child who, when she was ten years old, put a cat on layaway at the mall and rushed home to tell me I had four hours to pick it up.

Besides, the little guys were pretty cute, and I was in the market for a kitty or two. Teddy was the typical tuxedo cat with precise markings and white whiskers. Tessa sported black whiskers and gleamed like a small black leopard. It didn't take long for TNT (aka Teddy and Tessa) to settle in. Their sole competition was an elderly, crotchety Calico who only left my bedroom for food and litter-box activities.

By the end of the week, TNT discovered the kitty doors, one between the house and garage, the other between the garage and back yard. After two weeks, they'd leapt the six-foot fence enclosing the back yard to forage in the front yard. At the end of the month, they'd explored the pleasant suburban neighborhood of their new home.

Spring came, and along with it, Teddy's first gift to me — grass. It wasn't a mouthful of green blades chomped from the lawn, but a clump of grass complete with dangling roots and clots of dripping mud. While scrubbing mud off the carpet, I'd glance up to witness Teddy prancing along the back deck, head held high, another gigantic clump of grass clamped in his grinning jaws. Day after day, I tried to intercept his gifts before he reached the house, but far too often failed.

Fortunately, summer arrived, and the soggy ground dried up. Teddy turned to pursuits other than excavating my lawn. Once or twice a day, he dragged in his prizes: leaves and seedpods — some from species of plants that I didn't recognize — a sprouting daffodil bulb no doubt dug from someone's garden, whole walnuts and flowers, and the occasional piece of bark.

In the meantime, Tessa decided to specialize in earthworms. Often, I'd catch her scurrying inside with a fat, juicy earthworm twisting between her teeth. She carried it as carefully as a newborn kitten. Once in the house, she'd toss the worm high and pounce on it, pick it up and hurl it into the air, over and over again (okay, not so much like a newborn kitten).

If the ill-fated worm seemed viable, I'd slip it into a potted ficus tree in the family room, furrowing out a hiding place for it. Evidently, distressed earthworms make a noise beyond the range of human hearing, or perhaps they emit an unusual smell, because Tessa never failed to reclaim her coveted earthworm from the ficus pot.

By summer, TNT turned to quasi-criminal pursuits, stealing a brand-new gardening glove and a yellow feather duster, wrestled over the fence and maneuvered through the cat doors. A half-dozen socks. A fancy dish towel. A crumpled cigarette pack. A crisp five-dollar bill. A crawfish pilfered from someone's pond. It got so bad that I had to wait until dark to dash from the front door to my mailbox for fear that annoyed neighbors would accost me about my felonious felines.

As TNT got older, their hunting skills grew to include not only various vegetable matter and slow-moving worms but fleet-footed rodents. Being well-fed cats, they seldom desired to gnaw upon these interesting animals, but instead carried them lovingly into the house and deposited them at my feet.

With practice, my hunting skills grew as well. Armed with only a yardstick and an empty coffee can, I invariably captured the pitiful creatures, only to be faced with a moral dilemma: What should I do with a live rat brought into my house against its will?

Who knows what compels cats to offer up gifts? Is it gratitude for the good life we give them? Are they seeking parental approval, like toddlers handing their mothers bouquets of wilted weeds? Or are they trying to provide for us because we're obviously incapable of doing it for ourselves?

Feline behaviorists will no doubt develop a theory one day to explain it all. But to those of us who receive these proudly proffered gifts, it doesn't really matter. We already know the answer. We can read it in their eyes. We know our cats bring us gifts because they love us.

— Connie Goldsmith —

Day-Trippers

Cats do not have to be shown how to have a good time,
for they are unfailingly ingenious in that respect.
~James Mason

On a sunny morning in June, the Herb Society members arrive to tour my garden. Car doors thunk and lively voices fill the air as a dozen women stroll down the driveway. I run out to meet them, but Ringo is ahead of me, greeting them with enthusiastic meows. An orange tabby with handsome markings and an expressive tail, Ringo loves visitors, and they love him, stopping to pet him and tell him what a handsome fellow he is. Because he frequently vocalizes and also has white rings around his tail, I named him Ringo. Naturally, it followed that I'd call his orange tabby companion George.

This June morning, George leaves the welcoming duties to Ringo and hangs out in the back yard, napping in the shade of an apple tree.

Just the day before, my friend Steve had given me a big pot of catmint (Nepeta), with gray-green leaves and lavender flower spikes. Known for attracting bees and butterflies, it could make a lovely addition to the summer garden and add to the herbs I'd show the Herb Society folks. However, I looked at it with regret, knowing the best it would ever look was in the pot. Once I planted it in the garden, I knew the cats would eat it up.

I love my two orange tabbies, Ringo and George, but I was familiar with their appetites for catnip, and figured it would be the same with catmint. But Steve insisted that his cat, Dinah, had never bothered the catmint in his garden, so I summoned up enough hope to dig a hole, amend the soil, and plant the catmint. I wished it well and kept a beady eye on my two kitties, who strolled around nonchalantly, ignoring the new arrival.

I pictured the lavender catmint flowers billowing gracefully below my pink Bonica roses. This was Six Hills Giant catmint, so I anticipated voluminous growth and a refreshing minty scent. When Ringo and George and I retired indoors for the evening, the plant was looking great.

But today, on the morning of the tour, a sorry sight greets me. Gray-and-white Kit Kat, the neighbor's enormous cat, is lounging against the shredded remnants of catmint with a glazed look in her eyes. Rubbing lovingly against the pitiful stems, she makes it plain that she owns this special treat. I consider chasing her away, but why bother? The plant is a goner, and she might as well enjoy herself.

It isn't long before my two cats get the hang of it. George is first, having abandoned his nap in the shade to take little bites that prove to have a big effect. The Herb Society members come down the path to the back yard just in time to watch the show.

"I wonder if that stuff will have any effect on him," a woman in a floral dress muses. "If it were my cat, he'd probably get a little frisky."

"Well, George is pretty frisky to begin with, so I don't know if we'll be able to tell," I say.

Famous last words. As we watch, George leaps into midair, reaching for the sky. Next, he chases Kit Kat, easily twice his size, clear up the two-story sweetgum tree. He scrambles down with surprising grace and looks around as if asking for applause. Then he climbs to the top of the grape arbor, strutting back and forth tipsily. Walking along the wooden railing, he starts sailing off onto a grapevine, realizes it's not firm enough to stand on, and retreats backward to recover his footing. After a few hair-raising near-falls, I lift him down gently. He settles on the lawn where he licks his fur thoroughly as if to say, "Who me? I never would've fallen in a million years."

Ringo is last to sample the remaining crumbs of catmint. He sniffs it, nibbles it and rubs his head against the last stem standing. Soon, he has the same loose-limbed saunter as Kit Kat and George. He chases invisible butterflies, flying forward and sideways with a dancer's aplomb.

"Wow! You didn't tell us there'd be such entertaining cats in the garden," says a woman in a straw sunhat. "I'm getting some catmint for my garden!"

"Well, just as long as you don't mind it being demolished," mutters her friend in the floral dress.

"Well, how about we take a wander through the garden to see the roses and perennials?" I suggest. "We can even snip some herbs for your kitchens."

I bring paper bags and hand pruners to cut some samples for the women as we stroll. At first, only a few follow me. Most of them are more interested in watching the acrobatic cats. Eventually, Ringo and George wear themselves out, and we continue with our garden visit, checking out many varieties of oregano, rosemary, thyme, tarragon, and sage that thrive in the island beds. The visitors stop to pinch the herbs and savor their aroma. A few take photos and dictate notes into their phones.

I invite them to sit on the patio for iced tea and cookies. We look out on the garden and enjoy the long vista with colorful bellflowers and daylilies. The catmint is just a memory now, grazed to the last morsel.

"What should I plant under the pink roses that has lavender flowers? Anyone have ideas?" I ask.

So many possibilities are offered up—standard and dwarf Russian sage, various forms of flowering sage, delphiniums and asters... Pretty soon I'm excited to try some new plants, and the catmint is just a memory.

I walk the women to their cars, and as we say our goodbyes, I realize there is still plenty of time to go plant shopping.

The next week, a flurry of thank-you notes fills my mailbox, with a few kind words for my garden. But it's Ringo and George who get the lion's share of praise for their entertaining performance, thanks to the sacrificial catmint. I will send a thank-you note of my own to Steve, expressing gratitude from the cats for their psychedelic day trip.

—Barbara Blossom Ashmun—

75

The Pot Has Eyes

Most of us rather like our cats to have a streak
of wickedness. I should not feel quite easy in the
company of any cat that walked about the house
with a saintly expression.
~Beverly Nichols

From the minute we welcomed him home, we knew our kitten Tiki was going to keep us on our toes. In retrospect, perhaps adopting a jet-black cat whose fur perfectly matched our jet-black tile floors might not have been the wisest decision.

It took less than a week for Tiki to take full advantage of this oversight.

First, he began hiding in plain sight. He realized instantly that unless he moved and gave away his location, it was nearly impossible to see him once he hunkered down into a loaf position. We'd call his name and squint at the floor until we would finally spot an inky, fluffy circle standing out against the grout lines.

Once he knew we'd blown his cover, he'd pop up off the floor just long enough to arch his back at us like the Halloween silhouette of a witch's cat and then rocket off to find a new spot.

Quickly, it became his favorite game. As we tiptoed around trying to find him, my husband and I would take turns calling his name and saying aloud, "Is there a Tiki in this house? We can't find him anywhere!"

At first, he was a bit amateurish; he would leave clues. A tipped-over shoe. A closet door cracked open "just" enough. A cat-shaped lump under the bed comforters, wriggling with the excitement of waiting to be found.

But Tiki quickly stepped up his game and decided he was going pro. Let's put it this way: If the Cat Fanciers' Association ever adopts a "Best in Scaring Your Human" category, Tiki would take gold as the world champion.

For Tiki, plain hide-and-seek started to lose its luster. Adjustments had to be made. Experiments in "shock and awe" were conducted.

Tiki began hiding around doorframes, waiting until our feet were nearly at the threshold — and then, bam! From out of nowhere, there he would be, a black flash three feet in the air, paws fully extended like a cheerleader holding pom-poms, as he proceeded to scare the living daylights out of us!

He would hide for hours in the closet, wait for either my husband or me to come in, and then come flying out from behind the hanging clothes.

He began to materialize out of gym bags, purses, shopping bags, and from behind couch cushions, leaping in the air once we got close enough for him to scare us.

No place was safe. And I mean nowhere!

He'd hide in the bathtub — a place most cats write off as instant death, but not this daredevil. After being terrorized in the sanctity of my own bathroom, I tried to keep a watchful eye out and find Tiki first, but this willful little feline kept coming up with new hideouts.

But one morning in particular, he took the cake.

I had a busy day of housecleaning planned, and after running the vacuum cleaner on the upstairs rugs, I knew Tiki had hidden... somewhere. I made sure he wasn't trapped in a bedroom or bathroom, but he was nowhere to be found. Nervously, I picked through a pile of laundry, but nope. Not there either.

"Okay, well, he's somewhere in this house," I told myself, as I came down to the kitchen for my morning coffee.

I clicked on my phone and flicked through news headlines and social-media updates as I enjoyed my coffee. I called Tiki a few times and glanced in the living room, but I didn't see him.

"All right, crazy cat, suit yourself," I muttered, and finished the last of my coffee. I was just about to carry my mug over to the sink when I saw him.

Across the kitchen, within the dark recess of a large Dutch oven tilted on its side, a pair of copper eyes blinked at me!

I snorted and thanked my lucky stars I had my phone at the ready. I took several quick pictures and then texted one to my husband.

"Why did you just send me a picture of the dishes?" he wrote back immediately.

"The pot has eyes," I answered.

There weren't enough laughter emojis in the world that morning as I shared the image with family and friends, waiting until they too eventually saw the pair of mischievous, little eyes staring back in the photo.

I've checked behind a lot of doors and curtains since that day, and Tiki still loves nothing more than to come shooting out from his latest hiding spot, ready to razzle-dazzle us as he comes.

But as long as I live, I will never forget the morning that one of the pots in the kitchen blinked at me!

— Kristi Adams —

76

Our Water-Loving Kitty

Thousands have lived without love,
not one without water.
~W. H. Auden

I agreed to let my two daughters get a kitten if they met their end-of-year reading goals. We daydreamed about what we would name it as we crossed books off the required reading list from their school. Snowball, Sprinkles, and Fluffy were the top contenders. We talked about who would take care of the kitten's daily needs, ultimately deciding to divvy up the tasks so everyone had a turn. Everything appeared to be coming together perfectly — until we went to visit the kittens on adoption day.

It was supposed to be the picture-perfect moment all mamas dream of — two little girls smiling as they cuddled a little white fluff ball. I was prepared to post the photo on Instagram weeks before I even took it. But in the picture I actually took on that much-anticipated day, my younger daughter had a deep scowl on her face and my older daughter was crying. "Which one will we get, Mama? We love them all!" she cried. Clearly, I hadn't thought this through.

We went home with two kittens. I told myself I'd have twice the poo but half the kitty-sharing drama from the girls.

What I didn't know was how much entertainment one of the kittens would provide. She was the runt of the litter, and we named her Squeaky because her meow is barely audible. It is almost as if her vocal cords aren't fully developed, and her meow comes out as a quick, high-pitched squeak. But what she lacks in size and sound, she makes up for in personality and purr factor. This little kitty purrs like a well-oiled machine on overdrive, especially when she is soaking wet. She loves water!

We discovered this the first night we had her. While the other kitten, Clover, was hiding under the bed like a normal cat, Squeaky sat on the side of the tub as I gave my young daughters their evening bath. The girls were delighted she was there. She purred loudly and pawed at the water, intently watching the bath toys float around.

The next morning, I noticed her sitting on the counter as I washed my hair in the shower. Calmly, she closed her little eyes and purred loudly as I rinsed the shampoo out of my hair. It was as if just being in the steamy bathroom brought her peace in some way. Her sweet, furry face was the epitome of Zen mastery.

When I turned on the shower the next day, she came running and hopped in before it was even warm. I watched in disbelief as she played in the water, purring like a locomotive as it saturated her to the bone. She now showers with me every morning and often plays in the puddle near the drain long after I have turned off the water and am dressed.

A showering kitty seemed crazy enough until I heard my girls squealing with delight from the kitchen one evening. "Squeaky is in the sink!" they shouted. I ran downstairs and, sure enough, Squeaky was in the sink, purring away as she played with the stream of water coming from the faucet. I ran quickly to get my camera, worried I might miss this photo opportunity. Turns out, there was no need to rush. Squeaky loves water so much that she gets in the sink to help me wash dishes every day. Who knew that the runt of the litter, the extra kitten we brought home, would be such a delight?

— Kimberly Lowe —

The Diva

There are two means of refuge from the miseries of life:
music and cats.
~Albert Schweitzer

I was struggling through another year of college, but I was out shopping for dog food, and it happened to be Adoption Day. I had no intention of adopting a cat, but then she stuck her paw out through the kennel and I was a goner. She was nearly two years old and full of personality. Stocky and solid, my new tortoise-colored, shorthaired cat quickly became my best friend. Her cute pink nose inspired me to name her Francesca Rose. Within a few months, this morphed into Phronsie, named after the youngest and very devoted daughter in Margaret Sidney's timeless book series, *Five Little Peppers*.

I discovered Phronsie's singing talent on a Saturday morning. While cleaning the house, I popped a copy of *West Side Story* into the DVD player, hoping the iconic soundtrack would make sweeping and mopping a little more enjoyable. As a ballad began to play, I heard the distinctive sound of a loud meow. Worried something was wrong, I rushed into the living room, only to find Phronsie staring at the television screen. At first, I was concerned for her. The meow she was making was unlike any I'd heard from her before. As she continued, I listened closely. I realized there was a sort of melody to her meow. Was she trying to sing along with the music?

Dismissing her living-room performance as a fluke, I forgot about the incident. A few weeks later, I sat down to watch *The Wizard of Oz*. Within seconds of the opening chords of "Over the Rainbow," my musical-loving cat positioned herself in the center of the room and did her best to harmonize with Judy Garland. I couldn't believe my ears. I stopped the movie. Phronsie stopped singing. I pushed Play. The meowing began again like the encore performance of a dying diva in a famous opera.

Now convinced that Phronsie was truly attempting to sing, I put her performance skills to the test. We spent the next few hours listening to music together. Her silences let me know which songs she didn't like. Soon, I had narrowed her preferred set list down to a precious few, with "Over the Rainbow" being the clear favorite in the bunch.

I began to wonder if, in a past life, my cat was a Broadway star who loved the limelight then as much as she loved her catnip now. Nothing made her happier than a night of karaoke, featuring only her and her repertoire.

Most recently, I discovered that *Chicago* is her favorite musical, second only to *A Chorus Line*. Often, her meowing is so loud that I suspect she's trying to out-sing the original cast member, maybe dreaming of a starring role all her own. If allowed the chance, would she prefer to be center stage performing to a crowd of thousands? For now, she'll have to settle for an audience consisting solely of our household, including her canine and feline siblings, who seem to tolerate her talent at best.

Given that her entertainment value is quite high and her impromptu performances always elicit laughs and adoration from family and friends alike, I wonder if I even have a need for a television anymore, other than to watch *The Wizard of Oz* at Phronsie's insistence. If it were up to her, we'd spend every day listening to the dreamy sounds of Judy Garland records between bites of kibble, the occasional sprinkling of catnip, and a nap or two. After all, a star must have her rest if she's going to perform to the best of her ability.

— David-Matthew Barnes —

78

In a Flash

Anyone can learn how to communicate with animals if
they are open to the process and willing to practice.
~Karen A. Anderson

"**S**it!" I commanded, giving the appropriate hand signal for my voice command. Flash sat promptly. I smiled from ear-to-ear and then reached out and patted Flash on the head. "Who says you can't teach a cat to do tricks?"

Flash Dance Gordon was special right from the start. His mother was a pure white, bobtail Manx, as were four of his siblings. But Flash was orange, or ginger as they're sometimes called, and his tail was long, fluffy and very expressive.

I put my hand down flat on the floor. "Lie down." Flash lay down promptly, looking up at me with his big, round eyes, and his tail lashing back and forth on the carpet.

My grin got bigger. "That's two for two," I told him.

Then we practiced "Roll over," "Beg," "Speak," and "Fetch." Each time, he responded accordingly. When we got to "Fetch," Flash would run out and retrieve the wadded-up piece of notebook paper I'd written his trick list on and return it to me.

When he brought it back, I'd give him a small taste from the tube of cat hairball medicine, which happened to be made with cod liver oil. He loved that stuff!

We were going to put on a great show.

After I was sure he would perform all six of his tricks — either by voice, hand signal, or both — I invited over several friends.

Flash knew something was up when I put his little bowtie on him. That was as "dressed up" as I ever outfitted him, and he knew it was only for special dinners and treats.

My friends were all excited, and the chatter was loud and boisterous as they took seats in the rec room. One of them wanted to "lay odds" that the tricks were no more complicated than "Here's your food dish, now eat."

When they'd all settled in, I palmed the tube of fur-ball medicine in my left hand and placed the wadded-up paper ball on the coffee table near me. Then I set Flash in the center of the room and backed away a few feet. With my right hand, I gave him the command for "Sit."

Flash stared at a half-dozen faces now staring at him, tilting his head this way and that, and it looked like he was considering bolting from the room.

"Flash," I said in a no-nonsense voice, which usually got his attention. His eyes met mine, and I opened my left hand to show him his "reward."

"Flash. Sit." I gave the hand signal a second time.

Flash sat down promptly, then without further prompting, he lay down hastily, rolled over, sat up and begged, and meowed plaintively. Then he ran like a football linebacker expecting a pass — all without a single word or motion from me!

His audience clapped, cheered and laughed like crazy.

I shrugged and threw the crumpled paper ball toward him. He returned it, but I withheld the treat, and we started over.

"Flash. Sit." I gave the hand signal.

And again, Flash went through all six tricks — sit, lie down, roll over, beg, speak, and fetch — pausing just long enough between them for me to quickly call out the next one, albeit after the fact. My friends sat and cheered and laughed their heads off.

The third time through, I gave up, and Flash got his treat. Satisfied, he crawled under the couch, which was his way of saying, "Leave me alone now."

"I thought you said he did six tricks," said one of my friends.

"He did," I replied with a laugh. "I just never taught him to do them one at a time and only when commanded. We always did them in the same order."

My friends laughed. "Guess he taught you something today!"

"Guess he did," I said.

"Guess you two are not quite ready to go on the *Late Show with David Letterman*." She chuckled.

"Guess we're going to have to work on this a little more," I agreed.

But try as I might, I was never able to get Flash to do them one at a time, each on command, or even to do them in a different order. You can teach a cat to do tricks, but apparently, you can't undo the trick sequence or separate the learned behavior.

Flash Dance Gordon didn't care that we'd never be famous or on TV. He only cared that I never ran out of that hairball medicine. And I never did.

— Jan Bono —

79

Far Worse Things

Cats are inquisitive, but hate to admit it.
~Mason Cooley

The arrival of the chicks drew the terminally lazy cats from all corners of the house. Not at first, of course, but gradually as they became aware that something new was behind the closed door of the last room in the upstairs hallway.

Draco, the sleek, black, man-about-town, noticed the change first and sat himself down outside the door. His vigil attracted the attention of Little Kitty, evil genius mastermind, who raised her enormous orange bulk from the cushions of the back room to come sit beside him.

For Little Kitty to move for any reason other than the sound of kibble hitting the food bowl was unheard of, and so Luna, the small, white Siamese flower-child who always followed one of the other two on adventures, showed up shortly afterward. Last came The Nog (formally known as Egg Nog), the visionary-dreamer, dark brown tabby who lived in her own world and barely noticed that the other three lived in the same house. The Nog came and sniffed at the closed door, recognized it was not about to open any time soon, and went on her way. The other three remained.

My vet-tech daughter Emily got the little chicks from a veterinarian she worked with and chose my upstairs study as their nursery. I didn't mind as I rarely used the room anymore since most of my books were downstairs. I never thought the cats would pose any problem at all since their usual response to anything new in the house is to ignore it after about five minutes.

Years ago, when Emily brought home some rats, the cats parked themselves around the cage for, at most, twenty minutes before they became bored and sauntered off. I assumed they'd react the same way to the chicks.

I was wrong. And, as so often happens, it was only after the chicks were in my study that I found myself needing books from that room from time to time. I'd have to step over the Watchers, open the door carefully, and slip in fast before anyone else could get in or out. I'd repeat the process, usually with at least four books under my arm, while coming back out.

Sometimes, I'd pause at the end of the hall to watch the three of them sitting there. Occasionally, Draco would walk up to the door, put out his paw and push — just to check — before sitting back down. Luna took it further and would rub herself against the door and yowl loudly while Little Kitty, who was always the planner behind any event, sat back, seeming to scan the door and floor for signs of weakness.

While these three sat there every day, for at least an hour or two, The Nog would come and go from the back room to the water dish outside the bathroom. Gliding between the Watchers, she no longer cared what was behind the door since, obviously, no one was getting in. The enticing "cheeps" that made all their ears twitch were just a needless distraction from sleeping, so best ignored. Little Kitty, in obvious disagreement, finally decided that the best way in was to emulate what she had seen humans do. Hopping onto one of the bookcases in the hall near the study, she tried to turn the doorknob.

I only managed to witness this once when I was in the far bedroom with the door open. As soon as I said, "What do you think you're doing?" she jumped down and lumbered away in her usual way, pretending she didn't hear me. I know she tried this more than once, however, as I kept finding tufts of her fur on top of the bookcase.

This continued until the chicks were large enough to move outside to the coop, and the mystical door was opened at last. The three cats prowled in slowly, gazing about for the prey they had heard cheeping away at them for the past month, but found no one. Draco hopped into the now-empty plastic pen with Luna right behind him, while Little Kitty sat down on the floor and waited for their report. I'd never seen three more disappointed cats in my life. Afterward, they all wandered off to their own favorite spots and returned to their former lives of lolling on pillows.

They did not have a long break from the vigil, however, as Emily brought home three more chicks that went into the same room. Again, as before, the three cats set themselves up outside the door, and The Nog would slink past or between them on her way to the water bowl. The same scenario played out as before over the next month before those chicks also went outside and the disappointed cats again went creeping into the room.

This time, Emily cleaned the study thoroughly because her chick-growing days were done, but the cats seemed to interpret this as preparing for some new arrivals. Little Kitty took to sitting on the bed, Luna under it, and Draco in front of the Egyptian camel saddle in the corner. *The next time some cheeping creatures show up,* they seemed to think, *we are going to be on the right side of the door.* The Nog also visited the room, but finding nothing of interest in it, walked back out and returned to her spot in the back room.

After a few weeks, I found they were getting cat hair all over the books, and messing up the bed and cushions, so I evicted them all. I shut the door behind me after I cleaned it. The three of them made a great show of walking away like they didn't care, but as soon as I was out of sight, they returned to set up their vigil again. Two months later, with no sound coming from behind that door, Little Kitty or Luna could still be found occasionally sitting in front of the study. Draco, who hates being left out of anything, always made sure to show up at least once just in case.

I've tried to tell them there are no more chicks coming, but why should they believe me? I'm the guy who shooed them out of the room, who always slipped in and out, barring their way, who obviously wasn't an ally in getting at whatever had been in there making cheeping noises. So I've given up, and there they sit still. If there's one thing I've learned in life, it's that you'll never win an argument with a cat, and it's best not to try. And, really, if they're happy spending their days staring at a door, why ruin the fun? I know from experience they could be doing far worse things.

—Joshua J. Mark—

80

The Perfect Pair

You can't own a cat. The best you can do
is be partners.
~Sir Harry Swanson

I suspected something was up. I had found a little hole in the corner of a bag of flour, and later I found one in a bag of specialty coffee I had tucked in my pantry cabinet. I voiced my concerns to my husband Bill. "I think we have a mouse."

Bill, the eternal optimist, offered a different explanation. "I think it's just Sammie. You know how he likes to rummage through the closets. He probably got in there and poked a hole through the bags with one of his claws." Bill picked up our little orange tabby and brought him over to me for inspection. "See, his nails are getting long. It looks like time for a clipping."

Preferring my husband's thoughts over my own suspicions, I deferred to his explanation while he cradled Sammie, allowing me to clip his toenails. Under different circumstances, I might have been annoyed at the prospect of having to throw away a perfectly good sack of flour and an expensive pound of coffee. But with Sammie, all was overlooked.

I knew Sammie was something special the minute I laid eyes on him as he lounged in his cage at the animal shelter. "This is Sponge-Bob," the shelter adoption volunteer explained as she laid him in my outstretched arms. "He arrived here yesterday from his foster-care house."

I always did have a soft spot in my heart for orange tabbies, and my husband knew this all too well. While I didn't feel ready for a new addition so close to the loss of our previous cat, Bill was chomping at the bit for a new pet. The fact that we had wound up in front of the cage that housed the only orange tabby kitten in the shelter had been no coincidence. Bill had done his homework, and Sponge-Bob was irresistible. I nuzzled his head up to mine and, in nothing short of a Vulcan mind-meld like those performed by Mr. Spock on the original *Star Trek* TV series, the kitten communicated with me. "Take me home," he said. "I'm perfect for you."

Two days later, Sammie, as we re-named him, arrived at our home. We were an instant love match. When I bent to pet his head, he raised his paw and touched my hand. When I covered him in kisses, he answered by pressing his nose to my cheek. He came when I called him, followed me where I went, slept when I slept, and ate when I ate. Sammie and I were quite a pair, all right. So what if I had to throw away some flour and coffee? Sammie was worth it.

Yet one day, my little Sammie started to behave oddly. He no longer responded to my call, refusing to move from his vigil in front of the pantry door. One night, I found him sitting on top of the stove, his head pressed up against the wall. On another occasion, I found him with his paw stretched underneath my refrigerator. Strange behavior indeed.

Then, one night as I lay in bed just about to fall asleep, I heard the galloping of four cat paws down the hall, back up the hall, through the kitchen, back up the hall and into the bathroom. I jumped out of bed. "Sammie! What's going on?"

But Sammie would not respond. He sat still, his eyes keenly focused on the edge of the bathroom radiator. I bent to take a closer look. Two beady, little black eyes stared back at me.

"EEK! A MOUSE!"

I dashed out of the bathroom, shutting the door behind me. The mouse would have to be caught, but I couldn't bear the thought of hurting any animal, even an icky mouse. From the other side of the door, I heard more scrambling. *Sammie will have to take care of this one,* I thought. *I'll just go back to bed and let nature take its course.*

But I couldn't sleep. I waited in bed, listening to the cat-and-mouse bathroom battle for what seemed like several minutes until all was finally quiet. I looked over at Bill, sound asleep and snoring. *Well,* I thought, *I'll have to pull myself together and survey the carnage on my own.*

I grabbed some newspaper and a plastic bag from the kitchen and opened the bathroom door. There, I saw something I was not prepared to see: Sammie had the mouse cornered next to the bathtub with his nose pressed against him. *Wait. Is... he... kissing... him?*

Apparently, Sammie, like me, is more of a lover than a fighter. I shouldn't have been surprised. After all, my kitty was like me in so many ways. "Well, Sammie," I said, "you and I are going to have to figure out a humane way to rid our house of this mouse." And with that directive, Sammie sprang into action. I held the plastic bag open on one side of the stunned creature, and Sammie, perched on the other side, nudged him into it gently.

With the mouse safely inside the plastic bag, I slipped on a pair of flip-flops and walked the intruder out the front door, down the block and around the corner where I set him free under an oak tree. He looked up at me with confused yet grateful eyes, and then we both went our separate ways.

Back inside the house, Sammie sat looking rather proud of himself. I bent down to pet his head, and he reached his paw up to my face. "Sammie," I told him, "we make the perfect team."

Then I pressed my head to his. I swear I heard him respond, "Well, I told you so."

— Monica A. Andermann —

81

Walking Willy

Cats seem to go on the principle that it never does
any harm to ask for what you want.
~Joseph Wood Krutch

Willy and his sister Molly were the same size when they were kittens, but by the time they were a year old, he was more than twice as big as she was. In the warm weather, when the wood stove was cool, Willy loved to stretch along its top. Bits of him hung over the edge.

The stove was perched on a brick platform, giving Willy a good, out-of-the-way view of the world. From there he could watch the goings-on in the kitchen and the scurrying of squirrels or the flight of birds out the dining room windows. If he bothered to turn his head to the right, he could watch television.

One late summer day, when Willy was two years old, I was cutting a cantaloupe at the chopping block on the island counter in our kitchen. Willy left his perch on the wood stove and came over to me. He stretched his body upward, standing on his back legs beside me. His eyes and nose just reached to the top.

Willy had always been rather silent. Molly did all the talking for the two of them. But now, Willy mewed loudly. Really, it was more of a yowl, long and beseeching. He dropped to all fours and yowled again.

"Do you want some cantaloupe?" I asked. I cut a small piece and dropped it to him.

"YOOOOOWL," Willy said again. I dropped another piece.

He gobbled it up as fast as the first. As I turned to drop another small piece, Willy stood and took a step toward me, his eyes glued to the fruit.

Never before had a food, nor anything for that matter, made our big gray cat so animated and communicative. And, never before had I seen him stand on his hind legs.

I cut a few more small pieces and lifted one above Willy's head. Sure enough, he stood to reach it. I took a couple of steps back, still holding the fruit above his head. Our big gray cat walked toward me, on his hind legs, to get the juicy orange treat.

I think Willy could have qualified to appear on the "Stupid Pet Tricks" portion of *The Late Show with David Letterman*. His ability to walk across the entire kitchen on his back legs was impressive, and entertained many a friend and family.

For years I thought that Willy's penchant for cantaloupe set him apart as an atypical feline.

But in the age of "Google anything" I found that other cats are crazy for melons, too. Many of the same amino acids that are in meat are also present in melons. Those amino acids give off an odor that, to a cat, might smell like meat. That's the theory, anyway.

I wish we had taken a photo of Willy walking on two legs across the kitchen floor. But, alas, it was not quite yet the age of cell phones and constantly accessible cameras. It's an image that none of us will ever forget, though.

—Deb Biechler—

Learning to Love the Cat

82

Chicken Soup for the Soul

My Purrfect Match

*My relationship with cats has saved me from
a deadly, pervasive ignorance.*
~William S. Burroughs

t's morning. I know this because my cat is dragging her paw against my face, and the dagger extending from her middle digit just caught the corner of my mouth and hooked me like a trout.

I never wanted a cat.

All throughout my childhood, I longed for a dog — a buff Cocker Spaniel, specifically — so intensely that I became the default neighborhood pet sitter, piled my bed high with plush dogs, and even forged a typed letter to my parents from the ASPCA saying I'd make an ideal adopter. (The handwritten envelope gave me away.) My parents were staunchly opposed. "We travel too much for soccer and hockey tournaments," they reasoned. "You won't take care of it."

They were right. And the older I got, the more I realized it. Dogs were expensive, needy and impractical for a single, busy professional living in a tiny New York City apartment. Still, I considered myself a dog person — so much so that when a guy I had recently started dating told me he was a cat guy, I recoiled. A cat guy? I didn't grow up around cats, and I definitely didn't know any men who liked them. The only thing I knew about cats was that I was allergic to strays. And according to my dad, if I fed them, they would pee on our front porch.

This might be a deal-breaker, I told New Guy, and I meant it. I had gone through a difficult breakup the prior year that plunged me into my third major bout of depression, and I was preemptively trying to predict why this relationship would fail so I could save myself the heartache. Sure, he was witty and athletic, had good grammar and dimples, and wore the same Adidas Samba shoes I played indoor soccer in as a kid. But cats? That was a bridge too far.

Five years earlier, New Guy and his ex-girlfriend had adopted two kittens, Zelda and Oscar, but she ended up with both post-breakup when his schedule got too hectic. He missed his half of their fur-ball equation and was thinking about adopting another. *Okay,* I thought. *I'll consider this.*

The Kitty Loft, a pop-up shelter of sorts a block away from New Guy's Brooklyn apartment, was having an adoption event, so we stopped by. I lobbied for a kitten, but New Guy said he wanted an adult cat who would be playful but affectionate, independent but willing to curl up on his lap.

After surveying the scene, we spent some one-on-one time with Sir Ian Stanley, a slightly mangy-looking older male with a quirky personality who was a veteran of the shelter. We also met Otis, a mostly white shorthair with a creepy, cross-eyed glare that New Guy found hilarious. We told the volunteers we'd think it over.

We returned the following weekend. As New Guy spoke to the workers, I did a lap of the shelter. In the back, a little black paw reached out of a cage that wasn't there before. Her name was Bree, and she had recently been adopted and returned because of a runny nose. Although not a kitten, she was peanut-sized compared to the other cats and had big, marble-like blue-green eyes that popped against her shiny black coat. I stood my ground until New Guy and a volunteer came over, and then I put on my most desperate face. The volunteer opened the cage, and Bree crawled into my arms and up my chest, nuzzling her impossibly soft head against my neck. And then she started purring. "This one," I said to New Guy. "You have to get this one."

But he still wasn't ready to pull the trigger. His ex was possibly moving out of her current apartment, and when she heard New Guy was thinking about getting another cat, she suggested he take Zelda back. I was devastated. Not only was he not going to save Bree, but the cat he bought and raised with his ex was now going to be ours?

With time, I knew I could push aside the feelings of jealousy and insecurity, but I couldn't give up on Bree. "Should I adopt her?" I asked.

"Yes," said New Guy. "She would be good for you." Before I knew it, I was e-mailing my superintendent begging for permission to bring this pile of sweet-smelling fluff into my 150-square-foot studio and trying to figure out how I could afford to keep her fed and healthy when I was already living paycheck to paycheck. I e-mailed the shelter to see if she was still available.

By the next evening, she was hiding under my bed.

My bank account dipped as I bought eco-friendly litter, grain-free food, toys, brushes, and scratching posts, but adopting Bree paid off in spades. When I broke things off with New Guy after a guilt-inducing conversation with my ex-boyfriend, she let me cry into her coat. When I came to my senses the next day, she greeted him at the door. When I decided he was worth the chance, Bree moved into his apartment before I did. And when I was stuck inside it the next winter miserably working nights and weekends on a book, neither she nor he left my side.

And she's still with us now in California — standing on the bed I share with New Husband, mewing, purring, and begging for food with every bat of her paw. She has shown me that the only thing more rewarding than loving something — or someone else — is taking a chance that they'll love you back.

— Danielle Kosecki —

83

Nobody Moves In While I'm Away

Kittens can happen to anyone.
~Paul Gallico

"Someone else is living here now," I said to my husband as I stood in the kitchen doorway, blocking his way in.

My husband had been out of town on business for a week. He had just backed into the garage and was pulling his luggage out of the trunk of the car. He stopped in his tracks, cocked his head to the side, and asked, "What are you talking about?"

"I just want to warn you, things are not the same as when you left," I said. I tried not to smile.

"I've only been gone a week," he said. "What could've changed since we talked on the phone last night? And what do you mean 'someone else is living here'? It better not be your cousin. We agreed that's not a good idea."

He was standing on the step, luggage behind him, and trying to peer over my shoulders.

"Fine," I said. I moved away from the door so he could enter.

He set down his bags and looked around. "So, what's going on?"

At that point, I could no longer hold back my excitement. I took him by the arm and led him into the laundry room. A little gray kitten snuggled against his leg. He looked down. He looked at me. He looked down again and said, "What have you done?"

We took the kitten to the living room and watched him roll and play, while I explained how our new guest came to live with us. I was on a shopping trip with my sisters when we came across an animal adoption event on the sidewalk. The puppies were so adorable. We went inside the store to look at the other animals that were up for adoption, and that's when I saw him. All the other cats and kittens were at the front of their cages, as if they were saying, "Pick me! Pick me!" At first, I thought the cage at the end of the row was empty, but when I moved in closer, I saw a little bundle huddled in the corner. I asked to hold him, and he hasn't been inside a cage since.

My husband wasn't a cat person, but he soon became the cat's favorite person. Every evening, he got down on the floor and played with the kitten. One of their favorite games was hide-and-attack. My husband crouched behind the recliner, out of the cat's sight, and peeked ever so slowly around the corner. The cat went into hunting mode immediately, his eyes widened, tail fluffed out. I wasn't good at that game because I never knew the moment he would pounce. He surprised me every time, and I squealed like a child scared by a jack-in-the-box.

He was so smart. We brought in new toys, and the kitten loved accomplishing the tasks each required. Soon, we discovered that he loved sitting on the ledge of our two-story balcony over the living room. The first time we saw him up there, we yelled for him to stop as we ran up the stairs to rescue him. The inevitable finally happened, and he fell to the room below. I screamed. My husband came running into the room just in time to see the cat shaking his head and walking it off. After that, we installed a baby gate to preserve the remainder of his nine lives.

We both joked that we worked to keep up our cat's lifestyle. After all, he spent more time in our two-story house than we did. He slept when he wanted, ate when he was hungry, and got us up at whatever time in the morning he wanted to play. And although we have enjoyed having him added to our family, for a long time my husband jokingly gave me a warning whenever he went out of town: "Nobody moves in while I'm away."

—Vickie McEntire—

84

Say Again?

The world only goes round by misunderstanding.
~Charles Baudelaire

ancy and I met often at our community mailboxes. One day, after discussing the state of the world, we moved on to discussing our kids. And by kids, I mean our cats.

"I have three," she told me. "Mittens, Boots and Kitty."

Now, I have a thing about animal names. It seems to follow that if you give them silly or common names, you are likely to see them as silly or common.

"My girl's name is Phoebe," I stated, with a bit of snooty thrown in.

"That's an odd name," Nancy commented. "Don't think I've ever heard that before."

Well, I certainly don't think it's odd. In fact, I think it's an awesome cat name. I had toyed around with Chloe and Whitney when I took on this battered foster that a veterinarian had called me about. Eight years later, "The Phoebs," as she's nicknamed, is my companion, confidante and spider spotter. (When Phoebe freezes and stares off into the distance, I know without a shadow of a doubt that there is a bug about.)

I had Nancy over for coffee and pastries, and she seemed enamored with Phoebe. Nevertheless, she commented, "I still think her name is bizarre."

The following day, a notecard with a kitten entangled in yarn was propped on my door:

Dear Kathy,

Thank you so much for the lovely visit yesterday. Your apartment is so homey, and Feed Me is precious.

Best,
Nancy

—Kathleen A. Gemmell—

85

Lucky

People that don't like cats haven't met the right one yet.
~Deborah A. Edwards

My rough-and-tumble, cat-hating husband was on a construction job site. There was a lot of activity and heavy machinery. It was dusty, dirty and loud.

As the trucks leveled and compacted the ground, a little ball of fur walked out of a dust storm toward my husband. She was crying so loud that he thought she was hurt. He picked up the tiny ball and checked her out. She didn't look injured, just angry. He wondered where she came from and how she got there.

My husband searched the area for a mother cat or a litter of kittens. He couldn't find either. As he held her, he thought, *What the heck am I going to do with a kitten?* Being the nice guy that he is, he placed her in his work truck on an old shirt with a capful of water nearby. She lay there snuggled in his shirt and scent all day.

After work, he corralled a co-worker who knew about cats to go with him to Walmart and get whatever supplies a cat needs. He brought her home and set her up in the kitchen with food, water, a bed, and a litter box. We already had a toddler fence in place, so he felt sure she would be safe in the kitchen. Then, he went to bed.

In the middle of the night, he woke up to purring right by his cheek. She had climbed over the safety fence and found her way to the bedroom. Did I mention my husband hates cats? Well, even he could not resist the purring ball of fur. He let her stay there all night, and the rest is history. He became her human, and she became his cat.

Where was I? My son and I were visiting Grandma at the beach. We had lost our dog several months earlier, and because our son was a toddler we had decided to wait before getting a new puppy. Our vet had predicted that the right pet would come into our lives at the right time, anyway.

We came home to a husband who was a pushover for a lonely, little kitten. Although he won't admit it to this day, he is quite fond of the cat. She wakes up in the morning with him, greets him at the door after work, sits on his lap during the nightly news, and sleeps on him at night. He coos to her, scratches her head, plays string wars, and cuddles with her on the sofa. This big, strong man and this little cat. She is extremely loyal to him, and they are inseparable when he is home.

My son and I also fell in love with this tiny ball of fur. She played with my son, chasing whirling balls, pushing Thomas the Train all over the tracks, and hiding in boxes. As the seasons passed, they grew together, and their companionship evolved from her running from him to running to him. She now sleeps on his empty bed during the day, greets him when he comes home from college, and hangs outside in the back yard with him in the sunshine. My son does not have siblings, and Lucky has become a constant in his life.

Lucky is now seventeen, and our hearts break as we realize our time with her will be ending soon. She eats less and less. She moves slower and slower, and she has a hard time climbing stairs. We try to make her as comfortable as we can. We carry her up the stairs, feed her a special diet, and lift her onto the bed at night. But we can all sense she will be leaving our lives soon.

When she passes, we will miss her tremendously. This cat who came into our lives through a dust cloud has brought love and companionship. She watched over my son and melted my husband's heart. Our vet mentioned the right pet would come into our lives at the right time, and she did. My husband named her Lucky because she was able to walk through the chaos of a busy construction site with no injuries. I called her Lucky because she had found a good home. My son called her Lucky because he felt we were the lucky ones to have her. I think we were lucky all the way around!

— Sandra Martin —

86

Catastrophe

One must love a cat on its own terms.
~Paul Gray

Beavis was a rescue cat who came to our family from a broken home. At the time, I remember thinking that his attitude just might have been responsible for the break. His first three days in our house were spent under a bed hissing and spitting at anyone brave enough to venture near. Even the non-threatening offer of food or water provoked an aggressive response.

Eventually, after a number of weeks and a lot of patience, Beavis deigned to be in the same room as other family members, as long as he was given his space and wasn't approached directly.

His first visit to the vet was a nightmare. The poor man had to wear a thick leather apron and industrial-grade gloves before giving Beavis a routine examination. After the visit, the vet wrote in his notes that Beavis was a "very difficult" animal to deal with. At least he didn't ask us to change vets.

It was my bright idea to get him some companionship. Drawing on my "vast experience" as a cat person, I reckoned the cure for his antisocial behaviour would be some cat company. The second mistake I made was in encouraging my daughter and her friend to be the ones to choose a barn kitten from a local farmer. As it turned out, they couldn't decide which one to pick, so they compromised by choosing two kittens.

It turned out that Beavis was not pining for cat company, but rather came into his own as a kitten bully. The little guys were terrorised at every turn. We had gone from a one-catastrophe family to three. Beavis was unable to share food or even toilet facilities with the kittens. We spent more time keeping them apart than watching them interact. It looked as though we were destined to suffer long-term cat problems.

One day, Beavis was strutting his stuff through a particularly well-fitting door in our basement. He was not quite through when it closed sharply on his tail. He let out a blood-curdling squeal and took off to the farthest part of the house. Finally, we managed to corner him, carefully wrapped him in a large bath towel, and rushed him off to the vet. During this visit, he seemed much more subdued than previously, but we thought it was probably due to the tranquilizer administered on his arrival. The vet stitched up what could be saved of his tail and put a conical collar around his neck to stop him from worrying at the damaged area. He was a sad sight indeed. Imprisoned in his restrictive neckwear, the kittens were finally able to get up close and inspect him.

For three weeks, Beavis displayed a hangdog attitude. It was sad to see such a previously confident, dominant animal forced to retreat into himself. The whole family, including the kittens, felt sorry for him. He'd had a lot to cope with. Beavis was now unable to groom his beautiful orange coat, and feeding time often saw him chasing his food bowl around the kitchen floor in an attempt to eat as he did before the accident.

At the end of his neck-cone sentence, I caught up with him and held him closer than I had ever managed before. Anticipating the worst but hoping for the best, I removed the collar carefully. Beavis moved off a little way and stood for a few minutes looking around as if to ensure that the restriction was really gone. When he realised that this was his new reality, he walked straight over to me and nuzzled and licked my hand in gratitude.

From that day on, I lost a ferocious cat and gained a feline lap dog. His nature changed completely. Now he interacted well with all the family, even his kitten cousins. He was a reformed cat. I could now call him from the other end of the house, and he would trot over to see what I needed, just like a faithful little dog. Whenever I watched television, he would sit at my feet and purr loudly. Previously, I hadn't known he was even capable of purring.

Friends who had known the old Beavis could not believe the change. During his next trip to the vet, there was no longer a need for the vet to armour up. Beavis seemed happy to be examined and handled. He had changed into a big, furry orange teddy bear. The vet was even able to make a positive change to his notes on Beavis's behaviour.

I will never be sure whether it was the shock of the tail incident or the restrictions of the collar that changed his attitude. Either way, I believe he came to realise that people really cared about him. Happily, with his new outlook, he was with us for many years. I was even convinced that he learned a few words of greeting, which he shared with me each time I came into a room. Beavis turned out to be a wonderful mentor for the kittens, who absolutely adored him. And he taught us all a lesson about showing gratitude to those who care for us as we journey through our lives.

—James A. Gemmell—

87

Hedgehog

*The cat could very well be man's best friend
but would never stoop to admitting it.*
~Doug Larson

My wife and I arrived at our daughter's friend's house. We thanked the girl's parents for allowing our little girl to stay the weekend for a slumber party. We shared some small talk while the girls said their goodbyes.

And then it happened. "Dad!" exclaimed my daughter. "We found a kitten!"

I looked at my wife and said emphatically, "No."

But it was too late. The girls ran to the back porch and extracted the creature from a makeshift cardboard-box bed. They handed it to my wife, who then looked at me with pleading eyes. Before I could utter a word, she offered to take it home.

"There were others," said the girl's father, "but they were dead. Their mother was nowhere to be found."

I received another pleading look from my wife.

"We really don't need another cat," I mumbled. But I knew in my heart that, indeed, we now had another cat.

The kitten was handed to me craftily to pull at my heartstrings and, of course, to clinch the deal. He was a tiny critter who fit in the palm of my hand and weighed no more than a pound. He looked but a few days old. His spiky gray fur made him look like a baby hedgehog.

Learning to Love the Cat |

We took our new infant with us to the pet store and purchased kitten formula and several tiny bottles. On the way to the register, we picked up a little stuffed hedgehog for him as well.

For the next few weeks, we took turns feeding him just like a newborn infant. We put him over our shoulders when we were done and patted his little back until he burped. Then we rocked him to sleep and placed him in his small bed in the master bathroom where we isolated him from the others just in case he had brought any viruses home.

Every day during those two weeks, I went home at lunchtime. Quickly, I greeted our other cats and then nudged them away from the bathroom door as I squeezed in to see the new charge. He now had a name, Ollie, but he really didn't know that it was for him. Nonetheless, he wiggled his stump of a tail and rubbed up against me. I fed him, burped him and then gave him a hug. I tried to give him a kiss on the top of his head, but he squirmed to get away. His feral instinct was still strong, but I was beginning to imprint on his tiny mind. I was his mother!

"Alright, Ollie-Bollie!" I exclaimed. "I love you anyway." I placed him in his bed next to his furry hedgehog counterpart and returned to work.

As Ollie grew, his spikes turned into a silky, shorthaired smoky-gray coat. He had a beautiful white tuxedo chest and abdomen. All four feet were capped in identical white socks.

Finally, released from isolation, the cat assimilated well with the rest of our pride. He followed me all morning, every morning, as I prepared for work. He sat near the kitchen table and whined until I patted him on the head.

"Good boy, Ollie-Bird," I'd say, patting him once more. Then he'd be off on an adventure until it was time for me to leave. He knew when that was. He'd look me in the eye and meow. He'd plop himself belly-up on the floor and stare at me.

It was time for his morning massage.

So, with a sigh, I would put down my bag, lunch, and coffee to kneel on the floor and rub his belly. He'd flip to one side, and I'd scratch and rub down the length of his back. He'd flip to the other side, and I would repeat the process. Several times, he would flip. Finally, I had to tell him I was going to be late for work. We both stood. I smoothed out his fur and then headed for the door.

I always bent down and tried to kiss him on the head, but he just couldn't handle it and would jerk away. He'd always return seconds later for another pat.

Quickly, I would move to the door. "Bye, wife!" I'd holler. "Bye, Ollie!"

This became our daily ritual. Sometimes, in my rush to my busy world, I would get impatient and begrudgingly give him a quick backrub before darting off to work.

Every evening, though, as I unlocked the door and walked into the house, there was my devoted, forgiving little friend waiting for me.

At night, Ollie would jump up on the bed and wait for me to get situated on my back and under the covers. Then he would snuggle up next to my feet as I read. Once the lights were out, he would wriggle between my ankles and purr until we fell asleep.

Every morning when I awakened, he was there looking me in the eyes.

Our daughter has grown from the little girl at sleepovers to a fine, young college graduate making a name for herself in the world. She and my wife are still in love with every rescue kitten they encounter.

Ollie is now our oldest cat. His smoky-gray fur is now more frosty-gray in color. He still thinks that I am his mother.

Now that I am in my sixties, I am finally understanding that our time on this planet is limited. I realize that I will not be here forever.

Likewise, I realize the inevitable future for this loving cat who has adopted me and trusted me to take care of him for all these years. I know that eventually he will no longer be with me. Knowing that he chose me, even though I initially did not choose him, makes that realization even more profound.

He loves me.

I may not have much more time with him, so I've pledged to make what little time I do have left worthwhile in order to let him know that I love him, too.

I vow to give him the best backrub every morning — even if I am running late.

I promise to allow him to stay warm, snuggled between my feet in the middle of the night — even if I really want to turn over and lie on my side.

I assure him that I will greet him joyously at the door when I get home and thank him for being there to welcome me back into his day.

I guarantee him a great life until the end and promise him all the hugs in the world.

And, should he ever be open to it, I will kiss him on the head and say, "Gotcha! I love you, Ollie-Bollie!"

— Tim Ramsey —

88

Ode to Frankie Cat

No amount of time can erase the memory of a good cat,
and no amount of masking tape can ever totally
remove his fur from your couch.
~Leo Dworken

When I first met my husband, I knew in my gut,
that Joel was too perfect; there must be a "but."
Indeed, I was right. In his flat, there it sat:
His fat, furry roommate named Frankie. A cat.

I adored Joel's devotion — adopting a stray.
Committed and kind. I mean, what could I say?
My feelings on cats? Want the truth? Not a fan.
But willing to give it a shot for this man.

The problem was, each time I'd visit Joel's place,
my eyes felt as if they'd been peppered with mace.
My throat burned like fire, my nose turned bright red,
not to mention the thunderous throb in my head.

Though Joel was prepared to reverse the adoption,
I saw he was smitten. It wasn't an option.
Through sneezes I pouted, but knew in the end,
he couldn't abandon his four-footed friend.

I looked for a loophole, but found there was none.
So when we were wed, I acquired a son.
I went to the doctor, took meds every day.
I vacuumed like mad to keep dander at bay.

Humongous air filters invaded our house.
(Amazing the things we will do for a spouse!)
I learned I could live with the cat — from a distance.
And thus began years of compelled coexistence.

I turned a blind eye to the onslaught of hair —
on my couch, on my floor, on my pricy suede chair.
I always wore slippers; I just couldn't bear
my feet on the litter that spilled everywhere.

I envied friends' homes where you had half a chance
of sitting without getting fur on your pants.
And since Joel refused to declaw our dear child,
I watched Frankie shred every rug and just smiled.

For years, he and I were like ships in the night.
Clichéd but a phrase that described us just right.
The cat understood and stayed out of my way.
He knew to find Dad for a pat or some play.

Each night, Frankie snuggled in Joel's cozy lap,
and enjoyed a massage while he took a long nap.
Joel's love for that cat was ferociously real.
I frequently felt like a useless third wheel.

My two human children grew up with pure joy
for this cute, cuddly critter — their fun, fuzzy toy.
They tackled him daily; they pulled at his fur.
And Frankie, Lord bless him, would sit there and purr.

It's hard to believe fourteen years have flown past,
and I fear that this year could be poor Frankie's last.
In the past several months, he's become far too thin.
He's developed a tumor — a fight he can't win.

You'd probably think I'd be shouting, "Hooray!"
Yet my feelings are not black and white but more gray.
I've awaited this moment for so very long,
but now that it's here, it seems terribly wrong.

Yes, Frankie, it's true that we had a rough start,
but over the years, you have chipped at my heart.
With Joel and the children so often away,
you became my companion all day, every day.

And lately, when I've felt frustrated or fried,
it's you who comes over and sits by my side.
Though touching you still makes me break out in hives,
it's been pretty nice having you in our lives.

Despite all the damage, the hair on my seat,
the odorous litter that stuck to my feet,
you brought our home comfort and love, and for that,
I'll always be grateful to you, Frankie Cat.

— Rebecca Gardyn Levington —

89

Yin Yang

Perhaps it is because cats do not live by human patterns,
do not fit themselves into prescribed behavior,
that they are so united to creative people.
~Andre Norton

After my husband Harold and I got married, we settled into our first apartment and our life as newlyweds. Before we got married, we had agreed a cat would be a wonderful addition to our lives. We were only married three weeks when we decided that the time had come.

One Saturday morning, we went to our local animal shelter to pick out our new family member. We weren't looking for any particular type of cat. Age, sex, coloring or breed didn't matter to us. We just wanted a cat to fill our hearts and home with love. When we got to the shelter, we were informed we would have a good selection to pick from since the shelter was overflowing with cats. After walking down several aisles of cages and looking at all the sweet cats, we were overwhelmed.

"How can we pick just one cat when so many need homes?" I whispered to Harold. He nodded in agreement.

As we were nearing the end of the last aisle, I spied a little ball of fur wedged in the corner of a cage. The fur was half-white and half-black. The first thing that came to mind was that the sleeping cat resembled a yin-and-yang symbol.

"What unique markings," I blurted out. "Can I see this cat?"

"Actually, that is two kittens," the volunteer answered with a smile, informing us that they were both found in the back of an apartment complex two months prior and brought to the shelter. "They are inseparable," she continued.

She went on to tell us they were having a hard time finding a home for them because they felt it would be best for them to stay together.

As soon as the volunteer placed the kittens in our arms, we knew those fur balls would be ours. It was love at first sight.

"Now we don't have to pick just one!" I joked.

We didn't have to think of name choices. We knew what to name them instantly — Yin and Yang. It was Yin for the girl who had a solid, shiny black coat and Yang for the boy who was as white as snow.

From the moment we brought home our new kittens, they made themselves comfortable, sleeping together curled up like a perfectly fit puzzle. Unfortunately, they chose the most unusual place to sleep. Despite the fact they had a large, fluffy new cat bed, they slept intertwined together on my craft table, right smack in the middle. It didn't matter if they were lying on top of a drawing pad, pencils or glue sticks. They seemed perfectly comfortable. When they weren't sleeping, they played hockey with markers as they swiped them back and forth to each other.

I tried repeatedly to introduce them to their bed, enticing them with tiny kibbles of treats and toys. I even moved their bed right next to my craft table, hoping they felt it was close enough to feel comfortable. Nothing worked.

It was very difficult to be creative with Yin and Yang snoozing on the sharp pins or the wet paint of my latest masterpiece, so I tried scooting them over to the far end of the table as a compromise. "Okay, you can both stay on the table, as long as you stay on your end so I can work," I coaxed my stubborn kittens. I slid them over to the end of the table. Not a moment later, they slid right back to the middle.

This is just a phase they're going through, I thought, convinced they needed a little more time to get used to their new home.

By the third week, I came to the conclusion that no amount of coaxing, bribing or compromising would work. Yin and Yang made it perfectly clear that the center of my craft table was their spot. I was invading their space. They won! I surrendered and moved my crafts to the kitchen table.

"Okay, you win!" I said to them as I took the last craft off the table.

Once my supplies were relocated, I looked forward to a morning of crafting. I was working on a project to hang on our family-room wall, and I couldn't wait to get started. I felt optimistic that I would finally have ample room on the kitchen table without having to fight the fur balls for space. Taking inventory, I realized I was missing blue paint, so I made my way to the closet to get it, along with additional paintbrushes. Upon my return, right there, smack in the middle of the kitchen table, were my kittens, curled up in their infamous yin-and-yang sleeping position! "You've got to be kidding me," I laughed.

Then it dawned on me: Yin and Yang wanted to be close to me while I worked. Maybe it was a sense of security, or they just liked hanging out with me, their new mom. As quietly as possible, trying not to wake the sneaky little invaders, I moved everything back onto my craft table. Within minutes, Yin and Yang followed and settled down on their spot in the middle of the table.

With a defeated sigh but a smile in my heart, I took my spot at the end of the table, resigning myself to working my way around Yin and Yang.

"I see they won!" My husband laughed when he walked in and saw me cramped at the end of the table, with the kittens spread out sleeping peacefully in the middle.

I guess at that point we both must have laughed a little too loudly because Yin and Yang lifted their heads in unison and slowly sauntered over to my little corner of the table.

They planted themselves right on top of my unfinished project. Just before they closed their eyes once more, we caught a glimpse of their smug expressions, which we interpreted as victory. It was a victory we were more than happy to allow them in exchange for the laughter, love and companionship they provided in return.

— Dorann Weber —

90

Don't Count Your Chickens

Mistakes are part of the dues one pays for a full life.
~Sophia Loren

The jangle of the phone startled me. With all three boys at school, my husband tinkering in the workshop, and the critters napping, I figured I'd seize the opportunity to write undisturbed. So when the phone rang, I let the answering machine take the call.

"Mom, it's Christopher," my son cut in after the beep. "Mom, are you there?"

My heart skipped a beat at the sound of his voice. A litany of possibilities ran through my mind as I rushed to pick up the phone. Was he sick? Hurt? In trouble?

"Hey, Chris," I said, struggling to keep my voice calm. "What's wrong?"

"Nothing's wrong. I just wanted to know if it's okay if I bring home a chicken."

Several weeks ago, he'd told me about the chicks hatching in his science class's incubator, so I assumed he was referring to those chicks, which had, apparently, matured into full-grown chickens. Visions of fresh eggs and chickens pecking at the bugs in our back yard filled my mind. They would make a great addition to our home in the country.

"Bring home two of them, if possible," I suggested. "They'll be company for each other."

"Thanks Mom!" Christopher said, handing the phone to his teacher so she could confirm I was truly willing to take the critters.

Later on, as I drove the fifteen miles to school to pick up our twin boys, I realized I didn't have anything ready for the chickens. We have several cats and a dog, and we'd kept rabbits for a while, but chickens were altogether different. We would need a coop and chicken feed.

After pulling into the line in front of the school, I shut off the engine and texted my oldest son who works after school at the Missouri Farmers Association. I asked him to pick up whatever food and supplies might be necessary for two young chickens. I figured he would know what they needed or could ask one of his co-workers.

When the school doors opened, a horde of excited children poured from the building. This was their last day of school. Patiently, I waited for the crowd to thin out, assuming my teenage sons would be among the last to exit. Eventually, Benjamin pushed through the doors and ran down the steps. I gasped as he approached the car — with a black-and-white kitten nestled in the crook of his arm.

"That's not a chicken!" I said, as he climbed into the back seat.

Benjamin gave me this "Duh, Mom!" look and didn't even bother to respond. Instead, he hugged the kitten closer.

The front passenger door opened, and Christopher slid into the seat next to me. He was snuggling a tabby kitten.

"I thought you asked if you could bring home a chicken," I said.

"Mo-o-o-m! I said 'kitten,' not 'chicken.' Our teacher's cat had five kittens, and she needs to find homes for them. Can we still keep them?"

There wasn't much sense arguing. After all, I had already agreed to take them, although I'd misunderstood what "them" consisted of. That, coupled with the longing in both my sons' eyes, was enough to sway me.

"Yes, we can keep them," I said.

Reaching into my purse amid cheers from the boys, I retrieved my phone and sent a quick text to my oldest son asking him to cancel my request.

Apparently, I wouldn't be needing chicken feed anytime soon.

— Renée Vajko-Srch —

91

My Husband Did Not Want a Cat

*I had been told that the training procedure with cats
was difficult. It's not. Mine had me trained in two days.*
~Bill Dana

My husband did not want a cat. Our household was all set.
With one loud dog, two girls, three boys. Why add another pet?
My husband did not want a cat. We had dog hair galore.
Why sprinkle feline fur onto our clothes and chairs and floor?
My husband did not want a cat. They're snooty and aloof.
They scratch without a warning and don't listen to reproof.
My husband did not want a cat. They act like life's a bore.
The laps that most desire them they'll happily ignore.
My husband did not want a cat. They purr as if to boast
That once again they clawed the couch instead of scratching post.
My husband did not want a cat. They're fussy, mean, and proud,
Capricious, fat, and lazy beasts. That's it. No cats allowed.
But I had grown up liking cats, though some were independent.
I researched breeds to find one that was truly sweet and pleasant.
It had to be a longhaired cat; they always looked so pretty.
And one that wanted us around — a sociable kitty.
And with a four-year-old at home, the cat must be quite kind.
Patient, tolerant of noise, or it might lose its mind.
Then I found an ideal breed. "A Ragdoll's what we want!

They're gorgeous, calm, affectionate, and rather nonchalant.
They get along with kids and dogs and don't tend to be stuffy.
They're heavy cats with bright blue eyes — plus, they're oh-so-fluffy."
My husband still was unconvinced. "How much do Ragdolls cost?"
I said, "I'll use my mad money. Our budget won't be lost."
My husband asked, "Then who will do the cleaning of the litter?"
"Not you," I said. "We've got five kids to help care for this critter."
"But what of those with allergies who visit us at home?"
"That's fine. We'll just make sure we sweep and mop before they come."
My husband said he'd think on it. He still seemed somewhat wary.
But he surprised me with some books he'd got from the library.
He read them to our youngest — tales of kitties in their glory.
I guess he didn't quite equate cats now with purgatory.
We visited the shelter just to practice petting kittens.
Our daughters got all dreamy-eyed. My husband — nearly smitten.
Then finally the day arrived to pick up our new kitty.
We took the family on a drive three hours from the city.
We'd picked the last cute kitten with fawn fur and darkened nose,
A cuddly, pure-bred Ragdoll with blue eyes and white-mitt toes.
He didn't mind the car ride or sitting on kids' laps.
He yawned and stretched and arched his back, then curled up for catnaps.
Our dog was not a fan at first. She doubted we were sane,
For bringing in this fluffy runt to traipse on her domain.
But soon the kitten won her o'er. Together they would tussle.
Comically mismatched in size, but loving every scuffle.
Our children readily adored the quiet, fuzzy wonder.
Trailing strings and taking turns to make the kitty purr.
He didn't mind our youngest dressing him with her own clothes.
I'd find him lying on his back, paws up in sweet repose.
A kinder, gentler kitty I could never hope to find.
He'd captured all the hearts within our home including mine.
But the real surprise is what has happened to my spouse.
He now reaches for the cat once he's inside the house.
Now my husband loves the cat. And often, he gets carried,
Underneath my husband's arms. Is this the man I married?

Now my husband loves the cat and spoils Darcy rotten,
With egg yolk from his silver spoon — his former doubts forgotten.
Now my husband loves the cat. He beckons from his chair.
And doesn't seem to notice all the tawny-colored hair.
Now my husband loves the cat. Our home's a cozy corps,
of dog, two girls, three boys, a cat — who could ask for more?

— Katherine L. Mitchell —

Brave Cats

92

Six Legs Between Them

When I am feeling low all I have to do is watch my cat
and my courage returns.
~Charles Bukowski

When I got Primrose, she had an infected hind foot. She was a teenage cat and had been found wandering in a field. Spayed but not chipped, hungry but friendly, she was so happy to be rescued.

I took her to the vet where they lanced and cleaned the foot and put her on antibiotics. Unfortunately, the infection didn't respond to treatment and moved into the joint. A couple of weeks later, I was back at the vet with her getting some really bad news. Primrose was going to lose that leg.

As a cat parent and rescuer, it would be my first amputation of anything other than a tail. Primrose would be my first tripod. Although I knew people with tripod cats who said they all did great and that recovery from the surgery was not difficult, this was new to me. And scary.

Primrose got another round of antibiotics, and her surgery was scheduled for the next week. I took her home and put her back in her kennel, promising her for the umpteenth time that eventually she would get to be free again. She looked at me trustingly with huge brown eyes set in a pretty brown tabby face. She hadn't known me very long, but she knew she was safe with me. She knew I just wanted to help.

A few days later, it was Thanksgiving. That afternoon, I got a message about an injured kitten that had been found in a Burger King parking lot. I agreed to meet the lady who found her, and I went to pick up my new rescue.

She was about four months old. She was clean and looked healthy, but her right front leg was hanging limply. I was pretty sure she had been hit by a car. If so, she was lucky that she only had a broken leg! I named her Gillian. She was all black except for a white spot on her chest and she had beautiful golden eyes.

Primrose's surgery was scheduled for the next day, so when I took her in, Gillian went, too. After Primrose was checked in and taken back to a kennel, they turned their attention to Gillian. As I expected, an X-ray and exam showed that the leg was broken at the clavicle. I was shocked, though, to be told that the leg would have to be amputated. Holy wow! Back-to-back amputations and two tripod cats!

It was Friday, and Gillian's surgery was scheduled for the following Monday. She was given pain meds, and I took her home. She was a happy little thing, chirping and meowing at me almost constantly and purring in spite of the discomfort she had to be feeling.

I thought Primrose would need to stay overnight, but she was doing so well after her surgery that I got to pick her up that same day. I took her home and put her in a small kennel, figuring the less space she had to work with while she was learning her new balance, the better. Her leg had been amputated all the way up at the hip, so her weight distribution would feel completely different. The vet had told me that cats usually adapt better to losing a hind leg than a front leg, but watching poor Primrose weave back and forth, I wondered if that was true. Hopefully it was more due to the aftereffects of anesthesia than a portent of things to come!

Twenty-four hours later, she was doing much better. I grimaced when I saw her try to hop into her litter box and end up balanced on the edge. I had not considered that. She looked at me in consternation. She had no idea how to resolve the situation! I reached in and gently lifted her back half and set her remaining hind foot in the litter. As soon as she was done, I changed out that box for a shorter one.

Monday rolled around, and I took Gillian in for her surgery. She also did well and got to come home the same day. As with Primrose, I marveled at how clean and perfect the incision looked — hardly any swelling or inflammation at all!

The girls each had to go back two weeks later to have their sutures removed. By that time, they had both progressed more than I would ever have imagined. After the first few days, I let them out of their small kennels but kept them in the bathroom. One day, I went in, and Gillian jumped into my lap. Another time, I opened the door, and Primrose hopped over the baby gate like it wasn't there.

It only got better from there. Before long, they were both racing through the house and jumping on furniture. When they are in motion, I can't see what they are doing differently — how they are compensating for the missing limb. They are each as graceful as any other cat, as fast and agile. It's amazing!

The one real problem is one that had not even crossed my mind. Primrose lost a hind leg; cats use their back feet to scratch with, but it is totally instinctive. So when her ear itches, she tries to scratch it. Her hip twitches and jerks, but there is no leg and foot attached to scratch with, and she looks so bewildered and puzzled. "Why isn't it working? Why does it still itch?" I can't help but laugh and feel sorry for her at the same time. And then I scratch the ear for her. Sometimes, a girl just needs a little help.

At night, they sleep in my bedroom, Primrose tucked at my side and Gillian up on my pillow. They share me with my other current rescues and forever cats and get along well with everyone. They have sweet personalities and no bad habits.

I do not expect a missing leg to be a liability when it is time for them to find their forever homes. It might even be an asset! There is a growing trend of people wanting to adopt "special" animals; it's wonderful to see and be a part of. Rescue animals have often been neglected, abandoned, and sometimes abused. Some of them are like Primrose and Gillian, injured because they were out in the world all alone. I love it that I get to heal their wounds and soothe their souls, and then pass them along to someone who will love them forever.

Watching these girls romp and play, I often think about what an amazing world it would be if humans adapted to their shortcomings the way animals do. No self-pity. No whining. It's not even a "can-do attitude." They just deal with life as it is and move right along. Life is what we make it, and these little tripods are making it just fine!

— Linda Sabourin —

A Cloud in Our Hearts

*Maybe there's no actual magic in it, but when you
know what you hope for most and hold it like a light
within you, you can make things happen,
almost like magic.*
~Laini Taylor, Daughter of Smoke & Bone

"Don't you want to play with the dogs?" I called after my two sons as they darted around the corner toward the cat wing of the animal shelter.

"I want a cat!" called Nicholas over his shoulder.

"Me too!" yelled his younger brother, Robert, waving his arms.

I was going through a divorce and I hoped getting a family dog would lighten my children's hearts. My childhood dog had been a constant companion for me during tough times.

But the kids wanted a cat. I laughed as my boys cuddled two sweet, little kittens — a tabby called Huey and a snow-white kitty we named Cloud. *I definitely lost this battle,* I thought to myself as we went home with two little felines and left the barking dogs behind.

Huey and Cloud were part of the family immediately. The boys cleared toys off their windowsills so the cats could sit and look out, and I surrendered my laundry basket filled with fresh cotton towels for them to curl up in together. All summer long, Huey and Cloud kept my boys on the run outside, chasing birds and scaling trees, bringing a smile to their faces every day.

When Christmas came around, we added a stocking to our fireplace for the cats, and my boys made kitty lists for Santa that were longer than their own wish lists for toys. Despite the hectic time of the year, each day still began and ended with loving our cats.

"I have to give Cloud and Huey a hug goodnight," Robert exclaimed as he dodged my effort to get him up the stairs for bed on December twenty-third.

Continuing up the steps with Nicholas, I could hear Robert running loudly from one end of our small house to the other, searching for his pals. I loved how much he cared for our cats, but I was tired and needed the boys in bed so I could wrap Christmas presents.

Seeing a long delay tactic unfolding, I called over the railing, "Upstairs now!" in my most serious, I-mean-business voice.

"Mom!" Robert screamed back, causing the hairs on my arms to stand up. I darted back down the stairs with Nicholas close behind me.

We found Robert kneeling in the dark beside our Christmas tree, the blinking lights dancing green and red over his silhouette. Cloud was lying quietly in a puddle beneath the branches, nonresponsive to Robert as he softly stroked his soft white fur. Dropping to my knees, I reached under the tree and scooped Cloud into my arms.

"What's wrong with him?" Nicholas asked as both boys hovered over me. Cloud's eyes were open, but he gazed blankly past us. A heavy rasp vibrated through my hands, replacing his soft, musical kitten-motor purr.

"He wet himself." I tried to keep calm as I wrapped him in a blanket and hugged him close. "I think he's just cold."

"No, there's something wrong with him!" Robert yelled, angered by my calmness. "We have to bring him to the hospital."

"Robert, I don't know any animal hospitals open this late at night," I reasoned.

Cloud's breathing appeared to relax as I cuddled him, and he wiggled inside the warm blanket. "See, he's fine," I rationalized. "I'll bet he's just a little sick from drinking the Christmas tree water."

Cowering a few feet away, Huey edged over to us and began to sniff Cloud's fluffy head.

"Ee-owww." He let out a cold moan as his back stiffened, and fur shot up into alarmed spikes down his extended tail.

Huey agreed with Robert — Cloud needed help now! "Get me the laptop," I said to the boys. "I need to find an all-night animal hospital."

An hour later, we sat in the vet's office, waiting anxiously for the doctor to return with the results from Cloud's testing.

"Your cat has been electrocuted," she stated flatly as she sat down behind her desk. Robert tightened his grip on my leg, and Nicholas squeezed my hand as they both looked up at me with tear-stained cheeks.

"No," I blinked in confused disbelief. "I think he drank the Christmas tree water."

"He has a hole burned through the roof of his mouth," she continued, "in the shape of a Christmas tree bulb."

We spent the next day, Christmas Eve, driving back and forth from home to visit Cloud in the animal hospital as the doctor did all she could to save him. "Don't expect any response from him," she warned at each visit. Out of earshot from my boys, she whispered, "I don't think he has much longer."

Huey darted over to us each time we returned home, only to slink away disappointed that we hadn't brought his best friend home. As I placed presents under the tree late that night, my heart sank even lower when I noticed Huey's food bowl was still full, sitting on the floor beside Cloud's empty bowl. We all missed Cloud.

I tried to sound excited the next morning. "It's Christmas! Santa came last night."

"Let's go see Cloud," Robert said, ignoring his pile of gifts.

"Yeah, let's go," Nicholas agreed, stopping to cuddle with Huey on the kitchen floor. We all got dressed and headed back to the hospital.

"Merry Christmas, Cloud," Robert whispered, pressing his nose against the cool glass of the oxygen chamber where Cloud lay inside. The blue blanket under Cloud began to wriggle. He lifted his head and slowly opened his eyes, blinking away the morning light as he looked directly into Robert's eyes. *Purrrr,* his motor lightly rumbled.

"Cloud, you're back!" We all grabbed each other in joy and cheered, sparking a barking frenzy among the kenneled dogs at the other end of the room.

"It's a Christmas miracle," the vet said in disbelief, walking up from behind.

Four days later, we brought Cloud home. Huey sniffed him briefly and then pounced on him with delight, sending both cats rolling on their backs and swatting each other like it was any other day.

"Look what Santa brought you," the boys chimed as they finally tore through the cats' Christmas stocking still hanging over the fireplace. Nicholas tossed shiny balls into the air for Huey to leap after, and Robert raced through the house dragging a feather on a string for Cloud to chase. Huey and Cloud remained inseparable for the entire day until they fell asleep curled on top of each other in the laundry basket that night. It was a few days late, but a wave of happiness flowed through our house. It had turned into the most joyful Christmas ever. Although he has a permanent hole in the roof of his mouth, Cloud recovered, and so did our family.

Those two cats had filled my boys' hearts when they came into our home. Now they brought us together to understand gratitude and love better than any lesson I could have taught them — filling my heart with love and pride for all four of my precious little guys.

And to think I had wanted a dog…

— Laura Savino —

94

The Bat Fanatic

It always gives me a shiver when I see
a cat seeing what I can't see.
~Eleanor Farjeon

t was a mystery how the heavy, antique rocking chair turned itself upside down in the living room most nights. It took all my strength to set the upholstered chair upright in the mornings.

I never heard it happen, but I had my suspects, who would be placidly grooming themselves in a patch of sunlight when I saw them the next day. Ransom would occasionally turn his rough tongue to smooth Tootsie's yellow fur like he had since Toots was a kitten, licking until Toots folded his wide ears flat and growled a warning.

One night, I was awakened from a dream by a high-pitched clicking and the sound of the cats racing up and down the stairs. The hall nightlight dimly illuminated a winged creature swooping against our bedroom ceiling.

"Bat!" I screamed. I swept the covers over my head in a panic and pounded my husband's shoulder to wake him.

"What. What?" He flipped on the light and saw nothing. "There's no —"

About that time, the stealthy glider entered the bedroom for another pass. Unperturbed, Dear Husband rose from the sheets dressed only in his underwear, pulled the quilt from the bed and waited. So did Toots at the top of the steps. His large ears, almost bat-like themselves, twitched forward. With his body cocked and loaded, he readied to spring into action.

"Here it comes," my husband teased, tossing the quilt at me and making me scream again. Seconds later, the bat did appear. I ducked with another screech. Dear Husband yanked the remaining sheet from the bed, leaving me exposed, and threw it over the creature. Then its clicking began in earnest from beneath the sheet on the floor.

Toots followed Mark downstairs to witness the release. Though bats consume thousands of mosquitoes a night, I still didn't want one in my house. This one had obviously lost his way.

"Probably flew in on a wind current when we brought in the groceries," Dear Husband explained. I was skeptical but didn't say more.

"Oh, look. Tootsie's almost disappointed," I said, pointing to the little cat. He was patrolling the hallway, looking into nooks and crannies and the cracks on the ceiling. Before going back to bed, I turned all the lights on and tested the latch on the attic door. Solid.

"Some protector you are," I scoffed when I passed him curled in the hallway on my return from the bathroom.

The next morning, despite the chair being tipped back against the wall, I didn't connect the pieces.

That evening, we got home late. Walking in the porch doorway, I paused and checked the doorframe for any hanging bats. I waited to see if I could feel one swoosh past my ear. No bats. Usually, both cats greeted us at the door begging for supper this time of night. But no cats, either.

Inside, Toots didn't rise from the carpet where he lay. He watched us as we passed him to hang up coats and again to switch on lamps. Belly flat to the floor with his forearms curled beneath him, only his head swiveled to follow us. Ransom, perched on the back of the couch, watched Toots with great interest, too.

"What's up with them tonight?" I asked. "They look like they ate the canary."

I took a seat to unlace my boots. Toots rarely missed a chance to play with my laces, but he stayed rooted to the carpet. I wiggled the laces, feeling a bit concerned now. He merely blinked at my attempts. Then, lifting one shoulder only slightly, he bent to peek beneath his front arms before smiling back at me with a magical twitch to his grin.

Eerily, one by one, the hairs on my neck began to rise.

He settled in, pressing himself firmly into the carpet spreading his body weight out wider but not before he peeked again beneath his body. His Cheshire grin said it all.

"Mark," I whispered. "He's got something beneath him."

Dear Husband, much more concerned with his television episode than a cat, ignored me — until Tootsie lifted both shoulders before slamming himself flat to the rug.

"At least someone will catch a mouse around here," he joked to Ransom, whose only hunt involved a cat dish. The cat ignored him, now fixated on his buddy. This finally drew Mark's attention, too.

Even when Mark got up and stood above him, Toots didn't budge. Occasionally, he'd peek beneath himself again, happy as a hen sitting on a cache of chicks. Pulling the cat aside, neither of us expected to see a very weary, brown bat. Toots struggled frantically to secure his catch.

"Mark, rabies," I warned, trying not to crawl out of my skin at the sight of it. I grabbed a towel to cover my head. Somehow, this would help.

Every spring, one lone bat will find an opening, probably beneath the shingles, and slip inside to the attic. But two?

Now wearing leather gloves, Mark pushed aside the cat. Despite its fiendish expression, the frightened bat was barely breathing, though it struggled against Mark's attempts to gently unsnarl its claws from the carpet. Ticked, Tootsie circled Mark's feet, meowing great howls of protest as he followed him to the door. He returned, leaping into the upholstered chair and sending it rocking with his tantrum as if in slow motion. It tipped backward. Mystery solved.

"Good boy!" I said, catching the rocker in time. Then I sat down beside him, stroking him with praise. As I did, I felt his skin for any injuries, thankful his rabies shots were up to date. "What a fine hunter and protector you are, Tootsie. Fine indeed."

"We have a bat problem," I said emphatically to my husband when he returned.

"We don't have a bat problem," he replied, turning up the volume on the TV.

The next morning as I put on make-up, Tootsie joined me. He found the tall, wicker clothes hamper particularly interesting. Despite the roar of the blow dryer, he seemed entranced at the space where the hamper met the wall. Sitting like a sphinx, he smiled up at me and then back at the opening. Even wet, my neck hairs rose. Gingerly, I eased one corner of the hamper away from the wall while holding Toots back with my ankle.

I didn't have to turn it far to see that we definitely have a bat problem.

— Susan A. Hoffert —

95

A Special Independence Day

Who would believe such pleasure
from a wee ball o' fur?
~Irish Saying

My kids cheered as soon as they woke up on the Fourth of July. "It's Fireworks Day! How soon can we go downtown to watch them?"

"Guys, it's 7:00 a.m.," I said. "It has to be dark to watch fireworks."

"We have to wait all day?" They groaned. "This is going to be the slowest day in history."

"No, it won't. We'll have fun, and it will be time to go before you know it. Let's start by eating breakfast."

I made the kids' favorite breakfast: chocolate-chip pancakes. After we ate, I told each of the kids to pick four things they wanted to do to help pass the time until we could leave to watch the fireworks.

Jordan decided that he wanted to watch his favorite movie, play Battleship, and build with his Legos. "And for my fourth thing, I want to play with the dogs and Tigger," he said.

Julia also chose to watch a movie, play a game, and hang out with our pets. "And I want to bake cookies," she said.

Our day was filling up with fun activities that would pass the time until dark.

We settled in to watch the kids' movie choices, each with a pet on our laps. Then we had lunch and played some games.

"Can we bake the cookies now?" Julia asked.

I gathered the ingredients and showed Julia which ones to mix into the bowl. Tigger, our black cat, jumped onto the counter to watch.

"Sorry, Tig," Julia told him. "Cats can't eat chocolate-chip cookies." She looked down at the dogs — a Beagle and a Poodle mix — on the floor. "Dogs can't either."

Soon, the batter was mixed, spooned onto cookie sheets, and put into the oven.

"I can't wait to eat a million cookies," Jordan said.

"You can have two cookies," I told him.

"Two?" he whined and folded his arms.

"Two for now, Bud," I said firmly. "You can eat another one after we have dinner."

When the timer went off, I pulled the cookies from the oven and set them on the cooling racks.

"Let's play *Candy Land* while we're waiting for the cookies to be cool enough to eat," I suggested to Julia.

She nodded, and we headed upstairs to play.

An hour later, Jordan came upstairs, holding his stomach. "My tummy hurts," he groaned.

I sighed, already suspecting the cause. "Did you eat more than two cookies?"

He nodded.

"How many more?"

"A few."

But when I looked at the cooling racks, I estimated that he'd eaten half a dozen cookies. No wonder his stomach hurt.

Hours went by, and things only got worse. The stomachache turned to vomiting.

"Are we still going to go watch the fireworks?" Julia asked.

Sadly, I shook my head. "We can't go. Your brother is too sick."

"It's his fault he's sick. It's not fair that I have to miss the fireworks because he didn't follow the rules."

I rubbed her back. "You're right, honey. It's not fair. But your dad is out of town, so there's nothing I can do about it."

I got Jordan settled in his room with a blanket and a bucket, just in case.

Later, Julia and I ate her favorite dinner, but the yummy food didn't soften the sting of missing the fireworks.

When it got dark, we began to hear the loud booms of our town's fireworks display. Immediately, both of our dogs ran under the desk and huddled together. I could see them trembling.

"I'm sorry, boys," I said to them. "I know the Fourth of July isn't your favorite night."

"How come?" Julia asked. "Don't they like fireworks?"

I shook my head. "Beamer and Mugsy are afraid of fireworks. The noise scares them."

Julia's attention moved from the dogs hiding under the desk to the cat lying calmly on top of it. "Do cats like fireworks?"

"I don't know about all cats, but Tigger doesn't mind them."

Julia stroked the cat's head. "You're braver than the dogs," she told him.

We heard another boom from the fireworks. Tigger stretched his back legs and glanced at his canine friends under the desk. He was definitely enjoying being the brave one.

Julia and I sat on the couch. I rubbed her back and apologized again for her missing the fireworks.

She shrugged. "It's okay. Dad said we were going to a baseball game this weekend. There's always fireworks at the games."

"Thank you for understanding," I said, still rubbing her back.

Tigger jumped down off the desk and went underneath it where the dogs were.

"Oh, no! Tigger is afraid now, too," Julia said. "He's going to hide under the desk with Beamer and Mugsy."

Tigger snuggled down between the dogs. Slowly, he smoothed his paw down Mugsy's back. Then he did the same thing to Beamer.

"He's petting them, Mom!" Julia said. "He knows they're scared, and he's making them feel better."

"I think Tigger saw me rubbing your back, and we always rub his back, so he must've realized that would comfort the dogs."

Julia and I sat on the couch, listening to the fireworks, and watching our cat pet our dogs.

"This is way better than fireworks," Julia said. "Everyone has seen those. But how many people have seen a cat rub a dog's back?"

I smiled. "How many people have seen a cat rub two dogs' backs?"

As we watched, I noticed the dogs' trembling had lessened. Tigger's back rubs were visibly calming them.

When the loud noises ended, Tigger and the dogs came out from under the desk as though nothing unique or special had happened.

But Julia and I knew we'd never forget it.

That Independence Day, Tigger was not only brave, but he was kind when he didn't have to be.

And kindness is always worth remembering.

— Diane Stark —

96

Roger the Wonder Cat

*I have felt cats rubbing their faces against mine and
touching my cheek with claws carefully sheathed.
These things, to me, are expressions of love.*
~James Herriot

We had just lost our beloved Tortoiseshell of fourteen years, and it was clear that Tom Tom, our social tabby, was lonely. Although he always required a lot of attention, it had gotten to the point where he wouldn't let us out of his sight. When we had to leave him alone, Frank Sinatra would serve as the temporary fix for his broken heart. The smooth sounds of Ol' Blue Eyes would lull Tom Tom into a cat-nap, allowing us to sneak out the door.

I visited several shelters and conducted my own "interviews" in an attempt to find Tom Tom the perfect companion. During this intense screening process, I happened to meet "Roger" during a book signing on a "Caturday" at our local library. "Caturday" is a monthly children's reading event that partners with our local animal shelter. Adoptable cats are brought to the library and children improve their skills by reading aloud to the nonjudgmental animals. In turn, it helps prepare the cats for socialization and readies them for adoption.

The staff at the shelter encouraged me to visit the adoptable cats before the children arrived. I entered the conference room and sat in the middle of the floor, surrounded by cages of shy and timid cats. Leaning over to peer into the cage of a little gray kitten, I was startled by a deafening meow in my right ear, followed by an immediate furry and forceful head-butt that just about knocked me over!

I turned around to find the culprit: a little orange tabby cat sitting innocently beside me.

With another loud meow, he jumped into my lap and head-butted me again!

Collective laughter rang out from the shelter staff.

"We'd like you to meet Roger!" they announced.

This tiger-striped extrovert, who obviously had no concept of personal space, was allowed to roam free before the children arrived and was clearly different from all the other cats that cowered in their cages.

Even though he came off as a bit brash, he was still cute — but in an odd sort of way. The massive pointy ears on his little head made him look like a bat.

Giving it one more go, as if it were his last chance, he climbed up my chest, stared at me, and let out another ear-splitting meow. This was followed by the most powerful head-butt of them all. My glasses flew across the floor!

As the children lined up, Roger was placed into his cage. His persistent meows continued as his little orange paws reached out to me through the grate.

Needless to say, Roger won.

Within two weeks of joining our family, I noticed that Roger was eating less and appeared to be losing weight. I was puzzled because he had been found healthy in two separate vet checkups.

I made another appointment. After switching Roger's food, I was told to bring him back if he didn't improve in the next day or two. He resumed devouring the food and seemed to be doing fine. But then, a week later, I called the cats to eat. Tom Tom ran right in, but Roger didn't.

I found him lying lethargically in the living room, with what appeared to be burst blood vessels in both ears. I rushed him to the vet. It turned out that Roger had contracted cytauxzoonosis, a protozoal organism transmitted to cats by a tick bite.

The infection, commonly known as Bobcat Fever because its natural reservoir host is a bobcat, is rare for a domestic cat and almost always fatal. Once symptoms surface and the infection has progressed, the cat usually dies within a day or two. New antibiotics have been proven to increase a cat's chances of survival if caught within the early stages. Sadly, Roger's infection had advanced, as blood clots were already forming, organs were starting to shut down, his fever was increasing, and his blood sugar levels had soared to dangerous heights.

As rare as this infection was, the vet explained that, ironically, she had just treated another cat a month prior. That particular case wasn't as severe as Roger's, and that cat did recover. Then she explained that she had begun treating Roger with the leftover antibiotics.

Making no promises and again reiterating how grim things looked, the vet explained that she would continue to treat him through the night and would call me in the morning. She prepared me for the inevitable; he most likely wouldn't make it.

The next morning, Roger was showing small signs of improvement.

I asked to visit, and the vet agreed.

My heart broke as they carried Roger into the examination room. Wrapped in a blanket, he was laid on the table before me.

Silent tears streamed down my face as Roger lifted his head and steadied himself slowly to stand up.

Stepping forward with all the strength his weak little body could muster, he gave me a feeble head-butt before collapsing and curling up against my chest.

I cried harder.

How in the world had I managed to get myself so attached to this little cat in such a short amount of time?

The next day, he showed even more improvement.

With subsequent visits and intensive love and care, each day looked a little more hopeful than the last.

Before long, his IVs were removed!

After a three-week vet stay and the incredible care of one very dedicated veterinarian, Roger recovered.

His vet couldn't explain it. "It's a wonder he's even here!"

While things were looking up, one challenge still remained: Roger's blood sugar continued to run dangerously high.

Although extremely rare for a young cat, Roger was diagnosed with diabetes.

On top of caring so intensely for Roger, that same dedicated vet also had to deal with the fact that I was terrified of needles and scared to death to take him home!

Thankfully, we both survived.

After three months, Roger has successfully been weaned off insulin shots altogether. His diabetes is now controlled by a strict diet.

Roger is rather famous at the animal hospital and is often referred to as their miracle: "Roger the Wonder Cat!"

A miracle, indeed.

He's still vocal and struggles with personal space issues, but he never passes up the opportunity to give a loving head-butt to everyone, Tom Tom included.

Finally, he's a playful, happy, energetic kitty, who simply refused to give up.

On days when I find myself wanting to throw in the towel, along comes a daily head-butt to remind me otherwise. It's a reminder to never underestimate the power of love and perseverance.

— Valerie Archual —

97

Watson to the Rescue

Thank you… for gracing my life with your lovely presence,
for adding the sweet measure of your soul to my existence.
~Richard Matheson

Once upon a time, I thought squirrels were cute. I was charmed by their bright little eyes and adorable chatter. I was fascinated by the way they twitched their fluffy tails while turning an acorn over and over in their human-like hands.

How, I wondered, could anyone dislike a squirrel?

A divorce and a move from a farm to a house in the suburbs answered that question in a hurry. My new back yard was filled with many kinds of trees. Poplar. Pine. Sycamore. Sweetgum. And, most abundant of all, towering oaks, any squirrel's first choice for a playground. What the back yard didn't have was cats. All three of my farm cats — Burlap, Tiger, and Oreo — had stayed behind with my ex-husband because he had a barn filled with mice.

For the first time in a quarter-century, I was feline-free. And every squirrel in my new neighborhood knew it.

They swarmed my property. Built nests in my attic. Dominated my birdfeeders. Chewed holes in the screens of my screened-in porch. Partied in the eaves of my garage. Worst of all, the squirrels stripped some exposed wiring with their teeth and caused major electrical damage.

The time had come to declare war. I banged on the kitchen window and hollered every time a squirrel was in sight. I smeared the birdfeeder pole with Crisco. When that didn't deter them, I wrapped double-sided tape around the pole. I put several rubber snakes in the garage. I coated my porch posts with Tabasco sauce. I threatened to buy a BB gun.

The squirrels just laughed.

Clearly, I needed a cat. An aloof cat. A cat who wanted to spend the day outside, working, instead of curled up in my lap. A cat who didn't demand expensive canned cat food served in a crystal dish. A cat who was lean and lanky. A cat who understood that squirrels are Public Enemy Number One.

I scoured the "FREE TO A GOOD HOME" want ads in the newspaper. No cats. I visited the animal shelter. They had a couple of litters of cute but very young kittens, an elderly cat that was blind in one eye, and an overweight adult cat that had been declawed and was thus confined to the indoors for the rest of her life.

Needing to think things over, I went for a walk on Watson Road, a seldom-traveled rural road not far from where I live. There's a vacant barn situated right where the road curves and starts uphill. Near the gate is a sturdy tree stump that's perfect for sitting. I plopped down to rest for a minute before tackling the steep climb that lay ahead.

That's when I heard an unmistakable sound. "Meow… meow."

I knew for certain that this was no grown cat. Its cry was soft and high-pitched. *It's probably a feral kitten, wild and untouchable,* I told myself. *It won't come when I call.* But I called anyway. "Here… kitty, kitty, kitty." Out dashed the cutest gray tabby kitten I'd ever seen. White muzzle. White chest and belly. White paws. Pale green eyes in a perfectly triangular face.

The kitten ran straight toward me, so I picked it up and peeked under its tail. Boy cat. He purred and purred and purred. He looked scrawny but otherwise healthy. "Do you want to be my kitty?" I asked. He purred some more. "If you live with me, you'll have to learn to be a mighty squirrel hunter," I told him. That little cat looked me right in the eye, and I swear I saw him nod. What could I do but take him home?

Watson grew into a lean and lanky cat. A cat who's aloof enough to love the outdoors but also loves to curl up in my lap on cold winter nights. He's never once demanded expensive canned food in a crystal dish.

As to whether Watson is the answer to my squirrel problems, I'll say this: I no longer need Crisco or double-sided tape. Or rubber snakes. Or Tabasco sauce, except in the kitchen. I never had to buy that BB gun. The squirrels in my back yard still frolic and chatter in the treetops and turn acorns over and over in their human-like hands. But they don't come down to the ground. Not when my cat's anywhere around.

Watson the mighty hunter knows without a doubt that squirrels are Public Enemy Number One, and it's his job to scare them away.

—Jennie Moore Ivey—

98

Loving Blue Eyes

You don't run from the people who need you.
You fight for them. You fight beside them.
No matter the cost. No matter the risk.
~Rick Yancey, The Last Star

Blue Eyes showed up at our country home one December day. A large, cream-colored male cat, he was already an adult and had been roaming for who knew how long. I was not surprised when Blue Eyes tested positive for feline immunodeficiency virus (FIV), spread commonly by aggressive unneutered males through bite wounds. Since Blue Eyes was otherwise healthy and non-aggressive, we adopted him into our fur family.

For seven years, Blue Eyes spent his life the same way as our other rescued strays, living in a climate-controlled cattery in the barn. His health remained stable, and life was simple and good for Blue Eyes. Once a day, I trekked to the barn to feed, clean, and water the cats. Other times, I would go to the barn just to spend time with them.

All of that changed for Blue Eyes and me when he was diagnosed with diabetes. Twice a day after that, every morning and every night, I made a trip to the barn to give him an insulin injection. Administering the insulin proved no problem. With his cuddly friendliness, Blue Eyes didn't flinch at being stuck with a tiny needle. During the morning treatment, he took the injection in stride, more interested in his breakfast of dry kibble than in the slight pinch on the back of his neck right before I injected the insulin. At night, he appeared impatient to be done with the process, eagerly sniffing the air and leaping to the counter for the canned food that he knew awaited him.

With diabetes, it's important to give the insulin injections as near to the same time each day and ideally twelve hours apart. I played around with times, trying to find the best schedule for my life, seeking convenience and ease of routine because Blue Eyes didn't care what time he received his injections as long as food was involved.

After more than three years, I have settled on a 10:00 a.m./10:00 p.m. schedule. Choosing 10:00 a.m. means I can have my two or three cups of coffee and become fully awake before heading to the barn, but 10:00 at night can have drawbacks. Even if I'm tired, have cozied up in my chair with a book, don't feel well, have company, am still full from dinner, or have a hangnail, I still must go. I don't fuss or fret. I just stop whatever I'm doing, rise, fill the syringe, grab the canned food, put on my shoes, and walk to the barn. It can be a warm, starry night or freezing cold. A soft breeze might be blowing, or a foot of snow might be on the ground with wind howling around my ears. I've gone to the barn at night with icy rain slashing my cheeks, with storms and tornadoes threatening, with electricity and without.

Moving Blue Eyes from the barn to the house would make life easier for me, but not for Blue Eyes. We already have several house cats — territorial cats who would not welcome him. Besides, Blue Eyes has lived in the barn for years. It's his home. He has cat friends there. The stress of moving, even if only to the house, could further compromise his already compromised immune system.

So, Blue Eyes stays in the barn, and I travel like a postman back and forth every day, rain or shine, sleet or snow, delivering lifesaving insulin to him.

But why bother? Why trudge out into the sweltering heat or freezing cold twice a day when it would be so much easier to put him to sleep? Because of love, that's why. Love of his sweet nature even in the midst of terrible diseases, his gentleness, and his uncomplaining, accepting attitude of the circumstances. Blue Eyes didn't just show up on my doorstep randomly. Something bigger than the both of us guided him to me. He was meant to find me, and I was meant to care for him.

It hasn't just been diabetes either. A year after he joined us, Blue Eyes' itchy skin and constant scratching was diagnosed as demodectic mange. Finding Demodex mites on the skin of mammals is not uncommon, and the mites don't usually cause a problem unless the animal's immune system is compromised. Blue Eyes, with FIV and diabetes, hardly stood a chance against the mite invasion. The treatment involved multiple weekly trips to the vet and stinky lime sulphur dips.

The one and only time I saw Blue Eyes' positive attitude waver was in the third round of consecutive dips. That day, when I took out the carrier and set it on the floor, Blue Eyes actually ran and hid behind the sofa in one of the cat rooms. It broke my heart to haul him out and place him in the carrier, knowing what lay ahead at the vet clinic.

The third time he was diagnosed with Demodex mites, I almost gave up the fight. He looked miserable, and I knew I could not force him to go through another round of dips. For a cat who loved to be snuggled, who would wrap his paws around my neck and rub his head against my chin when I picked him up, I couldn't bear for him to run from me and hide. Yet, until an alternate treatment became available, dipping was the only recourse. Blue Eyes couldn't understand the connection between the dips and the relief it brought to his itchy skin. I had to look past any immediate distress we both felt and make the decision to put him again through the smelly, wet process of having a sulfur-and-lime solution poured over him and then leaving him to air dry. His itchiness mostly abated, and he seemed to have resigned himself to once-a-week dips.

Then, after learning to live with FIV, diabetes, and mites, a blood test revealed that Blue Eyes had developed hyperthyroidism, meaning more medication and monitoring.

If a medal of honor existed for the cat who has had the most diseases and health setbacks, and still faces each day with heroic resilience, Blue Eyes deserves it. Blue Eyes has lived with us for more than ten years. It's safe to say he's at least fifteen. Through all the diagnoses, medicines, injections, treatments, skin scrapings, dips, and tooth removals (he has maybe one tooth remaining), his loving spirit has never diminished.

As long as Blue Eyes continues to fight for his life, I'll be by his side. As long as he needs me to travel back and forth to the barn, twice a day, in all kinds of weather, I will. And when the day comes that his body and spirit say enough — when he needs me to be the strong one, the brave one, and let him go — I will.

Because that's what love is.

— Teresa Hoy —

99

Home Is Where the Cats Are

He has become a much better cat than I have a person.
With his gentle urgings, he made me realize that life
doesn't end just because one has a
few obstacles to overcome.
~Mary F. Graf

That February night began as usual — until we realized the house was on fire. My husband feared it would catch all at once. He gave me ten minutes to get dressed, gather the six cats, and get out.

We grabbed Pixie and Nick, but Taylor was another story. He had come from a hoarding situation, and in the six years we had him, he never allowed us to get close to him. That night, though, trust won the day. He had been in our home's largest room, in a corner chair farthest from the doorway, yet he let my husband walk across the floor toward him, lift him up, and place him in a carrier.

With three cats to go, my husband suggested I next grab Ollie, who was pacing around frantically. Instead, I ran upstairs for Chloe. She had been holing up under the bed in our room to protest our recent adoption of Nick, the newest member of our menagerie. I determined I would pull her out by her back foot if necessary, but when I walked into the room she was sitting by the door, waiting patiently for me to get to her. For once, she didn't grouse when I scooped her up. Once she was stowed away safely, I concentrated on Ollie. He was still in marathon mode, but when I threw him a treat, he stopped in mid-stride.

As my husband prepared to take Ollie outside, I looked frantically for Hobbes. He was nowhere to be found. Even though he felt bad about leaving Hobbes, my husband insisted we leave. He took Ollie to the car, which he had parked on one side of the driveway, while I started for the truck on the opposite side.

By then, I heard sirens, and I only hoped that the firefighters would save Hobbes. Behind me, my husband happened to glance inside as he walked past the front door. Who did he see framed in the doorway but Hobbes, peering through the glass as if wondering, "Why is everyone outside?" When my husband placed him in my arms, my relief knew no bounds. We had run out of carriers, so Hobbes sat on my lap, paws wrapped around my neck, for the entire four hours it took to bring the fire under control.

While the fire companies battled the blaze, a friend located an animal-friendly hotel we would move into later that night. Once the fire was contained, a fireman brought out a litter box and a tin of dry cat food, an act of kindness I won't soon forget.

When I went to check on the cats, they were relatively calm, considering that they had been shunted from a warm house to a cold car, and then surrounded by flashing lights, shouting voices, and fire engines furiously pumping water. Only Nick was truly distressed, to the point he was panting. He was an older cat with health issues who had been left on the street and then handed around for several months prior to living with us. I'm sure he thought he was being abandoned again. "It's okay, Nick," I said, attempting to reassure him. "We are going somewhere, but we're going together. You're part of a family now." On some level, he must have understood because he settled down soon, and his breathing returned to normal.

We arrived at the hotel around four in the morning, sailing past the front desk with six cat carriers piled on a luggage cart — three on the bottom and three on top. The night manager said he wouldn't soon forget the sight. We hadn't heard a peep from our cargo, but as we unlocked the door, Pixie started meowing. Soon, the rest of the crew decided that caterwauling in a hotel corridor in the wee hours of the morning was an excellent idea. We bundled them inside quickly to avoid getting thrown out with nowhere to go.

We lived in that hotel for seven months. Friends wondered how we managed so well. I don't deny that it was difficult at first; however, we quickly got back on track, mainly because the cats' routine was our routine as well. Feeding time at the zoo, tricking Nick into taking his pills, and ensuring the feline restrooms were up to snuff all had to be attended to no matter where we were living.

Just like at home, the cats provided us with many laughs. Nick developed a penchant for banging on the flap of the litter box when someone was using it and then tearing off. The time he ousted Taylor from the box was unforgettable. Taylor is a longhaired cat, and when he came into the living area, his hair stuck straight up like a porcupine and his eyes were slits. Since he was our resident pacifist, he didn't do anything but glare at Nick; we knew what he was thinking. Meanwhile, Nick innocently studied the walls and ceiling, as if he were checking to see if the paint job needed touching up.

I'm not saying that we were never discouraged, but the cats seemed to sense when things felt overwhelming. Often, one of them would cuddle in our laps or snuggle next to us when we needed comfort the most. A gentle touch of a paw or the soothing sound of a cat's purr allowed us to leave our troubles behind and enter a realm of calm, even if for a short while.

The way they adapted so seamlessly to their new living quarters was also a source of strength. We had gone from a large, two-story home to a much smaller environment. Yet if the cats felt that the setting was a bit odd, their attitude seemed to be that since everyone was accounted for, things couldn't be all bad. That mindset trickled down to us. We had lost a third of our home, but we had all gotten out safely. We had a warm place to live, and we had each other.

The cats became like family to the hotel staff, too. We only needed someone to come in weekly to change linens, but the cleaning people would often visit the cats on their break, a welcome respite from a taxing job. We also met a woman who came regularly to the hotel on business. She had recently lost her older cat and was thrilled to meet ours. On subsequent trips, she always stopped by to see them.

Finally, it was time to move back home. Being in the house was strange at first. It didn't seem as if we belonged. Even the cats appeared anxious and unsure of their new surroundings. It took a while, but we all settled in gradually, and our house once more felt like our home. If you asked the cats, though, home had been with us all along.

— Carolyn M. Trombe —

100

Angel in Cat's Clothing

When your kitty purrs to you, doesn't it break
your heart that you can't purr back?
~Candea Core-Starke

"Dust to dust, ashes to ashes... " My mother looked up at her youngest grandson, already over six feet tall, as he intoned the time-honored phrases. When he finished, her granddaughter stepped forward. Mother had to look up at her as well. Even if she stood straight, like she used to before she passed the age of seventy-eight, she was still the shortest one in the group. A tall north woods Minnesotan family, for sure.

Twenty years earlier, in the summer of 1986, Mother was visiting the Montana ranch where her daughter and family used to live before coming to Minnesota. Everyone had gone to the lake that day, as usual, leaving her at the house alone. She didn't mind. It gave her some time to reflect, catch up on some reading, and enjoy the scenery. She took a book and walked out the back door to the patio. The mountains showed their snowy caps over the expanse of fir and spruce trees that lined the lot behind the house. A bluebird called in the distance. She heard the breeze rustle through the branches as it whispered to her. "Come. Come walk in her forest."

She placed her book on the old wrought iron table that sat on the upper level of the patio, a popular meeting place for summer meals and entertainment and other activities. The lower patio that led to the paths into the woods could be reached by descending a steep tier of old railroad ties. Free or very inexpensive, they were the ideal landscaping material. Or so the family thought at the time.

As she lowered her foot to the second step, she hit a patch of black ooze, creosote brought to the surface by a summer thunderstorm that had swept through the area earlier that morning. Her right foot went in one direction, the left in the opposite direction. There were no railings to spoil the view, nothing to grab on to. She sailed and turned like a loose flag twisting in the wind and landed on the granite flagstones on her left side. That sickening splat is a sound she says she can still hear when she thinks of the incident.

She didn't know how long she lay there before she began to hear the buzzing. She opened one eye. Returning consciousness brought with it a searing pain, waves of electric shock coupled with stabs of volcanic heat. She cried out once. No one to hear her. How long had she lain here? What time was it? Would anyone be home soon? She tried to turn to look at the sky, but shooting pain stilled that effort.

Then she heard it again. BZZ, BZZ. The menacing sound grew louder. Out of the corner of her eye she saw misty yellow and black objects — one close by, and then another, and yet another. Bees! Her involuntary stiffening brought the electric shock waves back twofold.

She had never been tested for bee sting allergy, but all she could think of now was the time when she was a little girl. Some bee stings had put her in bed for several days. She couldn't hear what the doctor had said to her mother that day, but he left the house shaking his head. She was very ill, but she did manage to recover.

Bees. She had to get away somehow. She tried to turn. If she could just get to her knees… "Ohhhh!" She couldn't do it. Her movement seemed to disturb the bees even more. She squeezed her eyelids closed and tried to remain perfectly still. The humming vibrations seemed to permeate every pore. She even imagined she could feel hundreds of tiny wings against her cheek. She prayed as she tried to quell her rising panic.

Time slowed, like someone had turned down a faucet to a trickle. After what seemed like days, the buzzing began to taper off. Then she felt a flick of something soft against her face. Too large for a bee, at least she hoped so. She opened one eye again and saw a narrow strip of black and gold fur swishing back and forth. That strip led up to a mottled colored body and then a head with black pointed ears.

Katrina. The family's calico cat, not much more than a kitten, sat near her face, swatting almost leisurely at the bees. "Good Kitty," Mother murmured. The cat swished her tail once as if in response.

She passed in and out of consciousness for an undetermined amount of time that day, blessed moments of oblivion that kept her unaware of the pain. Each interlude of awareness affirmed that her furry angel was still with her. The faithful kitty never left her post and was still there when the family returned.

They rushed her to the hospital. "Hip crushed... Will have to replace... " Cocooned in her drug induced insulation, she barely registered the words and their meaning. Her daughter took care of the details. She went home a week later with a walker and pain meds.

Katrina was waiting for her, napping in the sun by the sliding glass doors in their bedroom. Her daughter pointed to the cat. "Saved your life, she did, that Katrina."

She nodded. Two of her grandchildren joined their mother. One of them looked at the cat and then at her." Why did you ever name her Katrina anyway? What kind of a name is that for a cat?"

She stared at the calico bundle of fur, now licking her paws. She couldn't remember. "Well, let's change it then. From now on her name is BeBee, because she saved me from the bees." Everyone agreed.

Katrina, renamed Bebee, lifted her head, looked at her and yawned. "Whatever," she seemed to say as she resumed her grooming. She had a new name and thanks to her my mother survived to bear a new hip.

That replacement lasted almost twenty years. So did BeBee. The hip started to wear out from the metal grating against the bone. It began to go downhill and so did BeBee, kind of like pet and mistress were linked. They told her it would be too traumatic to give her a new replacement now. The hip was too old and had suffered too much deterioration. The vet said the same thing about the cat. Mother held the cat in her arms while the vet gave her that last shot.

"Dust to dust, ashes to ashes… "

Her granddaughter knelt down, her long brown hair, curling naturally in ringlets, scattered over her shoulders as she placed the shoebox in the shallow hole. The evergreen trees, a birdbath and a row of birdhouses her daughter had collected over the years seemed an appropriate site for the final resting place of the old feline. A bluebird landed on the birdbath, watching respectfully. Or was it in relief?

We each threw a handful of dirt over the box. Her son-in-law and oldest grandson finished the job with a shovel and her daughter topped it off with a small hand painted sign that said simply, BeBee. As a tear rolled down her cheek, she remembered her bee-fighting angel in cat's clothing. She would miss her.

—Carolyn Donnell—

Xena — A Story of Courage

Just watching my cats can make me happy.
~Paula Cole

I n February 2019, our beautiful Maine Coon, Xena, suddenly lost the use of her back legs and bladder. My partner David and I were extremely concerned and took her straight to our vet, who booked her for X-rays, blood tests, and ultrasound scans. The results were inconclusive, but it looked as though Xena might have a problem with her spinal discs, which would probably be permanent. The vet gave her Gabapentin and taught me how to express her bladder. Then we took her home.

She was still a bright, happy cat, so we didn't want to put her to sleep, but it was heartbreaking to see her drag both back legs as she tried to walk. It seemed as though Xena would never walk again, barring a miracle.

Very early the following morning, our vet called to say that she had contacted the neurologist at the veterinary hospital in Derby, our nearest city. Chris, the neurologist, thought that Xena could have a tumour pressing on her spinal cord, and it might be operable. She would need an MRI to find out, which was expensive. But if he was right, there was a chance that Xena might regain the use of her legs. So, of course, we agreed instantly.

Within an hour, we received a phone call from Chris asking if we could bring Xena in that morning for the MRI. Later that day, he called with the results. He had been right. Xena had a tumour — a meningioma — that was pressing on her spinal cord. It was probably benign and would not grow back after removal. Chances of success were reasonably good, so Xena might walk again! We had hope, when we had thought there was none.

Xena was booked for surgery two days later. The operation was successful, and we went to see her later that day. She seemed tired, but pleased to see us and in much better shape than I would have been after a four-hour operation. Over the next few days, she regained some of the feeling in her back legs and could walk just a little when supported.

Soon afterward, when she was managing to use a litter tray, we took her home, armed with an array of medications plus instructions for her care. But we were warned that recovery would be long and slow. We had to keep her in a large cage, give her regular physiotherapy, and teach her how to walk again. And no one could say if Xena would actually regain the full use of her back legs. It was largely up to her, as cats, like people, react in different ways to this sort of trauma. Xena might be prepared to work with us and do everything required, or she might not. So we weren't expecting much, but we carried on doing as Chris had instructed.

For a few days, nothing much seemed to change. Then, just a week later, Xena amazed us all. Having not managed to support herself on her back legs at all, she suddenly stood up all by herself. I was so surprised that I thought I must have imagined it. But I hadn't, and soon she began to walk a little with her back supported. Encouraged, we booked her for some hydrotherapy, which was known to be a great help for dogs in this situation. Most cats panic if put in water, but our brave little cat astonished everyone, tolerating neck-deep water while walking on a treadmill.

When we saw Chris again, he was absolutely delighted with Xena's progress. Over the next few weeks, she moved from the cage to a room of her own, with all furniture removed so that she could not jump or climb and hurt herself. We continued with her hydrotherapy, and she became quite famous at the centre, as they had never had a cat who tolerated so much water-based activity. She also had her own Facebook page, with many people following this brave little cat who seemed determined to walk again against all odds. People said they were praying for her and wishing her well, and I'm sure it all helped.

Soon, she could manage the few steps out into our enclosed garden, though she still needed some help to walk properly without dragging her legs. Her determination was impressive. Despite probably still being in pain, she really wanted to walk again, play, and do all the things that cats should. Unfortunately she had to be confined to her own room for three months until healing was complete, but she put up with that too, along with all the medication and physiotherapy.

Some cats would have refused to take their pills, become upset at having their legs moved and rubbed, or been desperate to escape, but not our Xena. She seemed to understand. She was a model patient.

A couple of months later, David and I went on a much-needed holiday that we'd fully expected to have to cancel. But Xena was walking now, and to be safe we left her at the veterinary hospital's "Cat Hotel," where Chris assured us he would drop in and visit her regularly.

Two weeks later, we brought her home. It was now exactly three months since her surgery. Her operation site had healed, and we could allow her the full run of the house and garden. She was allowed to run, jump, and climb stairs... anything she wanted. And she soon proved she could do it all again. Xena was cured!

That was four months ago. Xena is now completely back to normal. Her fur has grown back, she has put on weight, and she is a healthy, happy cat again. We had thought she might be traumatised permanently by all that had happened to her. But this courageous, little cat simply brushed it all off and got on with living. She is a walking lesson in how to deal with adversity. A lot of people could learn from our Xena.

— Helen Krasner —

Meet Our Contributors

Melissa Abraham resides with her husband and their cat in south Louisiana. With a Bachelor of Arts in Modern Languages and a Graduate Translation Certificate in French, she is both a substitute teacher and a freelance translator of French, Spanish, and Italian documents. She is currently working on a fantasy novel.

Kristi Adams loves sharing the humorous side of life as a regular contributor to *Military Spouse* magazine, *Stars and Stripes*, and the *Chicken Soup for the Soul* series. She lives in Germany with her husband, serving on active duty, and their cat Tiki — who insists that everything is his show. Learn more at www.kristiadamsmedia.com.

Mary M. Alward has been published in both print and online venues. Her work has been published in the *Chicken Soup for the Soul* series, *Guideposts*, as well as others. She is the mother of a grown daughter and two grown grandsons, whom she enjoys spending time with. Mary enjoys reading, writing and other crafts and activities.

Monica A. Andermann lives and writes on Long Island where she shares a home with her husband Bill and their mouse-loving kitty Sammie. Her work has been included in such publications as *Guideposts*, *Ocean*, *Sasee* and *Woman's World* as well as many other titles in the *Chicken Soup for the Soul* series.

Kate E. Anderson hails from Northern Utah where she shares a home with four interesting little boys, a dashing husband, and one very special daughter. Kimber is now a teenager with lots to say and still has a deep love for animals, especially our seven chickens, various fish, and two very spoiled Beagles that sleep in Kimber's bed.

Valerie Archual is a children's author, a travel writer, and a previous contributor to the *Chicken Soup for the Soul* series. Aside from clicking away at the keys, she loves spending time with her family, which of course includes her two orange tabby cats, Tom Tom and Roger, (aka The Gingers!) Learn more at www.valeriearchual.com.

Barbara Blossom Ashmun is the author of seven books, most recently, *Love Letters to My Garden*. She gardens on an acre in Portland, OR and cherishes her cats.

T.J. Banks is the author of *Sketch People*, *A Time for Shadows*, *Catsong*, *Souleiado*, and *Houdini*, which the late writer and activist Cleveland Amory enthusiastically branded a winner. *Catsong* was the winner of the 2007 Merial Human-Animal Bond Award.

Rachel Evangeline Barham is a classically trained singer, voice teacher, author, and editor based in Washington, D.C. She cleans up for a concert, but her natural habitat is outside: observing birds and other critters, biking, or navigating her stand-up paddleboard. She lives with her spouse James and two black cats.

David-Matthew Barnes is an author, playwright, poet, and screenwriter. He writes in multiple genres, primarily young adult. His literary work has appeared in over one hundred publications. He earned an MFA in Creative Writing at Queens University of Charlotte in North Carolina.

Carolyn Barrett has lived in New Jersey her entire life and enjoys her work as an ultrasound technologist. She has four children and will soon become an empty nester. Carolyn enjoys music, flower gardening, the beach, antiquing, reading and writing. She is working on an inspirational book and blogs at www.lifeisnteasy.com.

Garrett Bauman and his wife Carol have taken in, at last count, nineteen cats. All but one were strays. His stories have been published in sixteen *Chicken Soup for the Soul* books and also in *Yankee*, *Sierra*, *The New York Times* and other publications. He has recently retired as a college professor and moved to South Carolina.

Retired kindergarten teacher **Deb Biechler** lives on five acres of wooded bliss with her partner Randy and dog Jessie. She has a beloved daughter, Hilary. Deb volunteers at the Necedah National Wildlife

Refuge and local library. In addition to freelance writing, she leads workshops on meditation and mindfulness.

Maureen Boyd Biro shares her home in the San Francisco Bay Area with her husband, Martin, and cats Hemingway (a.k.a Killer) and Sophia. A writer and dream teacher, Maureen is currently working on a book about dreaming with your pets. Learn more at lyricaldreaming. com.

Jeanne Blandford is a writer/editor who, along with her husband, is producing documentaries and creating children's books. When not in their Airstream looking for new material, they can be found running SafePet, a partnership between Outreach to Pets in Need (OPIN) and Domestic Violence Crisis Center (DVCC).

Jan Bono writes a cozy mystery series set on the SW Washington coast. She's also published five collections of humorous personal experience, two poetry chapbooks, nine one-act plays, a dinner theater play, and has written for magazines ranging from *Guideposts* to *Woman's World*. Learn more at www.JanBonoBooks.com.

Lori Kempf Bosko is a Canadian writer who loves animals, adventures, and Chicken Soup for the Soul! This is her third contribution to the *Chicken Soup for the Soul* series. When she's not busy writing, she enjoys spending time with friends and family — especially four fun, amazing young grandkids.

Jill Burns lives in the mountains of West Virginia with her wonderful family. She's a retired piano teacher and performer. She enjoys writing, music, gardening, nature, and spending time with her grandchildren.

Carrie Cannon is completing a Bachelor of Liberal Arts in Literature and Creative Writing at Harvard University, which is actually her hobby. Her full-time occupation is home educating four of her seven children. When she finds a rare, quiet moment she enjoys sitting in the sun with any of her eight cats.

Cynthia Carter-Trent enjoys inspiring her audience, be it through writing mysteries, romance, or short stories. When she's not writing, you can find her in the kitchen with her mom cooking up magic, outside exploring nature with her son, dogs and cat, or alone narrating audiobooks.

Nebula Award-nominated **Beth Cato** is the author of the *Clockwork Dagger* duology and the *Blood of Earth* trilogy from Harper Voyager. She's a Hanford, CA native transplanted to the Arizona desert, where she lives with her husband, son, and requisite cats. Learn more at BethCato.com and on Twitter @BethCato.

William Clark first took creative writing at Ball State University. He went to Ball State in Muncie, IN, for undergraduate and graduate work. He has written a nonfiction book and two novels: *A Light on the Path* and *Seeing Beyond the Shadows*.

Jeannie Clemens attended Tarleton State University. She has two children, six grandchildren and two great grandchildren. Jeannie is a retired school secretary in Texas who enjoys family, traveling, crafting, gardening, and creative writing.

Les Davies self-published his novel titled *Afraid of the Dark* under the name Sel Seivad. He has had a number of short stories published in anthologies and currently has a young adult novel being considered by a publisher.

Sergio Del Bianco has a background in fine arts and psychology. He is an artist and writer, interested in the intersection of art, psychology and the humanities. He resides in Europe with his spouse and growing family of rescue animals. E-mail him at sergiodelbianco@yahoo.com or through twitter @DelBianco97.

Emily Dill lives in Owensboro, KY with her husband Jason. They have two crazy black cats and are expecting their first child this summer. Emily has been featured in multiple short story collections and her local library journal and is now querying her first novel. She loves reading, sports, Disney, and video games.

Mackenzie Donegan received her Bachelor of Fine Arts from NSCAD University in Halifax, Nova Scotia. She currently works as an artist in Ottawa. She lives with her husband Matt and her Siamese cat Huxley. She enjoys exploring her creative side and hopes to continue to share her creations with the world.

Carolyn Donnell started writing again in 2003 thanks to a workshop through California Writers Club. Since then she has had short stories and poems published in various anthologies and two novels published under the name C. S. Donnell.

Kashana Douglas was born and raised in Ohio. She loves music, being creative and researching her many curiosities. Kashana has always loved animals and had quite a variety growing up. She married and moved to South Carolina where she resides with her husband, her calico cat and her teacup Chihuahua.

Judy Dykstra-Brown has lived in Mexico since 2001 and has published books of poetry, a memoir and several children's books, all available online. She is presently working on two additional children's books and memoirs about Africa and growing up in South Dakota. She writes daily in her blog at judydykstrabrown.com.

Rebecca Edmisten lives in Johnson City, TN and is delighted to be published a third time in the *Chicken Soup for the Soul* series. Becky is a veteran teacher of English and Theatre; she says that writing — especially nonfiction — is both a pleasure and a thrill. She looks forward to sharing "Bons Amis" with her students and readers of *Chicken Soup for the Soul: The Magic of Cats.*

Dr. Sheila Embry is a govie, author, pracademic, sister, aunt, cousin, and friend who loves to read, write, think, and laugh. An author with more than twenty-five years experience, her books can be found online.

Karleen Forwell is a stay-at-home mom whose career has changed to homeschooling, gardening and raising two amazing children. She lives in the Sierra Nevada Mountains and enjoys all that it entails. Attempting a simple life, she enjoys the brief, silent moments that writing grants her.

Dave Fox is a freelance travel writer, and a writing and life coach, based in Ho Chi Minh City, Vietnam. To learn more about his books, online writing workshops, and creativity coaching services visit Globejotting.com.

A father of two grown children and three grandchildren, **James A. Gemmell's** main hobbies are hiking, writing and guitar playing. Travel has always been an interest and seems to increase as time goes on. James has a love of all things Spanish and enjoys being in that country at every opportunity.

Kathleen A. Gemmell pens for an array of publications. She is also an animal welfare proponent, a psychology buff, and a connoisseur of fine pizza.

Connie Goldsmith is a retired RN, and a prolific writer of teen nonfiction health and science books, with twenty-five of them for Lerner Publishing's school and library imprint. She lives in the Sacramento, CA area and has a grown daughter, a son-in-law, and two amazing cats that keep her amused between writing projects.

Christine Grecsek is a member of the Society of Children's Book Writers and Illustrators, and her short fiction and poetry have been published in regional magazines and won several awards. Her heartfelt ode to peanut butter won her family a mixed case of gourmet nut butters. Sadly, none of them contained peanuts.

Liz SanFilippo Hall received her Master's in Humanities/Creative Writing from The University of Chicago. She's a freelance writer/editor, blogger at OopsAndDaisies.com, and aspiring kid lit author. Her hobbies include chasing her two young kids around, drawing, exploring the outdoors, and reading.

Bonnie Compton Hanson is an artist and speaker as well as the author or co-author of sixty-five books for adults and children, plus hundreds of articles, stories, and poems (including forty-three in the *Chicken Soup for the Soul* series). A former editor, she has also taught at several universities and writing conferences. And she loves children and pets!

Janet Haynie thanks freelance writer Sheri Zeck of Milan, IL for writing her story. Sheri's work has appeared in numerous *Chicken Soup for the Soul* books, *Guideposts*, *Angels on Earth* and *Farm and Ranch Living*. Sheri writes about her faith, family and adventures of raising three girls at www.sherizeck.com.

Helen Heavirland enjoys reading, international volunteering, hiking, observing wildlife, and watching the escapades of pets. A nurse, bookkeeper, and author, she especially enjoys writing stories and teaching others how to write theirs. Learn more at www.helenheavirland.com.

Susan A. Hoffert writes reflective stories of daily living, painting scenes to warm a reader's heart. She especially enjoys writing stories of faith inspired by the chickens of her coop. Dear Husband is her greatest support. Her stories appear in previous *Chicken Soup for the Soul* books and other anthologies.

Butch Holcombe lives his dream every day as a writer and is also the publisher of *American Digger* magazine. When not writing or working on the magazine, he enjoys spending time with his muse, Frankie, as well as Frank's adopted brothers and sisters. He enjoys hearing from readers at publisher@americandigger.com.

Teresa Hoy shares her country life with her husband and a fur family of rescued cats and dogs. Her stories have appeared in the *Chicken Soup for the Soul* series, *The Ultimate* books, *Rural Missouri* magazine, and *Guideposts*. In addition to writing, she enjoys reading, researching, volunteering, cooking, and traveling.

Debra I., a musician and teacher, is an adjunct music faculty at Notre Dame, Andrews University, and Indiana University South Bend. She lives in southwest Michigan with her husband Kenley, and the very spoiled MippyCat. She performs with several local groups. Her writing experience mainly includes symphony program notes.

Jeffree Wyn Itrich lives in the great state of Texas, where her family harks back four generations. She has written two novels, a children's book, and a cookbook, as well as numerous articles published in a wide range of online and print publications. In her spare time, she quilts, gardens, bakes, and rehabs old furniture.

Jennie Moore Ivey lives and writes in Tennessee. She is the author of numerous works of fiction and nonfiction, including stories in dozens of titles in the *Chicken Soup for the Soul* series. Learn more at jennieivey.com.

Michaele Jordan was born in Los Angeles, CA, educated in New York, and lives in Cincinnati. She's worked at a kennel, a Hebrew school and AT&T. She's a little odd. Now she writes, supervised by a long-suffering husband and two domineering cats. She usually writes fantastical fiction. Learn more at www.michaelejordan.com.

Danielle Kosecki is an award-winning journalist and the editor of *The Bicycling Big Book of Training*. She lives in Oakland, CA with her husband, three cats, three fish, and one Taiwanese rescue dog.

Helen Krasner has written several books and hundreds of magazine articles, on both cats and other subjects. She lives in Derbyshire, in the middle of the UK, along with her partner David and their five cats. This is the third story she has had published in the *Chicken Soup for the Soul* series.

Cheryl Krouse is retired after a long career as a banking executive. Since then, she has done rewarding volunteer work, refreshed her sewing and crafting skills, and is seen often at the public library and the beaches of Florida. She loves to write about life, experiences and optimism.

Alex Lester is an author from Toronto who volunteers in animal rescue, fostering and rehabilitation.

Rebecca Gardyn Levington is a poet, children's book author, and journalist with a particular penchant for penning punny, funny picture books and poems — primarily in rhyme. She lives in New Jersey with her husband and two sons. Visit her at www.RebeccaGardynLevington. com and on Twitter @WriterRebeccaGL.

Bobbie Jensen Lippman is a professional writer who lives in Seal Rock, OR with her cat Purrfect and a robot named Waldo. Bobbie's work has been published nationally and internationally. She writes a weekly human-interest column for the *News-Times* in Newport, OR. E-mail her at bobbisbeat@gmail.com.

Barbara LoMonaco is the Senior Editor for the *Chicken Soup for the Soul* series. She graduated from USC and has a teaching credential. She lives in Southern California where she is surrounded by boys: her husband, her three grown sons and her two grandsons. Thankfully, her three lovely daughters-in-law have diluted the mix somewhat, but the boys are still in the majority.

Kimberly Lowe is a cancer researcher, yoga enthusiast, and avid outdoor adventurer. She lives in the beautiful Pacific Northwest with her two spunky daughters and their gaggle of zany pets that continue to delight them in unexpected and hilarious ways.

Lisa Mackinder received her Bachelor of Arts degree at Western Michigan University. A freelance writer, she lives in Portage, MI with her husband and rescue animals. Besides writing, Lisa enjoys photography, painting, traveling, reading, running, hiking, biking, climbing and fishing. Learn more at lisamackinder.com.

Irene Maran is a freelance writer living at the Jersey shore with her cats and turtles. She currently writes two bi-weekly newspaper columns, runs a prompt writing group and is a professional storyteller. This grandmother of five enjoys sharing her humorous stories with adults and children.

Shawn Marie writes from her home in Central Pennsylvania with her children and her cats. She enjoys reading, art projects and gardening. E-mail her at shawnmariewrites@gmail.com.

Joshua J. Mark is an editor/director and writer for the online history site "Ancient History Encyclopedia." His nonfiction has also appeared in *Timeless Travels* and *History Ireland* magazines. The cats in this story continue to live and engage in far worse things after realizing no new chickens were coming to tantalize them.

Sandra Martin received her Bachelor of Arts in English from the University of Michigan in 1993. She currently works for a university in North Carolina where her son also attends college. She has published several stories in children's magazines and hopes to have a picture book published soon.

Debbi Mavity is retired from the Department of Defense and lives in West Virginia. She enjoys hiking with her Golden Retriever, Rizzo. Debbi has had stories published in *Chicken Soup for the Soul: Life Lessons from the Dog* and *Chicken Soup for the Soul: Laughter Is the Best Medicine*. Follow her on social media @MavsMutthouse.

Vickie McEntire won Georgia Author of the Year for her second children's book, *Little Bird and Myrtle Turtle*. This is her second story published in the *Chicken Soup for the Soul* series. She loves reading, writing, photography, and watching birds in her back yard. Follow her on Twitter @vickie_mcentire, Facebook @BooksbyVickie, and Instagram @booksbyvickie.

Sharon McGregor is a west coast transplant from the Canadian prairies. She has always shared her home with at least one dog or cat. She loves writing mystery cozies and humour, reading, traveling, and going for walks with her dog Clio.

Brook-Lynn Meijer lives in north-western Canada with her mom and dad, two younger sisters, two dogs and one cat. Brook-Lynn can often be found with her nose in a book, but the busy teenager's life also includes playing the piano, swimming and snowboarding.

Katherine L. Mitchell lives with her husband Jason, their five kiddos, bossy dog, and beautiful Ragdoll cat in Chattanooga, TN. Katherine holds a B.A. in Sociology and has written two children's books and a narrative nonfiction work available at www.katherineladnymitchell. com. She's currently working on a murder mystery series.

Terilynn Mitchell is a registered veterinary nurse who has cared for unadoptable animals for over twenty-five years. She has been previously published in the *Chicken Soup for the Soul* series, as well as other literary journals, and is a professional member of the Cat Writers Association. She is based in rural Northern California.

Ann Morrow is a writer, humorist and animal advocate. She and her husband currently reside in South Dakota, along with their two cats and three dogs. Ann is a frequent contributor to the *Chicken Soup for the Soul* series and is currently working on a middle grade novel.

Megan Nelson is an avid reader and writer with two English degrees and a well-used library card to her name. She and her husband are raising two wonderful boys under the watchful eyes of three cats. Megan is a previous contributor to the *Chicken Soup for the Soul* series.

Debi Schmitz Noriega has been writing since she learned to read. She has four grown children and six grandchildren. Her creativity led her to design craft and quilt patterns for multiple books and magazines since 1986. Debi enjoys being with family, writing and watching her husband drag race at tracks around the country.

Anne Oliver, a native of Bluefield, WV, holds bachelor's and master's degrees from the University of Georgia. She and her husband, George, reared three Army brats during his thirty-one years with the Army. (HOOAH!) She enjoys volunteering, reading, and looking forward to more great adventures. E-mail her at armygrl74@aol.com.

Jessica Parkinson grew up in Toronto and now lives in Scotland with her husband and three girls. She completed her MLitt in Creative Writing at the University of Glasgow. Jessica leads courses in creative writing for people experiencing mental health issues, with a focus on the enjoyment of writing.

Connie Kaseweter Pullen lives in rural Sandy, OR near her five children and several grandchildren. She earned a B.A. degree, with honors, at the University of Portland in 2006, with a double major in Psychology and Sociology. Connie enjoys writing, photography and exploring nature. E-mail her at MyGrandmaPullen@aol.com.

Tim Ramsey has been an educator since 1983. He has had stories published in six titles in the *Chicken Soup for the Soul* series. In addition, he has published *The Hugs on My Shirt*, a collection of stories from his work at school. He is currently owned by six cats.

Jessica Reed lives in the Catskill Mountains with an assortment of pets. She has a daughter, Willow and a son, River. Jessica has written many stories for *Guideposts* publications and *Hippocampus Magazine*. She has a monthly book review in *A Time and A Place Magazine*. Jessica enjoys reading, writing, and painting rocks.

Donna L. Roberts is a native upstate New Yorker who lives and works in Europe. She is a university professor and holds a Ph.D. in Psychology. Donna is an animal and human rights advocate and when she is researching or writing she can be found at her computer buried in rescue cats. E-mail her at donna_roberts13@yahoo.com.

Morgan Rondinelli is a blogger, biologist, and big fan of cats. She primarily blogs about mental health, and she co-runs the organization Not Alone Notes. Morgan earned her B.S. from University of Michigan in Ecology and Evolutionary Biology. She also adores the arts, which include reading, writing, dancing, and theater.

Carrie Roope is a writer and editor based in the UK where she lives with her husband Colin and two boys Alfie and Ollie. She is passionate about history and heritage, which fortunately the UK has in abundance, and enjoys taking her boys on historical adventures that she one day hopes to turn into a fiction book for children.

Jan Rottenberg, D.V.M. started her veterinary practice, Just Cats Veterinary Care in 1993. In addition to rescuing cats she enjoys reading and music and is currently re-learning piano. This is her first published story and she hopes to write others based on the very special animals that have enriched her life.

Linda Sabourin lives in Alma, AR with her brother Mike. They share their home with an ever-changing number of cats, most of whom come in through Linda's rescue, River Valley Cats. She tells people "It only took me fifty years to figure out what I want to be when I grow up. It was worth waiting for."

Nancy Saint John graduated from UNC-Chapel Hill and lives in California. She has worked as a librarian, publicist and radio broadcaster, winning numerous awards and an Emmy nomination. She also formed a puppet troupe and a music and storytelling show for children. Nancy is owned by three happy cats.

Laura Savino lives in Virginia with her two sons and two cats. Using her experience as an international pilot for United Airlines, Laura is a motivational speaker actively inspiring others to live a life that excites them. Learn more at LauraSavino747.com or connect with her on Twitter @BigPlanet747 and Instagram @LauraSavino747.

Nancy Sevilla is a mother and grandmother. She lives in Northern California and has been happily married for forty years. She and her husband love to camp with their family and two cats, Hunter and Buddy. This is her first attempt at writing and it's all because of her miracle cat, Hunter!

Lori Shepard retired from the Orlando Police Department in 2008. Since then she has traveled extensively, stopping long enough to adopt the brilliant cat Libby. Lori enjoys performing and teaching at a local improv theater. Currently she works part-time as a librarian, enjoying all things books.

Diane Stark is a wife, mother, and freelance writer. She is a frequent contributor to the *Chicken Soup for the Soul* series. She loves to write about the important things in life: her family and her faith.

Ronica Stromberg is a cat lover with four children's books published: *The Time-for-Bed Angel* (a bedtime story), *The Glass Inheritance* (a middle-school mystery), *A Shadow in the Dark* and *Living It Up to Live It Down* (both teen books). She manages a National Science Foundation program and writes in her spare time.

Carolyn M. Trombe lives in upstate New York with her husband

and six cats. She works for the New York State Education Department and enjoys swimming and reading. She is the author of *Dottie Wiltse Collins: Strikeout Queen of the All-American Girls Professional Baseball League*, the only biography about a player in the All-American Girls Professional Baseball League.

J. (Jim) Truluck began his bucket list early in life. Topping the list: become a sailor and see the world. The second was to be a park ranger. With these dreams fulfilled, he retired. However, he stays active as a volunteer naturalist and writing about his adventures for family and friends.

Renée Vajko-Srch is a regular contributor to the *Chicken Soup for the Soul* series. Her novel, *Hope for Joshua*, was published this year as well as her children's book, *It's Dark in the Ark*, which currently ranks as a #1 New Release on Amazon. She is currently writing a devotional for autism and special-needs families.

Pat Wahler is a Missouri native and proud contributor to sixteen titles in the *Chicken Soup for the Soul* series. Pat is the author of three novels and is currently at work on her next book under the supervision of two rescues: one bossy cat and a spoiled Pekingese-Poodle mix pup. Learn more at PatWahler.com.

Dorann Weber is a freelance photographer who lives in the Pine Barrens of South New Jersey with her family. She's a contributor for Getty Images. Her photos and verses have appeared on Hallmark cards and in magazines. Contributing stories for the *Chicken Soup for the Soul* series has ignited a passion for writing.

Susan C. Willett is a writer and blogger whose award-winning stories, poems, and humor appear in print and online, including her website LifeWithDogsAndCats.com. She shares her home with four cats and three dogs — all rescues. Follow them all on Facebook, Twitter @WithDogsAndCats, and Instagram @LifeWithDogsAndCats.

Linda J. Wright is an award-winning author as well as an animal activist and advocate. Her mysteries *Stolen*, *Sacrificed*, and *Seized* feature animal crimes investigator Kieran Yeats, and are based on her thirty-plus years on the front lines of animal activism. Learn more at www.lindajwright.com.

Meet Amy Newmark

Amy Newmark is the bestselling author, editor-in-chief, and publisher of the Chicken Soup for the Soul book series. Since 2008, she has published 168 new books, most of them national bestsellers in the U.S. and Canada, more than doubling the number of Chicken Soup for the Soul titles in print today. She is also the author of Simply Happy, a crash course in Chicken Soup for the Soul advice and wisdom that is filled with easy-to-implement, practical tips for enjoying a better life.

Amy is credited with revitalizing the Chicken Soup for the Soul brand, which has been a publishing industry phenomenon since the first book came out in 1993. By compiling inspirational and aspirational true stories curated from ordinary people who have had extraordinary experiences, Amy has kept the twenty-seven-year-old Chicken Soup for the Soul brand fresh and relevant.

Amy graduated magna cum laude from Harvard University where she majored in Portuguese and minored in French. She then embarked on a three-decade career as a Wall Street analyst, a hedge fund manager, and a corporate executive in the technology field. She is a Chartered Financial Analyst.

Her return to literary pursuits was inevitable, as her honors thesis in college involved traveling throughout Brazil's impoverished northeast region, collecting stories from regular people. She is delighted to have come full circle in her writing career — from collecting stories "from the people" in Brazil as a twenty-year-old to, three decades later, collecting stories "from the people" for Chicken Soup for the Soul.

When Amy and her husband Bill, the CEO of Chicken Soup for the Soul, are not working, they are visiting their four grown children and their grandchildren.

Follow Amy on Twitter @amynewmark. Listen to her free podcast — "Chicken Soup for the Soul with Amy Newmark" — on Apple Podcasts, Google Play, the Podcasts app on iPhone, or by using your favorite podcast app on other devices.

Thank You

We owe huge thanks to all of our contributors and fans. We received thousands of submissions for this popular topic, and we spent months reading all of them. Our editors Elaine Kimbler and Crescent LoMonaco and our Senior Editor Barbara LoMonaco read all of them and narrowed down the selection for Associate Publisher D'ette Corona and Publisher and Editor-in-Chief Amy Newmark.

Susan Heim did the first round of editing, D'ette chose the perfect quotations to put at the beginning of each story, and Amy edited the stories and shaped the final manuscript.

As we finished our work, D'ette Corona continued to be Amy's right-hand woman in working with all our wonderful writers. Barbara LoMonaco and Mary Fisher, along with Elaine Kimbler, jumped in at the end to proof, proof, proof. And yes, there will always be typos anyway, so feel free to let us know about them at webmaster@ chickensoupforthesoul.com, and we will correct them in future printings.

The whole publishing team deserves a hand, including our Senior Director of Marketing Maureen Peltier, our Vice President of Production Victor Cataldo, and our graphic designer Daniel Zaccari, who turned our manuscript into this beautiful, entertaining book.

About
American Humane

American Humane is the country's first national humane organization, founded in 1877 and committed to ensuring the safety, welfare, and wellbeing of all animals. For more than 140 years, American Humane has been first to serve in promoting the welfare and safety of animals and strengthening the bond between animals and people. American Humane's initiatives are designed to help whenever and wherever animals are in need of rescue, shelter, protection, or security.

With remarkably effective programs and the highest efficiency ratio of any national humane group for the stewardship of donor dollars, the nonprofit has earned Charity Navigator's top "4-Star" rating, has been named a "Top-Rated Charity" by CharityWatch and a "Best Charity" by Consumer Reports, and achieved the prestigious "Gold Level" charity designation from GuideStar.

American Humane is first to serve animals around the world, striving to ensure their safety, welfare and humane treatment—from rescuing animals in disasters to ensuring that animals are humanely treated. One of its best-known programs is the "No Animals Were Harmed®" animals-in-entertainment certification, which appears during the end credits of films and TV shows, and today monitors some 1,000 productions yearly with an outstanding safety record.

American Humane's farm animal welfare program helps ensure the humane treatment of nearly a billion farm animals, the largest animal welfare program of its kind. And recently, the historic nonprofit launched the American Humane Conservation program, an innovative initiative helping ensure the humane treatment of animals around the globe in zoos and aquariums.

Continuing its longstanding efforts to strengthen the healing power of the human-animal bond, American Humane pairs veterans struggling to cope with the invisible wounds of war with highly-trained service dogs, and spearheaded a groundbreaking clinical trial that provided for the first time scientific substantiation for the effectiveness of animal-assisted therapy (AAT) for children with cancer and their families.

To learn more about American Humane, visit americanhumane. org and follow them on Facebook, Instagram, and Twitter.

AMERICAN★HUMANE
FIRST TO SERVE®

Editor's Note: Chicken Soup for the Soul and American Humane have created *Humane Heroes*, a FREE new series of e-books and companion curricula for elementary, middle and high schoolers. Through 36 inspirational stories of animal rescue, rehabilitation, and humane conservation being performed at the world's leading zoological institutions, and 18 easy-to-follow lesson plans, *Humane Heroes* provides highly engaging free reading materials that also encourage young people to appreciate and protect Earth's disappearing species. To download the free e-books and learn about the program, please visit www.chickensoup.com/ah.

Sharing Happiness, Inspiration, and Hope

Real people sharing real stories, every day, all over the world. In 2007, USA Today named Chicken Soup for the Soul one of the five most memorable books in the last quarter-century. With over 100 million books sold to date in the U.S. and Canada alone, more than 250 titles in print, and translations into nearly fifty languages, "chicken soup for the soul®" is one of the world's best-known phrases.

Today, twenty-seven years after we first began sharing happiness, inspiration and hope through our books, we continue to delight our readers with new titles, but have also evolved beyond the bookshelves with super premium pet food, television shows, a podcast, video journalism from aplus.com, licensed products, and free movies and TV shows on our Popcornflix and Crackle apps. We are busy "changing the world one story at a time®." Thanks for reading!

Share with Us

We all have had Chicken Soup for the Soul moments in our lives. If you would like to share your story or poem with millions of people around the world, go to chickensoup.com and click on Submit Your Story. You may be able to help another reader and become a published author at the same time. Some of our past contributors have launched writing and speaking careers from the publication of their stories in our books!

We only accept story submissions via our website. They are no longer accepted via mail or fax. Visit our website, www.chickensoup.com, and click on Submit Your Story for our writing guidelines and a list of topics we are working on.

To contact us regarding other matters, please send us an e-mail through webmaster@chickensoupforthesoul.com, or fax or write us at:

Chicken Soup for the Soul
P.O. Box 700
Cos Cob, CT 06807-0700
Fax: 203-861-7194

One more note from your friends at Chicken Soup for the Soul: Occasionally, we receive an unsolicited book manuscript from one of our readers, and we would like to respectfully inform you that we do not accept unsolicited manuscripts, and we must discard the ones that appear.

Changing lives one story at a time®
www.chickensoup.com